ROBERT BROWN, a twenty-one-year-old Scotsman, arrived on Vancouver Island in 1863 for the purpose of collecting seeds, roots, and plants for the Botanical Association of Edinburgh. It soon became apparent, however, that he was not content with being a mere gatherer of specimens, and his relations with his sponsor rapidly soured. So when the opportunity arose in 1864 to head the Vancouver Island Exploring Expedition, Brown eagerly accepted the position as its commander.

During the four and a half months of the expedition, Brown kept a journal which is published here for the first time. It is remarkable for its record of life on Vancouver Island over a century ago and its description of the island's pristine wilderness as well as for its proposals for future economic development. The accounts of agricultural settlements at Cowichan, Chemainus, and Comox and of the coal-mining town of Nanaimo are among the earliest available.

The Vancouver Island Exploring Expedition did not venture north of Comox, but it crossed the island at several points, often by new routes, and in the process left its mark by giving place names to several locations. The expedition's most celebrated achievement was the discovery of gold on the Leech River, named after the second-in-command, which resulted in a short but sensational gold rush.

Robert Brown was exceptionally interested in the way of life of the native people. His entries on land reserve policies and on the failure to settle land claims are especially pertinent today. Excerpts from his related writings, among them one of the earliest records of a potlatch (at Alberni) and a collection of Indian myths and legends display an appreciation unusual at that time.

Most of the known drawings of the expedition by Frederick Whymper, the artist who travelled with the expedition, are included in the book, giving a contemporary view of many sites and revealing some of the hardships the explorers encountered. A checklist of Brown's other writings on the northwest coast completes the book.

JOHN HAYMAN is an associate professor in the Department of English at the University of Victoria.

1 Robert Brown, photograph taken in Victoria by G.R. Fardon, 1865
(PABC 2395)

ROBERT BROWN

and the

VANCOUVER ISLAND

EXPLORING EXPEDITION

Edited by John Hayman

UNIVERSITY OF BRITISH COLUMBIA PRESS
VANCOUVER 1989

LP

© THE UNIVERSITY OF BRITISH COLUMBIA PRESS 1989
All rights reserved
Designed by Robin Ward
Typeset by Pickwick
Printed in Canada
ISBN 0-7748-0322-3

Canadian Cataloguing in Publication Data
Brown, Robert, 1842–1895.
Robert Brown and the Vancouver Island Exploring Expedition

(Recollections of the pioneers of British Columbia ; 8)
Bibliography: p.
Includes index.
ISBN 0-7748-0322-3

1. Vancouver Island Exploring Expedition
(1864 : B.C.). 2. Vancouver Island (B.C.) –
Discovery and exploration. 3. Vancouver
Island (B.C.) – Description and travel. 4.
Botany – British Columbia – Vancouver Island.
5. Indians of North America – British Columbia –
Vancouver Island. 6. Brown, Robert, 1842–1895.
I. Hayman, John, 1935–   II. Title.
III. Series.
FC3844.4.B76 1989   917.11'34042   C89-091142-8
F1089.V3B76 1989

*Publication of this book has been financially assisted by the
Government of British Columbia through the British Columbia
Heritage Trust and British Columbia Lotteries.*

05/15/91

FOR CISCA

CONTENTS

ILLUSTRATIONS AND MAPS

Numbers in parentheses following the illustrations listed below refer to numbers in Appendix 2. Unless otherwise noted, all illustrations are by Frederick Whymper.

MAPS

PREFACE

WHEN ROBERT BROWN was about to leave Victoria in the summer of 1866, after a sojourn on the northwest coast of a little more than three years, the *British Colonist* (Victoria) remarked:

> *We shall be sorry to part with the Doctor, not alone for the selfish reason that he is good for numerous interesting news-items, so long as he remains in the country; but because the Colony will lose a valuable man, who has done more towards exploring its unknown regions, unfolding its natural resources, and drawing attention to the latent wealth of the Island, than any other man in it; and because society will lose an affable and intelligent gentleman. (6 August 1866)*

Brown prudently cut out this newspaper article and pasted it into his scrapbook, presumably for possible use as a testimonial. His position as Commander of the Vancouver Island Exploring Expedition (VIEE) in 1864 certainly had brought him considerable local publicity, and he had himself remarked in his journal on his birthday in 1865 on having achieved "a colonial fame at 23."

Despite this status as a celebrity, Brown has not subsequently been given much attention—even though he left his mark by the most obvious act of giving place names to many locations on Vancouver Island. It is perhaps understandable that Brown's unpublished journals in the Provincial Archives of British Columbia (PABC) should have been rarely introduced into accounts of the period. In the five notebooks concerned with the 1864 expedition, Brown's handwriting (as well as that of his copyist) is rather daunting. The only sustained consideration of these journals is that provided by Andrea J. Walker in an unpublished BA Honours thesis written for the Department of History at the University of Victoria. It is more surprising that Brown's copious publications should have been largely passed over. Admittedly, many of these writings appeared anonymously in nineteenth-century periodicals and anthologies which are not readily accessible. Moreover, Brown was not a specialist. Though he could claim some standing as a biologist, he was also interested in geology, ethnology, social history, economics, linguistics, and literature. Perhaps the specialists of our own time have found it difficult to accommodate so broad an interest.

The emphasis in the present selection of Brown's writings is on Brown the explorer and ethnographer. To provide a context for his expedition journal of 1864, his newspaper article on previous explorations on Vancouver Island ("The Land We Live In") is first presented. To illustrate the journal of the expedition, I have included the drawings of Frederick Whymper, the expedition's travelling artist. Earlier writers on Whymper apparently have been unaware of his drawings in the Beinecke Library at Yale University, the Royal Geographical Society Library in London, and the Scott Polar Institute, Cambridge. With the exception of a few drawings, which are too faint for reproduction, all the known drawings by Whymper of the expedition are included here, in some instances in the form of the engravings which were made from them, and detailed information about them is given in Appendix 2. The final two extracts, from *Races of Mankind*, reveal Brown as an ethnographer. His account of a potlach at Alberni and his presentation of Indian myths are among the earliest of such records and display an attempt at understanding exceptional at this time. The checklist of Brown's published writings on the northwest coast (Appendix 1) indicates that the present volume is a modest sampling of his writings. In particular, his contribution to biology, while apparent from his exploration journal, needs to be considered further. The present volume may suggest, then, other aspects of Brown's writings that are well worth discovering.

For permission to publish previously unpublished papers of Robert Brown, I am grateful to John A. Bovey, Provincial Archivist of British

Columbia and D.M. Henderson, Regius Keeper of Royal Botanic Garden, Edinburgh. For permission to publish drawings of Frederick Whymper, I am grateful to G. Miles, Curator, Western Americana, Beinecke Rare Book and Manuscript Library, Yale University; C. Kelly, Archivist of the Royal Geographical Society; and R.K. Headland, Archivist of the Scott Polar Research Institute, University of Cambridge. The following have kindly responded to my letters of enquiry: J.T.D. Hall, Special Collections, Edinburgh University Librarian; R. Michel, Archivist at McGill University; Karl-Heinz Jügelt, Direktor of Universitätsbibliothek, Wilhem-Pieck-Universität Rostock; and M. Westrup of Rigsarkivet, Copenhagen. Colleen Donnelly has typed the manuscript with her customary patience and skill. The staffs of Special Collections, McPherson Library, University of Victoria, and the Library of the Provincial Archives of British Columbia have been most helpful. Thanks are also due to S. Pettit, S. Jackman, R. Mackie, and D. Bertz for reading my earlier drafts on this topic; to J.C. Fredeman, Senior Editor of the University of British Columbia Press, for her sustained interest in the project, and to J. Wilson, Managing Editor, for her careful copy-editing. Research was assisted by a University of Victoria Research Grant.

ROBERT BROWN

and the

VANCOUVER ISLAND

EXPLORING EXPEDITION

INTRODUCTION

WHEN ROBERT BROWN arrived in Victoria in the spring of 1863 at the age of twenty-two, he was well qualified for his position as a botanical collector. Indeed, he was perhaps overqualified, and the difficulties that developed in his relationship with his sponsor, the British Columbia Botanical Association of Edinburgh, grew out of different notions about his status and primary duties.

The son of a farmer, Robert Brown was born on 23 March 1842, at Camster, Caithness, in the remote northeast of Scotland.[1] The family subsequently moved to Coldstream, Berwickshire, apparently on account of the father's ill health, and this move brought Robert Brown closer to centres for study. Between 1858 and 1862, he registered for four sessions at the University of Edinburgh, during which period he was awarded a silver medal for a collection of British marine algae and an essay on their "medicinal and economic value," and a prize for his "Essay on the Comparative Merits of the Linnean and Jussieuean Systems of Botanical Classification."[2] Later, he was to remark of this phase of his life: "Trained from an early period ... to scientific pursuits, during my studies in the University of Edinburgh, I devoted especial attention to Botany and its allied sciences, with a view to adopting a scientific career."[3] Granted this sense of his life, it is understandable that Brown should have later resisted the definition of himself as a mere "seed-collector."

He seems, however, to have been a restless undergraduate, eager to explore the world rather than settle in a library or laboratory. In a letter of 31 December 1860 to Professor John Hutton Balfour, he noted his intention not to take examinations the following April, but to extend his studies by travel—"in the study of my favourite pursuits of Natural History and Natural Phenomena."[4] Specifically, he planned to travel on the *Narwhal*, on its seal and whale hunts. To arrange this passage, he was to travel as a surgeon—"though the duties of a Surgeon," he remarked, "are merely nominal."

In early March 1861, Brown sailed from Dundee on a two-month venture "to the extreme Northern Isles of Zetland, and the seas in the vicinity of Iceland, Jan Mayen, and Spitzbergen."[5] Following a rapid turnaround at Dundee, he set off again for a whale hunt which took him to northern Greenland. In October, he was discharged from his nominal duties, with a rating of "V.G.,"[6] and turned again to his university studies.

By the summer of 1862, Brown was once more intent on travel, and an opportunity occurred when the British Columbia Botanical Association of Edinburgh met to reorganize its "Botanical Expedition to Oregon." This expedition had been initiated in 1850 with the appointment of John Jeffrey as a collector, but it had been dormant since 1854, following "the inattention of Jeffrey and his consequent dismissal."[7] The Association now set about raising new subscriptions, and when it showed interest in having Brown as its new collector, he indicated his readiness to set out immediately. Prudently, however, the committee decided that it would be more appropriate for Brown to leave the following spring, by which time subscriptions might also have increased.

In the formal appointment of Brown on 23 February 1863, his mission was flatly described. He was to "collect Seeds, Roots and Plants . . . for the space of three years."[8] Later, Brown was to describe his assignment as a "botanical examination,"[9] but there is no justification for this more scientific description in the terms of the appointment. Neither was his salary particularly encouraging. In addition to some unspecified expense payments, he was to receive £80 for the first year, with possible increases to £100 and £120 in subsequent years if subscriptions permitted.[10]

On 2 March 1863, Brown sailed from Southampton for the West Indies, and after crossing the Isthmus of Panama by train, he travelled by sea to San Francisco. Here he found that a steamer to Victoria had just left and he had to wait for ten days—an interval that his sponsor felt to be regrettably expensive. On 6 May, Brown finally arrived at Victoria.

His first letter to his sponsor is not extant, but it apparently caused some uneasiness, since one committee member noted in reply that Brown seemed to view the social position of the collector as superior to what they had imagined.[11] There is probably a reference here to Brown's accounts of dinners with Governor James Douglas, who had "received [him] very kindly" (Journal, 9 May 1863), and Gilbert Malcolm Sproat, manager of the sawmill at Alberni and a Justice of the Peace, who arranged the opening stage of Brown's first expedition by providing passage to Alberni on the company's schooner.

Brown arrived at Alberni on 25 May 1863 and the following day travelled on to a lake "not found on the map" which he named Sproat Lake. Subsequently, he sailed on the trading vessel *Codfish* down Alberni Inlet and along the west coast to Ucluelet, Clayoquot, Ahousat, and Nootka Island. Along the way, he "botanised"—and concluded at Nootka that many plants there had been "apparently introduced by whites" (19 June 1863). For almost three weeks, the *Codfish* traded at various settlements along the coast before returning to Alberni. Brown then explored Sproat Lake further and courteously named some of the surrounding mountains after his Scottish sponsors. Subsequently, he moved on to Great Central Lake, but heavy rain prevented him from discovering the length of the lake, and he returned to Alberni and sailed for Victoria on 6 July. Back in Victoria, he reported on his exploration to Governor Douglas and was interviewed by the local press, which was especially interested in his visit to Nootka.[12] "Found myself somewhat of a hero," he noted in his journal (9 July 1863).

Towards the end of July, Brown set off for the United States mainland. He crossed the Strait of Juan de Fuca to Port Angeles and then journeyed to Port Townsend and Whidbey Island. In addition, he travelled by canoe up the Snohomish River and detoured to the Snoqualmie River in order to view the falls. He then decided to travel, on horseback and with Indian guides, over an Indian trail to Seattle. Throughout this excursion, he was alert to new plants, and he experienced "horrible vexation" when the best of his seeds were "utterly ruined" when they were drenched in crossing a river. From Seattle, Brown returned to Victoria at the end of August, by way of Port Ludlow and Port Townsend.

Two days later, on 1 September 1863, he again set out for the mainland, this time with the intention of travelling up the Fraser River. After a week of rather desultory botanizing around New Westminister, he set out for Lillooet, where he stayed for just over a week. He was back in Victoria towards the end of September and attended to packing his seed collection for dispatch to Scotland.

By now it was mid-October, but Brown apparently thought there was time for one further excursion before settling down for the winter. He therefore set out for Alberni again, apparently with the aim of discovering the length of Great Central Lake. On 22 October he arrived at the lakehead, having discovered that the lake was about eighteen miles in length, rather than the forty or fifty miles that it was reputed to be. Finally, after more than a week of "incessant rain" at Alberni, he decided to return to Victoria to "put through the winter."

Brown's journal for these winter months indicates a fairly active social life. There are several references to visits to the theatre, among them one which compares the theatre to the "San Francisco melodeum, consisting of nigger melody and witticism with occasionally small acts with abundance of double allusions and showing of legs" (25 November 1863). He also visited a newly opened "Squaw Dance House," noting that it was "filled nightly with Indian women and miners" (18 December 1863). In addition, he briefly refers to meeting such leading local citizens as John Todd, a former Hudson's Bay Company Chief Factor, "a grand old man ... of the regular Astoria type" (27 November 1863); Captain William Henry McNeill, "the famous trader" (12 January 1864), who had been active on the coast since 1831; Bishop George Hills (1 January 1864); and Arthur Fellows (17 January 1864), a hardware merchant, married to the daughter of Sir Rowland Hill.

Despite such occasional social pleasures, however, Brown found the winter a difficult period. The rainfall was exceptionally heavy during these months, and as Brown was to remark, "the miserable almost continual rain of a Vancouver [Island] winter is not calculated to improve one's health."[13] His funds were also very limited, and his relationship with his sponsor uncertain.

In his letter of 20 February 1864 to the Botanical Association, Brown therefore attempted to clarify his position. Acutely disturbed by feeling that he was receiving insufficient support, he urged that he be sent funds for his next expedition. "Travellers can now no longer travel in the [Hudson's Bay] Co. hunting grounds—living in their forts and travelling with their Brigades at little or no expense." A hurt pride perhaps displays itself as he reflected further on his salary of £80 for the first year: "I am compelled to admit that not every Indian would 'pack' my blankets for that sum per annum—and any miner would tell me in no stinted language—that working at that figure is 'played out'." Quietly reminding his sponsors that they had more than a seed collector in their employ, he further remarked: "I have rescued from oblivion and compiled vocabularies of no less than 10 *distinct* Indian languages (beside dialects) unknown to Philologists." But perhaps Brown was also aware that this enterprise would not impress, for he continued by noting that he had "collected natural specimens which independently of their Scientific Value would if disposed of after being described go far to pay my winter's expenses." In conclusion, he remarked: "I am well aware the Expn. is not for the advancement of scientific Botany, and though this must necessarily receive my attention I will take care that the Assocn's main objectives are *never* neglected." The committee, however, did not find this promise convincing. In response, the Secretary stressed that "the great object of the general body of Subscribers" was the acquisition of seeds—"without regard to such things as have merely botanical interest" (29 April 1864).

By the spring of 1864, the committee had, in fact, become dismayed at not having received any seeds. Brown had promised in his letter of 20 February to send some by the "next mail," but when the committee had still not received any by mid-May, it contemplated dismissing him. "I need not say," the secretary wrote on 16 May, "how much disappointment is felt by the whole subscribers that now, after a twelvemonth have elapsed since you entered on the duties of your mission, they are yet without any results." The slowness of the mail ensured that Brown was not aware of the extent of the Association's dissatisfaction with his conduct until much later, but in the spring of 1864 his position was problematic enough. Without funds for an independent exploration and resentful of the Botanical Association's view of him as a mere seed-collector, he seized the chance of gaining a new sponsor: the Vancouver Island Exploring Expedition (VIEE).

The VIEE of 1864 was not the first attempt to explore Vancouver Island, but much still remained to be discovered. As Alexander Rattray had disarmingly remarked in *Vancouver Island and British Columbia. Where they are; What they are; and What they may become* ... (London 1862), any account of the island at that date was necessarily "incomplete and unsatisfactory" because of "unhappily imperfect knowledge." "A large part of it remains to be explored," he noted. "Our knowledge, indeed ... is limited to that comparatively small portion of its southern extremity which is bounded on the north by Port San Juan and Nanaimo."[14]

Consequently, there were frequent calls in the early 1860s for further exploration. In the *British Colonist* of 8 June 1863, for example, the editor declared himself "struck with the vast amount we have yet to learn concerning the country." With naïve assurance he continued: "There is every inducement for men who are at leisure, or who can afford to take it, to start off during our lovely summer months on a ramble across the country, setting out from one coast and crossing to the other. The distance is nowhere very great and could be accomplished in a very short time by easy stages." This same writer suggested that the government might aid by providing supplies for the explorers. In its estimates for 1863, the government had, in fact, already established $6,000 "for the purpose of enabling a geological survey."[15] This amount was not expended, but in the following year $5,000 was again allocated (*British Colonist*, 4 February). For various reasons, an exploration was by this time being viewed as essential.

The optimism occasioned by the gold rushes of 1858 and 1861 had by now passed. Victoria had established itself as a supply centre for the mainland, and it had in 1860 reinforced this position by becoming a free port. But it was questionable how sustaining this measure would be, partly because of the opposition voiced by agricultural settlers who were experiencing difficulty competing with suppliers from the mainland. The Pre-Emption Proclamation of 1861 had stimulated agricultural settlement at Cowichan and Comox, since by this procedure settlers might take up unsurveyed land prior to arranging payment to the government, and as Governor Douglas observed in his address to the Colonial Legislature on 4 January 1863, the amount of land either sold or pre-empted in 1862 was almost double that in 1861. It was in this context that he spoke of "the great importance of providing a Geological Survey of the Colony."[16]

The prospect of gold discovery also animated many of those who supported exploration. In 1862, a writer in the 16 March *British Colonist* had resoundingly suggested that the "practical men" on an exploration might "set the question at rest whether our island is auriferous or argentiferous or both." In 1863, gold discoveries at Goldstream, close to Victoria, encouraged fresh hopes. As Brown was to discover, this fascination with gold was for most supporters of exploration the unspoken but fundamental motive.

There were reasons enough, then, why it was appropriate to launch an exploring expedition in the mid-1860s. The one remaining requirement was an official sponsor, and such a figure emerged with the arrival of Arthur Edward Kennedy as governor on 25 March 1864. On a visit to the diggings at Goldstream on 20 April he pledged official support for an exploration by a government contribution of two dollars for every dollar contributed by the general public.

A week later, some of Victoria's leading citizens formed a committee to organize an expedition. To arouse interest and financial support, the committee then arranged a public meeting for 10 May, and Brown was among those who attended. In exemplary fashion, he spoke briefly and to the point, referring his listeners to the newspaper articles in which he had recently outlined existing knowledge of the island and his own explorations of the previous year.[17] Later, on 20 May, the *Evening Express* (Victoria) published the detailed report of his second journey of 1863 which Brown had addressed to the Botanical Association of Edinburgh. In introducing this, the editor noted: "Dr. Brown's scientific mission has not been confined to any branch of work, but includes Geography, Zoology, Geology, and Ethnology." Brown was just as assured in his formal application for the position of commander of the expedition: "I am willing to undertake such work as would fall to the lot of a Botanist, Zoologist, & Geologist & am able to furnish an accurate & complete report upon the topography, soil, timber & resources, with such observations as might not be deputed to a professional Surveyor who would of necessity accompany such an Expedition as Second Officer."[18]

On 1 June 1864, the committee formally appointed Brown as commander, declaring that it had "full confidence in [his] capacity, zeal, and integrity."[19] Brown, however, seems to have been aware that his Scottish sponsor might question the propriety of his taking on this new role. In a letter of explanation (7 June) he therefore noted that he had been not only appointed as a commander with "despotic power" but also given "the (honorary) rank of Agent Government & a Magistrate." "So that in future," he pointedly remarked, "I will travel with power & not as the poor unknown plant hunter of last year." In addition, his expedition would not cost the Association anything, and he would have "a strong escort" which included an assistant to collect seeds. Unfortunately, the committee in Edinburgh was not impressed by these considerations. In reply (25 July), the secretary described Brown's letter as "a most unsatisfactory Communication." "It now appears," the secretary remarked, "that you have accepted another situation . . . utterly incompatible with the duty which you owe to this association." Clearly Brown had complicated his already difficult relationship with his Scottish sponsor.

As to the "strong escort" provided by the expedition, Brown himself described it in rather different terms in other contexts. "A queer looking lot," he remarked on one occasion, and "wondrously motley" on another.[20]

As travelling artist, the committee selected Frederick Whymper (1838–1901), the son of Josiah Wood Whymper, a well-known English wood-engraver, and the brother of Edward Whymper, a celebrated Alpinist. Frederick Whymper had arrived on Vancouver Island in the fall of 1862. The following year, he had travelled to the Cariboo, and in the spring of 1864 he had joined the road builders who

2 Frederick Whymper, *Victoria* (C–1572 Public Archives Canada). The view is of the Inner Harbour, the Legislative Buildings (or "birdcages"), with the Olympic Mountains in the background.

were working inland from Bute Inlet. He had left this group just before it was massacred by Chilcotin Indians, and he consequently attracted some publicity upon his return to Victoria in May 1864, just when the committee was about to make its appointments. Again, Brown may not have been strictly accurate when he later described Whymper as "an artist ... who has for some time past been more familiar with the gold-miner's pick than with the painter's palette,"[21] but Whymper was no effete aesthete. His published account of part of the expedition in *Travel and Adventure in the Territory of Alaska* (1868) suggests that he relished physical danger, and he managed to complete over thirty drawings on the expedition, often under the most difficult circumstances.[22]

Two other members of the group had served earlier in the Royal Engineers, the corps that had recently been disbanded: John Meade, who had arrived in Victoria as a lance corporal in 1858,[23] and Lieutenant Peter John Leech (1826-99), who was appointed second-in-command at a monthly salary of $100.[24] (All other members were paid $60.) There were also two university graduates: Henry Thomas Lewis, a graduate of Cambridge University, who declared in his application that he was "a practical farmer," an experienced gold miner, and "a good shot,"[25] and Alexander Barnston (b. 1838), a graduate of McGill University, who described himself as "well habituated to the hardships & dangers of a life in the woods."[26] The committee's relatively disinterested quest for knowledge is possibly reflected by the appointment of John Buttle (1838-1908), a former student of Sir William Hooker at the Royal Botanic Gardens at Kew and a botanist on the British-North American Boundary Commission. (In 1865, Buttle was appointed commander of a further expedition on the island, and it was during this exploration that he explored the lake that now bears his name.) John Foley was a more narrowly practical choice: he described himself as "thoroughly acquainted with quartz and copper mining and bush travel," and Whymper said of him that he "knew more of gold and its whereabouts than any five other men."[27] Finally, there was Ranald Macdonald (1824-94), undoubtedly the most colourful and entertaining of the group. His father was a Hudson's Bay Company chief trader and his mother a daughter of Com-Comly, a Chinook Indian chief. As a young man, he had pursued a picaresque career which had included almost a year in Japan, nominally as a prisoner. Eventually, after a visit to the Australian goldfields, he had returned to the northwest coast. At forty, he was the oldest of the explorers, but his persistent high spirits made him, according to Brown, a popular member of the group.[28]

On 7 June 1864, the exploration party left Victoria aboard the gunboat H.M.S. *Grappler* for Cowichan, where about a hundred settlers had arrived two years previously, and it was here that the group gained a significant additional member: Tomo Antoine.[29] "His father was an Iroquois *voyageur* from Canada," Brown wrote, "his mother a Chinook from the Columbia River. He had for forty years moved about over the country among Hudson Bay forts and hunting stations—*voyageur*, farmer, hunter, trapper—possibly worse."[30] By this ominous conclusion, Brown is probably referring to the suspicion that Tomo had a year earlier murdered his wife. (He had been acquitted on insufficient evidence.)[31] Brown, however, recognized Tomo's value. He had travelled on most of the previous explorations on the island;[32] he was a good linguist; and, despite having only one arm, he was a celebrated hunter. Brown did not regret his decision to employ Tomo. On the contrary, he was later to remark that without Tomo's assistance "the map of Vancouver [Island] would have been a sorry blank yet, and the first Exploring Expedition a forgotten affair."[33]

When the group proceeded up the Cowichan River it was also assisted by Kakalatza, a joint chief of the Somenos, and after a week's trek, during which the group divided between land and river parties, it arrived at Cowichan Lake. The days devoted to exploring the lake and its environs were perhaps the most agreeable part of the expedition. Shortly after arriving there, Brown noted in his journal the "Great News!" that gold had been discovered on a creek leading into the lake (17 June) and subsequently he was also able to report on "a hill of quartz" and "a perfect Mountain of Copper ore & Ironstone" (20 June). Later Brown remarked as well on the natural beauty of the region—of the forest "fragrant with ... piny odour," and of the woodpeckers, grouse, hummingbirds, and eagles. "These were halcyon days," he recorded. "The woods echoed with our joyous laugh and song, and the hills with the reports of the hunter's rifle; there was nothing to make us uneasy."[34]

Granted the high spirits of the explorers, it was perhaps unfortunate that Brown should have thought it advisable to divide the group at this point, but he recognized that the expedition might cover more territory by this procedure. Accordingly, Leech was made commander of a group that was to travel from the south side of the lake to Port

San Juan. Brown's party, meanwhile, would travel from the western end of the lake, follow the Nitinat River to the coast, and then reunite with Leech's party at Port San Juan, where the VIEE Committee had arranged to send supplies.

It was at Port San Juan that Brown seems first to have felt that the sponsoring committee in Victoria was not treating the explorers generously. On arrival there, he found that the expected supplies had not been delivered, and he did not realize that the supply ship had been forced to turn back by heavy seas. Subsequently, when the supplies arrived a few days later, there was an accompanying dispatch urging that Brown should exercise "the strictest economy ... consistent with the comfort of yourself and those under your command."[35] These references to "economy" and "comfort" seem to have riled Brown. Leech's party had just experienced an especially tortuous route, having been forced by dense and mountainous terrain to bushwhack some forty miles to cover a distance on the map of about half that distance. In his dispatch to the committee, Brown therefore referred to "the Herculean labour of penetrating the country ... in nearly every respect the country most difficult to be penetrated of any in the world." With chilling composure, he remarked further: "Your admonition about being economical of the provisions is somewhat uncalled for; for as you are well aware at the outside they are totally inadequate for our wants unless we killed game."[36]

After travelling along the coast to Sooke and entrusting the expedition to Leech, Brown set out on 13 July with Barnston for Victoria—in part to confront the VIEE Committee and clarify his relationship with it. It seems, however, that the attempt at clarification failed and that Brown became increasingly disturbed by the committee's preoccupation with the discovery of gold. Finally, on 16 July, he expostulated with it:

> *Though in deference to the wishes of the body of our people, I have ordered that the greatest portion of our attention should be devoted to minerals, yet at the same time, minerals only form in conjunction with geography, timber & Agricultural lands, &c, &c—one of several subjects to which our attention is to be devoted. We are not a "prospecting expedition" any more than we are a party of loggers, seeking sites for camps, or farmers looking for land, & whenever the expedition*

diverges wholly into either of these subjects I must request of
you to relieve me of my charge to make way for some more
fitting director.[37]

Even more pressing was Brown's need to clarify his position with
his Edinburgh sponsor. At Port San Juan he had received a letter
urging him to concentrate on collecting seeds and requesting that he
account for his activities by sending back his journal. On arriving in
Victoria, he found a further letter (dated 16 May) which indicated
that "unless full and satisfactory explanation of his conduct [was
forthcoming] ... the Committee would be under the necessity of
recalling his appointment."

On 18 July—two days after his expostulation to the Victoria committee—he responded to these communications from Edinburgh in
an eighteen-page letter that constituted his *de profundis*. Moving
between resentment and contrition, he began by declaring that he
had been unjustly treated. "You have already condemned me without
hearing me," he asserted. Sorrowfully, he agreed to return to his
starting-point—that of seed-collecting. True, he had earlier supposed
that his task was of "more than a mere commercial character," but the
order that he collect "hogs heads casks of seeds" had now revealed his
thorough misconception. Of his acceptance of this humble role, he
continued: "It was like death to me, but it was done." In separate
letters to members of the sponsoring committee, he implored them
not to abandon him. "Do not I pray you Dr Balfour loose [sic] faith in
me—else I will loose confidence in myself & break down under my
sorrows.... I am only 22 years. You thought me older I daresay." This
appeal to his young age is especially poignant, and it suggests that
Brown not only demanded much of himself but felt the strain of
others' expectations. He was, in fact, the youngest man on the expedition by several years; Leech, the second-in-command, was more than
fifteen years older.

Unfortunately, the emotional tone of these letters had the opposite
effect to that intended by Brown. One member of the committee
reacted "with the utmost disgust" and wrote to the secretary: "The
man is an idiot, and his letters are such a rigmarole of nonsense he
must have been drunk when he wrote them."[38] Certainly, Brown had
reason to feel dismayed. Reluctantly, he had been forced to recognize
that his sponsors in Edinburgh viewed him simply as a seed-collector,
and he had hoped that the committee in Victoria would be more

enlightened and encourage a more liberal exploration. However, he had gradually come to realize that it viewed him as the leader of a gold-prospecting party. By trying to serve two masters, he had not gained in status but merely confirmed his humble standing.

There was yet another irony: it was during Brown's absence from the expedition, while he was visiting Victoria, that the explorers, under Leech's leadership, made their most sensational discovery—a discovery that was to lead to the island's most celebrated gold rush and to imperil further the progress of the expedition itself.

When Brown set out from Victoria to join the exploration party at Cowichan, he had no idea that the explorers had made a significant gold discovery on a branch of the Sooke River that they had named after Leech. At Cowichan, however, he found that the explorers were "wild with excitement," and he acknowledged that "the coarse gold was enough to excite anyone" (26 July).

Brown now feared that members of the exploration group might defect and seek their fortunes on the banks of the Leech River, and he became the more anxious when dissension among the men forced him to dismiss John Foley. Dismayed at the possibility of the exploration's collapse, Brown urged in a dispatch to the VIEE Committee (31 July): "Treat all who bring no certificate of service to you as deserters & give them no pay whatever."

On 1 August, the expedition set out for Nanaimo, and Brown was prudent in then dividing the group for further exploration. His own group was to journey by sea to Comox and then cross the island to Alberni. Leech's group was to journey to Cowichan Lake by way of the Nanaimo Lakes and reunite with Brown at Alberni.

Again, Leech's group had the more hazardous route. When they reached Cowichan Lake, Buttle noted that they had "little else left but tea, sugar & flour & not a good deal of that" (29 August). Their subsequent hardship is indicated by the names of their camps: Hungry Creek, Starvation Creek, and Misery Creek. Finally, they had resolved that they would eat their dog, and escaped this dreadful necessity by unexpectedly arriving at Sarita Lake and catching a few trout.

Brown, on the other hand, had an agreeable canoe trip along the coast to Comox and was treated there as a dignitary by the settlers who had arrived in the area just a year or two before. As a rejoinder to the gold discovery on the Leech River, Brown was also delighted to report the discovery of a coal seam near the junction of Puntledge

River with a river that Brown was happy to have named after him.
"People I'm sure will be a little incredulous," Meade remarked, "when
told of seams 100 feet long and a thickness from 1 foot to 6 feet but
nevertheless it is a truth" (2 September). The subsequent journey up
the Puntledge to Comox Lake was not without difficulties, since the
group now travelled without Indian guides in a canoe that proved
unwieldy, but the journey provided a novel experience—the hunting
of beaver.

At Alberni, where they arrived on 24 September, the exploration
virtually ended, apart from some excursions along the canal (or inlet)
itself.[39] Summer was almost over; uneasy relations with Indians along
the west coast made exploration there hazardous; and the explorers
themselves were, as Barnston noted, "pretty well tired of forest life"
(21 October). In addition, Brown recognized that he should now
attend to seed-collecting for his Edinburgh sponsor. On 14 October,
he therefore decided to set out for Victoria, and on the same day he
received notice of recall by way of a ship docking at Alberni.

The exploration party now planned to cross the island, from Alberni to Qualicum River, on a trail that was reportedly well established. Brown had been assured that it was "beautiful . . . like a turn-
pike," but the explorers found otherwise. For part of the crossing,
Brown recorded, "our way lay over nothing but drifts of fallen timber,
along which we 'cooned it,' like squirrels, never during the whole
distance touching mother earth."[40] After arriving finally at the coast,
they travelled by canoe to Nanaimo and there boarded the *Grappler*
for the journey to Victoria. On 21 October, after an expedition of
almost four and a half months, they arrived back on the gunboat in
which they had set out.

On their return, the explorers found that they had become local
celebrities, and Brown, as commander, was the subject of special
attention. The *Victoria Daily Chronicle* declared that "to the ability,
energy, and untiring industry of Mr. Brown is, in a great measure, due
the brilliant success which has attended the exploring Expedition"
(26 October). On the same day that this praise was published, Brown
called on Governor Kennedy. "Had a most flattering reception & long
talk of a couple hours," he noted in his journal. A month later, the
expedition gathered further attention with the opening of an exhibition of Whymper's drawings. "I attended a short time to explain,"
Brown remarked in his journal (24 November). There was even talk

of an official dinner in honour of the explorers, but Brown declined. "Money is scarce," he prudently noted (2 January 1865).

Among the expedition's achievements, the discovery of gold on a branch of the Sooke River and the subsequent establishment of Leechtown was undoubtedly the most immediately remarkable. At the conclusion of the expedition, Brown learned from the Victoria postmaster that an estimated $ 100,000 had been taken from the area and that about 400 men were still active there. Throughout the winter, work continued sporadically at the diggings, and in his journal for 2 January 1865, Brown observed: "the general cry is 'What would the town have been without Leech River'." Shortly before returning to Britain in 1866, Brown visited the area and found it "a settled district with embryo towns, good trails, [and] stores." "I slept in a Hotel of two stories," he noted, "where I was entertained with a sumptuous dinner."[41] However, Brown had also to admit that the gold was "very scattered," and by this time discoveries at Big Bend had attracted the floating population of miners.

The failure to develop a coal mine on Browns River was probably more disappointing to Brown.[42] He had, however, always stressed that the exploration was essentially a fact-finding mission. On being appointed commander, he had declared to the committee: "I neither promise prairies, nor mines, nor yet a Goshen—a land flowing with milk & honey—but *I will try*. We are searching for truth & that we will find."[43]

Brown's subsequent publication of his findings is, indeed, his major achievement. The first publication, *Vancouver Island. Exploration 1864*, was a twenty-seven-page official report that was published in April 1865. In this publication, Brown outlined the exploration route, the mineral and agricultural potential of different regions, and the place-names he had established. Again, the press response was enthusiastic. Following a summary of the report, the *British Colonist* remarked: "That these results are well worth the money which was expended on their undertaking, no person, we are sure, in the community will attempt to deny" (21 April 1865).

Brown's Scottish sponsor was not, however, so readily satisfied. On completion of the expedition, Brown discovered that the Botanical Association had given power of attorney for its business to Dr. William Fraser Tolmie, formerly chief factor of the Hudson's Bay Company in Victoria and now a member of the Legislative Assembly.

Brown was incensed by this apparent lack of confidence. A commander himself, he resented having an authority placed over him. With a sense of hurt pride, he arranged to send his seed collection to Edinburgh, and accompanied this dispatch with the offer of his resignation.[44]

He had for some time been contemplating a "popular" account of his travels, to be accompanied by chromolithographs of Whymper's drawings. "From the nature of the book," he remarked to his sponsor (21 October 1864), "it is certain to be a paying concern." Towards the close of the year, he also saw another possibility for independence in the colonial government's proposal to create a Superintendent of Indian Affairs. But this position was not established by the government estimates in 1865, and Brown was relieved when the Botanical Association did not accept his resignation. The secretary reported that Brown's most recent dispatch (7 January 1865) had been "of a more business like style and of a less offensive temper than ... past communications," and it even published part of his "descriptive catalogue" for its subscribers.

All the same, the winter of 1864-5 was difficult for Brown, mainly because of a lack of financial support. He was therefore interested to find in the government estimates for 1865 that $1,500 had been allocated for the explorers. This amount was not, however, immediately distributed, and on 24 February, Brown noted in his journal: "I have not drawn a cent all winter." A month later, he remarked that he was living on sherry and eggs. His twenty-third birthday, 23 March, was therefore a day of reckoning—but, despite his continued financial difficulties, he reviewed his career with some satisfaction. "Though I have not done one tittle of what I might have done," he remarked, "yet when compared with some of my College Contemporaries this is not so bad—a colonial fame at 23." Finally, on 18 April, the government bonus was distributed. "Govt paid my quantum of $400," Brown noted in his journal. "Paid off all my Bills."

A month later, Brown set out on an expedition, mainly in Washington and Oregon. In a later summary of his travels, he wrote: "I left for Oregon, travelling along the banks of the Columbia and Willamette Rivers, penetrating the Cascade Mountains into the wild and only partially explored region of Eastern Oregon and Idaho, and returning by way of the Siskiyou and Sierra Nevada Mountains to San Francisco, California, in October 1865."[45] His return to Victoria "with a large and valuable collection" was remarked on in the *British*

Colonist on 16 October, where it was also noted that he was about to head north to collect more seeds.

It is increasingly apparent, however, that Brown was becoming as much an explorer as a botanical collector. In fact, he described himself as such in the spring of 1866, following another winter in Victoria, when he remarked that he felt "almost sick of the hum-drum everyday life of the hibernating period of an Explorer."[46] Even as he wrote this, he was about to set out with a group of coal miners for the Queen Charlotte Islands.

On this journey, Brown passed among the Gulf Islands (4–6 March 1866) and stopped several days at New Westminster (8–13 March), where he encountered miners going to the goldfields at Big Bend. Then he travelled along the east coast of Vancouver Island to Fort Rupert (22 March), and spent his birthday the following day writing an essay entitled "An Apology for the Indians," in which he argued that prostitution and drunkenness had been brought among them by "the vilest of whisky sellers ... or traders with no regard for aught but their own gain."[47] Finally, he arrived at "Skidegate Town" (31 March), having briefly visited Bella Bella on the way.

On his return journey, Brown stopped at Fort Rupert, near the northern end of Vancouver Island, and then crossed the island in the company of two Koskeemo Indians to Quatsino Sound. He declared the Koskeemo Indians to be "the only remaining Indian tribe in the country [he] had not visited or seen," and it therefore seemed to him fitting that he should finally visit them at this late point in his northwest sojourn.[48]

By 20 May 1866, Brown was back in Victoria, eager to discover whether his appointment with the Botanical Association had been extended beyond the original contract for a three-year period. However, it was at about this same time that his Scottish sponsor was deciding to end its support. The Association had been dissatisfied by the seeds from 1865, finding them almost all "rotten ... their vegetative power destroyed" (9 May). Subsequently, the Association was even more brutal. In a letter of 30 May, the secretary declared: "The results of the mission have proved so unsatisfactory that the greater part of the 3rd years subscription is in arrears and with nothing to distribute, we can get little in." The last box, the secretary noted, contained "only a mass of corruption." Consequently, it had been decided unanimously that Brown's services should be discontinued.

Brown now had time for only one further expedition, and this was

a venture quite unrelated to botanical collecting. With E.T. Coleman,
the artist and writer, he attempted in July 1866 an ascent of the
previously unclimbed Mount Baker. Unfortunately, after journeying
some forty miles up the Skagit River, they encountered "an un-
friendly tribe of Indians" and the expedition had to be abandoned.[49]

Brown's continuing interest in travel is reflected in his route
home—"visiting on the way California, Nicaragua, (which I crossed
from the Pacific to the Atlantic,) the West Indies, and the Eastern
States and Provinces of North America."[50] Following a winter's study
divided among Edinburgh, Kew Gardens, and the British Museum,
Brown then set out in April 1867 from Copenhagen with Edward
Whymper on an expedition to Greenland, "making extensive series
of observations and collections, not only in Botany, but in the allied
sciences of Zoology, &c."[51] The British Colonist continued to follow
Brown's progress and reprinted from The Scotsman a report on this
venture. Brown was, the Colonist noted, "nominally of Edinburgh,
and an alumnus of the University, yet ... [with] the most cosmopoli-
tan of reputations" (28 January 1868).

Brown also displayed some inclination to settle. In 1868, he became
a candidate for the Chair of Botany at the Royal College of Science in
Ireland. In Testimonials in Favour of Robert Brown (1868), more
than thirty testimonials were included, many of them from eminent
botanists. Joseph Dalton Hooker, Director of the Royal Gardens at
Kew, testified to "the great service which you have rendered to Botanical Science by your collections and research."[52] John Hutton Balfour, Regius Professor of Medicine and Botany at the University of
Edinburgh, described him as "a zealous Naturalist" and "a fluent
speaker."[53] Isaac Anderson-Henry, former President of the Botanical
Society, rather more circumspectly referred to him as "a Botanist and
Naturalist of no mean order [who] enjoys the advantage of easy,
pleasing manners, and gentlemanly bearing and address."[54] Of special
interest is the testimony of Gilbert Sproat. Referring to the VIEE he
remarked: "I can testify to the activity, tact, and good humour displayed by Mr Brown in the management of the Expedition, under
difficult circumstances.... Socially and personally, Mr Brown's character is all that could be desired in a gentleman and man of science."[55]

Regrettably, this array of testimonials was unsuccessful. Brown
was not appointed to the Chair. Instead he became an occasional
lecturer in natural history at the School of Arts and the Heriot-Watt
college in Edinburgh and at the Andersonian Institute in Glasgow. In

1873, he was an unsuccessful candidate for the Chair of Botany at the University of Edinburgh, and according to a later witness, this was "a disappointment which he cannot be said to have entirely surmounted."[56]

Brown was also unsuccessful in finding a publisher for the "popular" account of his travels. "The interest in the Northwest is barely sufficient to bring out a separate work of travels," he remarked in a letter to Mrs. Fellows of Victoria in 1870.[57] The previous year he had published his "Memoir on the Geography of the Interior of Vancouver Island" in a German translation.[58] No doubt it was gratifying to be awarded a doctorate for this publication by the University of Rostock, but it must also have been disappointing that no British publisher was forthcoming. Subsequently, Brown ranged between two very different forms of publication: scientific reports for learned journals and sensational sketches for popular magazines. Hovering uncertainly between these two extremes were autobiographical travel accounts that swayed towards fiction. Altogether his corpus was immense.[59]

In *Testimonials* (1868), he appended a list of his papers and reports published by scientific societies which ran to forty-one items,[60] and in a memoir published soon after his death, A.J. Wilson noted that "from first to last the total mounts to several hundreds."[61] These scholarly publications venture among botany, zoology, ornithology, geology, geography, and ethnology. Their most noticeable recurring concern is Brown's interest in the practical use of the natural phenomena he describes.

Brown's articles in popular magazines are quite varied. A few are concerned with colonial society: with the excitement of mail day in Victoria, or with "putting through the winter" in Victoria following a summer in the goldfields or on an expedition. More frequently, however, Brown wrote about Indians: about the changing status of the chief in Indian society or about battles between rival tribes. In these popular pieces, Brown does not attempt to present Indian life with the sympathetic understanding that he displayed elsewhere. In his journal, for example, he several times criticized those who characterized the Indian as an idle malcontent. These critics, he maintained, had not seen beyond the degenerates loitering around the outskirts of Victoria. In his popular pieces, however, the Indian is almost invariably depicted as mercenary, vindictive, and treacherous. No doubt Brown could introduce suspense and danger by this approach, but it seems also that he might have been fulfilling popular expectation.

Perhaps Brown's most rewarding writings are among those that aimed to combine instruction and entertainment. Certainly he came to be associated with those works of "popular education" that were considered so improving in the Victorian era. His contributions to H.W. Bates's *Illustrated Travels: A Record of Discovery, Geography, and Adventure* (1869–75) indicate well the scope of such writing. In early numbers of this compendium, he presented in four parts a fairly detailed account of the expedition's progress to Port San Juan—but at this point he broke off. His later contributions to *Illustrated Travels* are pieces of fiction, rather complicatedly connected with actual events on the expedition. Of these, "In Pawn in an Indian Village" is his most ambitious story, and its plot again emphasizes the meanness and treachery of the Indians.[62]

These different approaches and attitudes are also reflected in *The Races of Mankind* (1873–6), especially in its account of Indian life. In his detailed account of a "potlatch" near Alberni, Brown writes as an astute and appreciative observer (see pp. 157–75 below). In contrast, his account of the crossing of the VIEE from Alberni to Qualicum is explicitly included to provide "a picture of Indian life—treachery, duplicity, and uncertainty—more graphic than could have been given by the author in any other form."[63]

By the mid-1870s, Brown needed the income that these publications provided. He had been forced to recognize that he would be unable to gain a footing in the academic world, and his need for a steadier income had become more acute. For in 1875, he had married Kristiane Augusta Maria Eleonora Rudmose, the daughter of a teacher who resided at Ferslev, near Copenhagen.[64] The following year, Brown joined the staff of *The Echo* and moved to London. Subsequently, in 1878, he became a member of the editorial staff of *The Standard* (London), and he continued to work on this newspaper until his death in 1895.

It is difficult to feel that Brown's capacities were fully engaged by his works of popular education or by his journalism, and his later years seem to have been those of a disappointed and driven man. According to A.J. Wilson, he was determined that his children would not suffer from financial hardship, and he devoted himself to popular writings to achieve this end.[65] But Brown's youthful energy seems also to have become a debilitating compulsion to work. "He never learned to play," Wilson noted. "To be completely idle for a day even became, latterly, irksome, almost irritating to him. His fingers itched to hold the pen, to handle a book."[66]

In later life, Brown reflected nostalgically on his youthful years on the west coast. In *Countries of the World* (1876–81), for example, his account of the trek from Sooke to Victoria covered about ten pages—the same number in which he treats all of Alaska, Washington, Idaho, and California. Caught between the demands of popular journalism and scholarly reporting, he seems to have recalled with especial pleasure the peacefulness of the region: "It is a true summer morning. All is still."[67] And, a page later, with almost the incantatory power of repetition: "It is still early morning, and few sounds disturb the calm stillness of the solitary scene. The sweet tinkle of the cattle bells, as their owners crop the fern in the woods, strikes our ear through the fog." Working under the constant threat of deadlines, Brown wrote in "Mail Day in the West" of that single day, once a fortnight, when all business stopped and Victorians recognized their link with the world at large. As he recalled that day, however, it was the town's position as a place apart that appealed to him. Similarly, when he reflected on the expedition, memories of hunger, disappointment, and dissension slipped from his mind; it was the camaraderie that he recalled—"the early friendship which united us all [and which] has never been dissolved."[68]

*3 **Robert Brown**, photograph, inscribed on reverse: "Aug. 1874 Copenhagen" (PABC 2396)

Granted the way Brown reflected on his experience on Vancouver Island, it is agreeable to discover that he was not entirely forgotten in Victoria, even almost thirty years after he had left the area. In 1894, a year before his death, he received from Dr. C.F. Newcombe a letter in which Newcombe requested that he send him copies of his articles on British Columbia. Brown was unable to oblige, since he had not systematically kept copies, but he clearly found pleasure in recalling his years on the northwest coast. "There was a time," he replied, "when everything about British Columbia interested me. I passed in that region some of the most instructive years of my early manhood at a time when I did not know six people in it who had any knowledge of or interest in Natural History."[69]

Fittingly, Brown's final, posthumous publication was concerned with Vancouver Island. This contribution consisted of the introduction and explanatory notes for an edition of *The Adventures of John Jewitt* (1896). In this edition Brown drew freely on his own experience on Vancouver Island, almost ninety years after Jewitt had been held captive there. Again, it is the remoteness of the region that Brown contemplated. "A more solitary shore," he reflected, "so far as white men are concerned, it would be hard to imagine."[70] His different journeys seem by this time to have merged in his memory; on the same page, he wrote of spending "part of a pleasant summer in cruising along the western shores of Vancouver Island" (1863) and of his journey into "the still little known, but at that time almost entirely unexplored interior" (1864).[71] But personal reminiscence is also checked by his duties as an editor. In particular, he was concerned to provide details about the so-called "Aht" tribes of the west coast. Indeed, he remarked that his introduction was primarily intended "as a slight contribution to the meagre chronicles of a dying race."[72] Close to death himself, Brown seems to recognize that his life has come full circle. Earlier, as an explorer, he had tended to view things with a glad eye to future development. Now he is content to look back.

NOTES

1 In addition to sources of biographical information cited in subsequent notes, biographies of Robert Brown are contained in the following: *Dictionary of National Biography* 1 (Supplement 1901), 302–3; *Journal of Royal Geographical Society* 6 (1895): 577–8; *Standard* [London], 28 Oct. 1895; and *Times* [London], 29 Oct. 1895. Quotations from Brown's journals, 1863–6 (Brown Collection, I, 17 and II, 1, 2, 3, Provincial Archives of British Columbia [PABC]) are followed in the text by the date in parenthesis.
2 Brown to Henry Cole, 1 Oct. 1868, *Testimonials in Favour of Robert Brown ... Candidate for the Chair of Botany in the Royal College of Science for Ireland* (Edinburgh 1868), iii–iv.
3 *Testimonials*, iii.
4 British Columbia Botanical Association Papers, III, No. 466, Royal Botanic Garden of Edinburgh (RBGE).

5 *Testimonials*, iv. Brown's journal during these voyages is in the Scott Polar Research Institute, Cambridge. His published account of the region is in *The Countries of the World* (London: Cassell, Petter, and Galpin, n.d.), 79–145. This publication first appeared in serial form between 1876 and 1881 (according to the British Library Catalogue). Page references throughout are to an undated edition in my possession.

6 Certificate of Discharge, 16 Dec. 1861, Brown Collection, I, 1, PABC.

7 Minute Book, Botanical Expedition to Oregon, 2nd Expedition, 24 Mar. 1854, RBGE, I. Subsequent difficulties between Brown and the British Columbia Botanical Association may have in part resulted from the Association's earlier disappointment. See J.T. Johnstone, "John Jeffrey and the Oregon Expedition," *Notes from the Royal Botanic Garden Edinburgh* 20 (1949):1–53, and Harold R. Fletcher and William H. Brown, *The Royal Botanic Garden Edinburgh 1670–1970* (Edinburgh: Her Majesty's Stationery Office 1970), 136.

8 Minute of Agreement, RBGE, II, 6.

9 *Testimonials*, iv.

10 Minute of Agreement, RBGE, II, 6. In *Vancouver Island and British Columbia: Their History, Resources, and Prospects* (London: Longman 1865), Matthew Macfie remarked that "in all cases labour commands at least three times the remuneration it does in England, and often much more than that" (499). Among his examples, he listed the monthly wages of bakers (£8–12), butchers (£12–16), and lumbermen(£10).

11 Secretary to Brown, 27 July 1863, RBGE, I, No. 8. References to the secretary's letters to Brown are subsequently indicated in the text by date.

12 *British Colonist* [Victoria], 13 July 1863.

13 Brown to British Columbia Botanical Association, 20 Feb. 1864, RBGE, II, No. 4. References to Brown's letters to the Association are subsequently indicated in the text by date.

14 P. 3. Rattray received second prize for his essay in a contest sponsored by the Colonial Government. (Charles Forbes won the first prize of £50 for his glowing account, *Vancouver Island: Its Resources and Capabilities as a Colony* [Victoria: Colonial Government 1862].)

15 *Journals of the Colonial Legislature*, ed. James Hendrickson (Victoria: Provincial Archives of British Columbia 1980) I, 104.

16 *Journals*, ed. Hendrickson, I, 104.

17 "The Land We Live In," *Victoria Daily Chronicle*, 8 and 10 May 1864. See pp. 29–34 below.

18 Brown Collection, III, 9, PABC.

19 Ibid., I, 3, PABC.

20 "Journey of the Expedition across Vancouver Island," in *Illustrated Travels: A Record of Discovery, Geography, and Adventure*, ed. H.W. Bates (London: Cassell, Petter, and Galpin [1869]), 1, 254, and *Countries of the World*, 274.

21 *Illustrated Travels* 1, 254.

22 For further biographical information, see Helen Bergen Peters, *Painting during the Colonial Period in British Columbia 1845–1871* (Victoria: Maltwood Art Museum 1979), 75–7; Berenice Gilmore, *Artists Overland* (Burnaby: Burnaby Art Gallery 1980), 49, 58–9; Maria Tippett and Douglas Cole, *From Desolation to Splendour: Changing Perceptions of the British Columbia Landscape* (Toronto: Clarke, Irwin 1977), 40–3; and *British Colonist*, 25 Dec. 1901, 6. For a list of drawings made by Whymper on the expedition, see Appendix 2, pp. 205–8 below.

23 See Frances M. Woodward, "The Influence of the Royal Engineers on the Development of British Columbia," *BC Studies* 24 (Winter 1974–5):3–52. It is noted

      there that Meade "appears to have died or left B.C. before Nov. 1907" (45).

24 Leech was the only member of the expedition party who subsequently settled in Victoria. He became manager of the Hudson's Bay Company store in Esquimalt and the city engineer.

25 Brown Collection, III, 9, PABC. (Other applications cited here are from this collection.) Lewis matriculated from Queen's College, Cambridge, Michaelmas term, 1853, and moved to Saint John's College, 29 Jan. 1856. He graduated in 1859 (*Alumni Cantabrigienses* 2, 4 [Cambridge: Cambridge University Press 1951], 162).

26 Alexander Barnston matriculated from McGill University in 1854 (Matriculation Register, Record Group 7, c. 117) and received degrees in Arts in 1857 and Applied Science in 1859 (McGill University, *Directory of Graduates*).

27 *Travel and Adventure in the Territory of Alaska* (London: John Murray 1868), 58.

28 For further information, see *Ranald MacDonald*, ed. William S. Lewis and Naojiro Murakami (Spokane 1923).

29 He was also known as Tomo Omtamy and Thomas Anthony. Governor Douglas referred to him as Thomas William Anthony (and subsequently as Thomas Williams and William Anthony) when intent on describing him as "a British subject settled in the Cowegin Country," after Tomo had been shot in the arm and chest by a Somenos Indian: quoted in W.H. Olsen, *Water over the Wheel* (Chemainus, B.C.: Chemainus Valley Historical Society 1963), 17. Brown's spelling of the name varies, but I have used throughout his most common form: Tomo.

30 *Illustrated Travels* 1, 275.

31 *British Colonist*, 14 Aug. 1863.

32 Tomo had been a member of Adam Horne's expedition from Qualicum to Alberni in 1856 and a member of Pemberton's expedition from Cowichan to Nitinat in 1857. A detailed account of Pemberton's journey is provided by a participant: Captain T. Sherlock Gooch, "Across Vancouver's Island," *Colburn's United Service Magazine* 116 (1886): 517-41 and 117 (1887): 27-40. Of Tomo, Gooch wrote: "About forty-five years old, he was a slight, actively built man, with a dark, copper-coloured face, lit up by keen, intelligent eyes. Although of pure Iroquois blood, he had, by long association, acquired the habits and manners of the halfbreeds . . . By birth an Indian of Lower Canada, he spoke the French dialect of that province well, and also English, and many Indian languages" (524). For further details on these and other expeditions in which Tomo participated, see "The Land We Live In," notes 2 and 4, and *Journal*, notes 54 and 64.

33 *Illustrated Travels* 1, 275.

34 Ibid., 1, 304.

35 Brown Collection, III, 8, PABC.

36 Dispatch No. 3, 3 July 1864, Brown Collection, III, 1, PABC. Subsequent references to Brown's dispatches to the VIEE Committee are indicated in the text by date.

37 Brown Collection, III, 2, PABC.

38 Sir William Gibson Craig to the secretary, 10 Sept. 1864, RBGE, II, Misc. Letters.

39 The final entry in Brown's extant journal is 14 Sept. For an account of his presence at a potlatch near Alberni, see pp. 157-75 below.

40 *The Races of Mankind*, 6 vols. (London: Cassell, Petter, and Galpin 1873), 1, 44.

41 "Memoir on the Geography of the Interior of Vancouver Island" (holograph), Brown Collection, I, 10, 40, PABC.

42 A letter in the *British Colonist* (25 Jan. 1865) remarked: "Can you tell us, Mr Editor, if anything has been done about the coal mines discovered in the settlement by the Government Exploring party? Since Dr. Brown's report we have heard nothing." Applications for mining rights were made by several parties

(Colonial Correspondence, F215, F612, PABC), but these proposals were not carried through.

43 Brown Collection, III, 2, PABC.
44 In his letter of 7 Jan. 1865, Brown described the collection as follows: "47 paper parcels of seeds, 39 cloth sacks, of seeds of forest trees, &c; 1 Bundle dried plants, 3 specimens of wood with invoice and descriptive catalogue of the same." Brown's Edinburgh sponsors were not, however, finally satisfied by his achievement as a seed-collector. In an article entitled "On the Discoveries of Mr. John Jeffrey and Mr. Robert Brown ...," *Transactions of the Botanical Society* [Edinburgh] 11 (1872), it is remarked: "The second mission ... was not so profitable to its promoters as the first; seeds of comparatively few plants were introduced" (333).
45 *Testimonials*, v. For a detailed account of parts of this expedition, see *Countries of the World*, 286–300 and "A Journey across the Cascade Mountains into Eastern Oregon and a Description of Idaho Territory," *Proceedings of the Royal Geographical Society* 11 (1867):84–93.
46 "The Land of the Hydahs," Brown Collection, typed transcript, IV, 1, PABC.
47 Ibid., 32.
48 "At Home among the Koskeemo Indians," *Field Quarterly and Magazine Review* 3 (1871):180.
49 E.T. Coleman, "Mountaineering in the Pacific," *Harper's Magazine* 39 (1869):794. Coleman's successful ascent of Mount Baker in 1868 is described in this article (793–817). See also John Hayman, "Where Flowers Forever Bloom: A Victorian Artist on the West Coast," *The Beaver* 66:2 (1986):27–36.
50 *Testimonials*, vi.
51 Ibid., vii.
52 Ibid., 1.
53 Ibid., 2.
54 Ibid., 15.
55 Ibid., 17.
56 [A.J. Wilson], "In Memory," *The Adventures of John Jewitt* (London: Clement Wilson 1896), 8.
57 Brown Collection, III, 11, PABC.
58 Brown's *Memoir* has not been published in English. The German translation was published as *Das Innere der Vancouver-Insel* in A. Petermann's *Mittheilungen aus Justus Perthes' Geographischer Anstalt* (1869), Jan., pp. 1–10 and Mar., pp. 85–95. On the cover of the holograph, Brown has written: "This is the M.S. from which Dr. Petermann made that trans." (Brown Collection, I, 10, PABC).
59 A Checklist of Brown's publications concerned with the northwest coast may be found in Appendix 1, pp. 201–4 below.
60 pp.ix–xiii.
61 *Adventures of Jewitt* (1896), 8.
62 The title of this story refers to the Indians' belief that they will not be attacked when they hold captive a lost explorer, and they also await a trader from whom they plan to demand payment for their hospitality.
63 *Races of Mankind*, 47.
64 Brown may have met his future wife in 1869 before or after his journey to Greenland. In a letter of 24 Jan. 1870 to Mrs. Fellows, he wrote of his visit to Copenhagen: "I ... almost fell in love with a fair-haired Viking's daughter. Indeed I verily believe I would if I had been rich enough to ask the distinguished old Baron her not over amiable father for his 'one fair daughter & none other child'" (Brown Collection, III, 11, PABC).
65 *Adventures of Jewitt* (1896), 6. Robert Brown's sons attained the academic hon-

ours that the father aimed for: Thomas Rudmose-Brown (1878–1942) was Professor of French at the University of Dublin, and Robert Neal Rudmose-Brown (1879–1957) was Professor of Geography at the University of Sheffield.

66 Ibid., 7.
67 *Countries of the World*, 275.
68 *Illustrated Travels*, 1, 351.
69 Brown to Newcombe, 17 Nov. 1894, Newcombe Family Papers, 46, 2, PABC.
70 *Adventures of Jewitt*, 15.
71 Ibid., 13.
72 Ibid., 28.

I

THE LAND WE LIVE IN

This article by Robert Brown appeared in two parts in the Victoria Daily Chronicle, 8 *and* 10 *May 1864 at a strategic moment—when the VIEE was being organized and a leader was about to be chosen. The article provides a succinct account of what was known of the interior of the island at this time and of Brown's own travels in 1863. Brown acknowledged authorship of the article in a scrapbook which contains a clipping of it* (Brown Collection, I, 2, PABC).

VICTORIA, MAY 4TH, 1864.

Editors Daily Chronicle:—I am glad to see that the desire for a more extensive knowledge of the general features of the interior of this Island is at length assuming a material shape, and that the present season will probably put us in possession of more information regarding its real character than we have hitherto collected from all sources. That the committee may be in a better position to judge which are the points they should first direct their attention to, I will, as shortly as I can, recount what has already been ascertained, and I believe that much of what I shall state is only known to a few persons in the Island, and I think it will be of some interest to nearly all your readers. The members of the committee will certainly be able to expend the funds at their command to more advantage if they first

make themselves acquainted with all that is known regarding the
geography of the partially explored details of the country.

FIRST, it is a very mistaken idea to suppose that the Island has not
been crossed in several places, though indeed our maps seem to have
derived very little benefit from such journey. Commencing from the
South it is unnecessary to speak of the districts lying on the coast,
such as Victoria, Esquimalt, Lake, Metchosin, Highland, Saanich,
Cowichan, etc., all of which, as far as the few miles lying on the
seaboard and eligible for settlement by an agricultural population,
have been either surveyed (more or less by the Government officers)
or investigated by reconoissances sufficiently accurate for all ordinary
purposes, and very much superior to what could be bestowed on the
rest of the Island by any exploring party.[1]

In September, 1857, by command of the late Governor (the then
Mr. Douglas), the present Surveyor General made a journey up the
great Cowichan River to a large lake in the interior [Cowichan Lake],
and from that to the coast, at what is generally known as False
Nitinat.[2] His journey occupied 15 days, though only a short distance
was gone over, so very difficult was the travel, and owing to an
accident damaging some of his instruments, his observations were of
the most trivial nature. Between Somenos Plains and the other large
lake he found many lands eligible for settlement, but requiring to be
cleared; soil good, game, fish and timber; surrounding country of a
cheerful character, and often grand. The same remarks will apply to
the land in the vicinity of the Great Lake. The rest of the district was
for the most part rocky or mountainous. It is worthy of note that
gold-bearing rocks were met with in the mountains, and sandstone,
with small seams of coal in, about Nitinat. He noticed in the inlet one
large cliff of blueish primitive limestone.

This journey has not, as far as I am aware, been made since then by
any individual whose report is unquestioned, and the whole tract is
worthy of renewed and thorough examination.

2. Lieut. Mayne, R.N., crossed the Island a few years ago, when
attached to H.M.S. Hecate, starting somewhere near Barclay Sound
and coming out near Departure Bay.[3] The particulars I have not
before me, but I believe it resulted in nothing of importance—dense
woods and swamps being the general character of the country over
which his journey extended.

3. At the head of the Alberni canal is a trail to Quallicom river, a
little above Nanaimo. This is the best known, and indeed the only one

which can be called a traveled trail. It is frequently crossed by Indians, and by the men at the Alberni mills. It was first traveled by the Hudson Bay Co.'s traders from Nanaimo, and subsequently reported on by Mr. Pemberton.[4] The track is partly by land and partly by water, (Horne's Lake and Quallicom River.) It measures about 18 miles; soil gravelly, and the trail lying for most part through burnt wood. A ridge of mountains occupies the middle of the island here, running in the direction of its length, but not unbroken in their elevation. A better road might be cut to the south of Horne's Lake. It is merely (of course as they all are,) an Indian trail, and impossible to be followed without a guide.

A trail branches off from this to Comox, occasionally passed over by one or two of the Opischesnat [Opetchesaht] Indians, who are married to Comox women, but now more rarely than formerly, a deadly feud existing between the Barclay Sound and Comox and Nanaimo natives—the latter a few years ago having come over the trail, and nearly exterminated three tribes. The triangular piece of country bounded by Pemberton's Cowichan Lake Exploration, the Alberni canal, and the Alberni-Quallicom trail is totally unknown, with the exception of a strip on the coast, comprehending the Nanaimo districts, which has been described roughly in the reports of the Crown Lands Committee, and slightly portrayed on the District maps and the Admiralty charts.[5] Doubtless it is rich in coal and other minerals.

4. Though the one I am about to mention can scarcely be called a *trans-insular* trail, yet as the exploration opened up a large portion of the island hitherto unexamined, it is most worthy of note, and before long will be more fully described in all its minutiae in another place by the explorer, Dr. Robert Brown. He ascended a river at the head of the Alberni canal, and arrived at a many-armed lake [Sproat Lake], about 18 to 21 miles long in its longest axis. At the head of the longest arm, he found it to be fed by a large river,[6] which he ascended for some distance, but had to return through shear starvation. The Indians told him it flowed out of a large lake in the vicinity of the country of the Clayo-quots, and that they sometimes ascended it. They told him that by it Clay-o-quot Sound could be reached in two "Suns." This Lake (a very beautiful one) was for the most part bordered by low lying timbered land, the soil excellent, with good exposure. The river by which he ascended was studded on both banks with the villages of two tribes, the Opis Chesaats and Shes-haats, and bordered by several small prairies, covered with fern, which is a sign of good land. The

river abounds in salmon and beaver. Several large creeks flow in, along the banks of one of which is a large track of good open land, the principal hunting ground of the Indians. This creek would afford good water power for mills of any description. The feeding river flows for a considerable way through flat thickly wooded land, subject to inundations, soil good, timber mostly hemlock, (*Abies Bridgei,*) and Douglas pine, (*Pinus Douglasii*) with a little yew, (*Taxus Lindleyana*). In other places high trap banks. Though the time of the year, in which he discovered it, was the end of June, 1863, yet in many places snow was lying on the ground, not owing to any great elevation of the land, but to its being shaded by snow peaked mountains, very grand, no doubt, but which will not conduce much to its value for settlement. The timber however is very fine, and we believe Messrs. Anderson & Co. of Alberni, intend establishing logging camps both on the river and Lake.[7] He describes some curiously carved rocks in this lake, the work of Indians in remote, halcyon days, before the pale face's axe sounded in their woods.[8] Subsequently he reached what was previously known as the Central lake, by an Indian trail of four miles through open woods, swampy in many places, but so level that a wagon road could be very easily constructed. Last November, on his return from British Columbia, he succeeded in reaching the head of the lake, and found it neither 45 nor 50 miles, as formerly reported by vague Indian report, but only 18.[9] It is fed by a stream, apparently from the mountains, and emptied by a very winding and rapid river, which was named by the Doctor, *Stamp's* river,[10] flowing into the *Somass* river, emptying the first lake, named by him *Sproat's*, or Clecot lake. The banks are steep, rocky, or densely wooded, but in nearly every place so steep that the explorer found it a matter of some difficulty to camp. The timber is indifferent in quality. In fact the "great Central lake" is a great imposition on the good citizens of Vancouver Island. Both lakes have several pretty bays and wooded islands. The shores abound in game, and the waters with trout. They are totally unconnected with each other, and were only dimly and vaguely known previously to this exploration.

From Barclay Sound to the famous Nootka Sound, and from the Nimpish river on the East coast to Quallicum river, nothing is known of this large portion of the island, if we except the thin strip of the Comox (properly "Comoucs") country, and that but vaguely. A line drawn through the centre of this district would run across the widest

portion of this Island, through most of the West and the greater
portion of the Eastern coast would run through a wild uninhabited
region of mountainous appearance. Falling into the Tlupana arm of
Nootka Sound, is a river, following which in a north-easterly direction, travellers come to a lake (Lake Kanus) where the outlying fishing villages of the Nimpish Indians are situated. Falling out of this is
a rapid river, falling again into a lake (T'sllelth), which empties itself
by the Nimpish river, a little south of Fort Rupert. This exploration
was made in 1852 by Mr. Moffatt, an officer in the Hudson Bay Co.,
(now in charge of Fort Simpson, B.C.) but seems to be almost forgotten, and not entered on any official map, (with the exception of one by
Mr. Pemberton).[11] He found no land untimbered. The lumber was
however, observed to be of the finest description, and there being
abundant water privileges, spars could be floated down to the sea
without difficulty, a fact worthy of noting, at a time when spars are
not to be had in such abundance as formerly; and there being now
such a demand for them, every year is decreasing their number. He
heard a report of a tribe of Indians, called the Saa-Kaalicks, living on
a river near his track, and from the report being so circumstantial and
having been subsequently repeated, there appears to be no doubt of
the report being true. From their accounts of the Southern Indians
having been to war against them, he supposes a trail right through
the Island to near Victoria. Will no bold spirit settle it?

Nootka Island is said to be very finely watered, though hitherto no
one has cared to penetrate it. There is a quantity of good open land
round Friendly cove and the Indians report copper in the vicinity.
Notwithstanding the great excitement which once arose regarding
this harbour, and that the possession of it long ago almost created a
war between England and Spain, it has nearly died out of the memory
of the people.

6. Another trail (water nearly all the way) connects this (?) and
lands you at Kai-o-quot Sound, north of Nootka. This was traveled by
Lieut. Hankin and Dr. Wood, R.N.[12]

7. The Inlet of Koskeemo penetrates to within a few miles of the
other side of the Island, the remaining land distances being from 8 to
10 miles, mostly through swamps, and very unpleasant to travel
through, from this point to Cape Scott and Nimpish. Nothing is
known of the interior, though there is a probability now that Stewart
& Co. have commenced working their mills at Koskeemo,[13] and a

company have opened coal mines in McNeil's harbour,[14] that something more may be known by this time next year.

Such is a short outline of the principal facts in reference to our sea girt home. I have discussed them under the heads transinsular trails, as affording highways (rude, forsooth, but explorers must not be fastidious,) for more particular explorations to branch off from, and from the tops of the mountains round which, as from as many Pisgahs, the explorers might observe the country at their feet.

I have not spoken of the numerous smaller Indian paths, which might be termed "private trails," such as the one from Grappler Creek, in Barclay Sound, to Cape Beal, &c.; nor yet of the numerous lakes, which, by Indian report, fill every valley, and out of which a hundred streams flow. In a country difficult to be traveled, these lakes will yet form valuable means of communication, and in explorations, would form easy and useful inlets to the country, independent of the value which would result from the geographical exploration of them.

To mention them, would be to go over every district in the Island. For sake of illustration a few may be noticed. Off Stamp's River, there is said to be a large lake. Again, in Nahumet Bay, Alberni Canal, a river flows, on which the *Ucluluets* have a fishing village in the autumn, and is affirmed to flow out of a large lake.[15] In *Ouchleclousit* [Uchucklesaht] Harbor, off the same inlet, a little river flows (not over a hundred yards in length), out of a large lake, or perhaps chain of lakes, connecting with the one in the vicinity of Nahumet Bay.[16] Again, in Na-muk-amis Bay, in Barclay Sound, the river which flows in the bay through Sarita Valley is said to empty a lake [Sarita Lake]. Indeed, 9/10ths of the streams in this country and British Columbia flow out of lakes, which are in their turn fed by other streams. You cannot ascend a mile without looking down upon many a quiet lake in the valley not expected to exist, and I have no doubt but that Vancouver Island will be found to be one congerie of lakes and streams, affording excellent water power.

Apologising for the space which I have occupied in your columns, I will only add, that in furnishing this information I have no private object to serve. I am anxious to see a well organized expedition sent out, and even should I be a member of the party, it will be as a volunteer and not as a salaried servant.

Yours,
                GEOGRAPHICUS

NOTES

1 Colonel Walter Colquhoun Grant became the first surveyor on Vancouver
   Island for Hudson's Bay Company in 1849, but he made only a rudimentary
   survey of the Company's holdings in the vicinity of Victoria. He was succeeded in 1851 by Joseph Despard Pemberton (1821-93). In 1858, Pemberton became the Colonial Surveyor, and from 1860 to 1864 he was Surveyor-
   General of Vancouver Island. In these capacities he was responsible (together
   with B.W. Pearse) for the surveys Brown notices here. See also W.E. Ireland,
   "Pioneer Surveyors of Vancouver Island," *Report of Proceedings of 46th
   Annual General Meeting of Corporation of B.C. Land Surveyors* (1951):47-
   51.
2 In *Facts and Figures Relating to Vancouver Island and British Columbia*
   (London: Longman 1860), J.D. Pemberton published his letter to Governor
   Douglas (dated 12 November 1857), under the title "From Cowichan Harbour to Nitinat" (149-50).
3 Commander R.C. Mayne, "Route in Exploring a Road from Albernie Canal
   to Nanaimo, in Vancouver Island, in May, 1861, with a Track Chart," *Journal
   of Royal Geographical Society* 32 (1862): 529-35.
4 See W.W. Walkem, "Adam Horne's Trip across Vancouver Island [1856],"
   Stories of Early British Columbia (Vancouver: New Advertiser 1914), 37-51.
   J.D. Pemberton's account of his own crossing—to which Brown is indebted
   here—is included in *Facts and Figures*, 147-8.
5 The Committee on Crown Lands was established by the colonial legislature
   on 18 September 1863 (*Journals*, ed. Hendrickson, 3.13). Brown included
   newspaper clippings concerned with the committee in his journal. Brown
   may also refer here to Oliver Wells, *Vancouver's Island: Survey of the Districts of Nanaimo and Cowichan Valley* (London: Groombridge 1859).
6 Brown named this river after a member of the expedition party: Charles
   Taylor. According to Captain John T. Walbran, Taylor was "the first settler
   who essayed, in 1863-1864, to start a homestead on the left bank of the
   Somass" (*British Columbia Coast Names 1592-1906* [1909; Vancouver:
   Douglas & McIntyre 1971], 15).
7 In 1862, Anderson & Company, a British company, formally took over the
   mills at Alberni. By early 1863 there was concern about the amount of
   accessible timber in the region, and the operation extended to Sproat Lake.
   Despite this extension, the mill ceased operation during the winter of 1864-
   5. See also W. Kaye Lamb, "Early Lumbering on Vancouver Island. Part II:
   1855-1866," *B.C. Historical Quarterly* 2 (1938): 95-121.
8 See Beth and Ray Hill, *Indian Petroglyphs of the Pacific Northwest* (Seattle:
   University of Washington Press 1974), 120-1.
9 B.W. Pearse had reported to the Committee on Crown Lands (30 November
   1863) that Great Central Lake was "some thirty miles long." Brown included
   a clipping of this newspaper report in a scrapbook, and he added marginally:
   "The 'Central Lake' I have been to the head of it. It is only about 18 Miles
   long" (Brown Collection, I, 1, 47). Earlier in "Mr. Robert Brown's Botanical
   Expedition to British Columbia," Brown had himself described Great Central Lake as forty-five miles long (*The Scottish Farmer*, 7 Oct. 1863). In his
   scrapbook, he added the notation: "On the information of Capt. Stamp. Not
   so—only 18 miles" (Brown Collection, I, 16, 83-8).
10 Edward Stamp (1814-72) arrived on the northwest coast in 1857 and established sawmills at Alberni in 1860. For further details, see *Dictionary of*

Canadian Biography 10 (Toronto: University of Toronto Press 1972), 664.

11 Hamilton Moffatt, "Journal of a Tour across Vancouver Island to Nootka Sound via Nimkish River in the Year 1852," in Pemberton, *Facts and Figures*, 143-7.

12 "Exploration of Lieut. Hankin and Dr. Wood of H.M.S. *Hecate*, from Kyuquot Inlet on the West Coast, to Nimkish River, Fort Rupert," *British Colonist* [Victoria], 13 Dec. 1862.

13 In a report, "From Quatsino," the recent visit of W.R. Meldrum of Stewart, Meldrum & Company is noted, and the establishment of a settlement in the region is also described (*British Colonist*, 28 Feb. 1863). However, there is no record of a mill in Lamb, "Early Lumbering on Vancouver Island," 31-53 and 95-121.

14 Coal had been discovered at Suquash, near Port McNeill in 1835 (Walbran, *British Columbia Coast Names*, 393). Brown later remarked that the Hudson's Bay Company had once mined it, and that following an inactive period another company planned to develop the mine ("On the Geographical Distribution and Physical Characteristics of the Coal-Fields of the North Pacific Coast," *Transactions of the Geological Society* [Edinburgh] (1869): 13).

15 In October 1864, a contingent from VIEE explored Nahmint River and Lake. They had been told that Sproat and Johnston had earlier ascended the river but had not reached the lake, and they subsequently saw the tree blazed on 2 September 1863 by these explorers.

16 In a scrapbook, Brown noted: "Capt. Henderson (March 9/64) has just discovered a large lake at head of Ouchilouchilesch Harbour emptied by a River a few yards long" (Brown Collection, I, 16, 162, PABC). A contingent from VIEE explored the lake in 1864, and Brown subsequently named it Henderson Lake.

2

JOURNAL of the
VANCOUVER ISLAND
EXPLORING EXPEDITION 1864

Brown intended that his journal should provide the VIEE Committee and the colonial authorities with a more detailed account of the expedition than was possible in his dispatches. In addition, he used it to justify his actions. Meticulously, he explained his choice of routes and his practice of dividing the group into separate parties—and on at least one occasion, when challenged by Indians about colonial intrusion, he even seems intent on displaying his loyalty to colonial values. The journal was not, however, simply written for the VIEE Committee and the ruling order. Brown also seems to have recognized that it would be useful as a basis for his intended publication concerned with the exploration. His "Memoir on the Geography of the Interior of Vancouver Island" (1868) is, in fact, a radically abridged version of his journal, without the immediacy, vivid detail, and personal reflections of the journal.

On completion of the expedition, Brown's journal and those of other expeditionary members were deposited with the Colonial Secretary, and Brown seems also to have had copies made of the five notebooks containing his journal. As it happened, this was a fortunate precaution, since only Volume I of the original journal has survived. This volume, stamped "Library, Legislative Assembly, Victoria, B.C.," is now in the PABC (Brown Collection, ADD MS 794, III, 10), and it provides the text here for the period it covers (7–20 June). For the remainder of the expedition, I have used the copy. This copy, together with the journals of other members of the expedition, and

Map 1 Vancouver Island
published with translation
of Robert Brown's *"Memoir
of the Geography of the
Interior of Vancouver
Island"*

*much additional material relating to Brown, was acquired by the
PABC in 1960, when it was purchased from H.E. Heinemann of
Montreal, who had apparently received it from Brown's sister.*

*Brown has noted on the title-page of Volume I of the transcribed
version that it is a "true copy," and there are indications of correc-
tions that he made in it and even a notation that he could not understand the transcript at one point. However, a comparison of the copy
with the section of the original that has survived reveals that Brown
did not read the copy with consistent care, since errors of transcrip-
tion remain. I have occasionally emended the copy when it seems that
the copyist is responsible for some error in spelling. Enough of
Brown's writing exists in holograph for one to be confident that he
knew how to spell, and there is no reason to impose his copyist's
failings on him. Brown's own inconsistencies in spelling have been
retained without comment, when no obscurity results from them, but
I have regularized some variously spelt proper names (e.g., Macdonald and Tomo). Current spellings of place-names—together with
all other additions—are presented within square brackets. Angle
brackets indicate passages in either the original or the copy which
have been crossed out by Brown.*

*Brown's punctuation is often imprecise. He uses commas, dashes,
and periods indiscriminately. I have retained his frequent uses of the
dash, since this seems to suggest the pace of his writing, but I have
introduced periods at the close of sentences. To avoid confusion, I
have also sparingly added a comma, a dash, or an apostrophe at
points when Brown's haste has apparently resulted in his omitting
them, and I have also rendered in full most of his abbreviations.*

VANCOUVER ISLAND EXPLORING EXPEDITION

Tuesday June 7 [1864]. Everything now in readiness & the gunboat in
the harbour. Set off in HMS "Grappler" Lieut Verney[1] at 12 o'clock. A
considerable number of people assembled to witness our departure.
His Excellency Gov. Kennedy[2] rode down. Drew the men up in a row
& addressed them briefly—enjoining upon them now the eyes of the
whole Colony, soon of all America, would be upon them. Much was
looked for from them & to do so there must be first implicit obedience to their Commander for nowhere more than in camp were the
qualities of men tested unless indeed it be in a ship. "You have all

been selected for your individual & personal qualities. See not that we are deceived in you. I am glad to see such enterprize in this colony. Mr. Brown & gentlemen, I wish you God speed, and that you may return all safe crowned with the glorious laurels of a bold successful traveller." We immediately went on board, and many were the shakes of hands we got, & as we slowly steamed out of the harbour we were cheered & repeatedly cheered by the crowd until our scarlet shirted body disappeared around Arbutus covered Ogden Point.

Weather very wet. Arrived at Cowichan: anchored near Harris House at 6 p.m. very wet & miserable. Went ashore immediately with Mr. Barnston. Saw Harris who is a sort of Indian agent.[3] He was rather drunk. Talked about Journey. Not very sober in his ideas. Immense liar. Spoke about drills. Found he [had] none suitable, only a small hammer & crowbar, but have with us a sharp chisel and heavy hammer which will do as we cannot develop mines—only test—& if miners wish they can send a regularly equipped party afterwards. On coming on board found some things had got damaged. Repaired them. Saw also Jean Lemon a French voyageur who keeps "Cowichan Hotel."[4] Saw a map drawn by the notorious Iroquois "Tomo" of the Great Lake.[5] Talked with him [Jean Lemon] and his pretty half-breed daughter until 10. Pulled on board by Mr. Ladler[6] calling in at Harris on way for some things. Very wet. Slept in a sort of Box above Engine room with Barnston.

Wednesday June 8 [1864]. Very wet this morning. Indians from Roman Catholic Mission, sent by Bishop Demers[7] who came up with us, came to take us to Somenos, but so very wet that wishing to make at least a fair start I told them to go back & come back early tomorrow morning if fair & they did not previously see me at the Mission. Secured Flour bags—two in each of the drill bags I got made—overhauled things & of course like all expeditions something wanting, but worst of all through no neglect of mine, though I had been assured that they had been put on board, the two large axes, 20 lb of biscuit and portion of our salt had been omitted.[8] Weather clearing up a little. Employed in making tracings of several maps in Mr. Verney's possession. Requested Lieut. Leech to make arrangements for Camp. Appointed Foley cook until Sunday. Mr. Whymper took a sketch of the Bay. Most of the Indians (Clemandots) [Clemclemaluts] are now absent getting game up in the Saanich & Victoria neighbourhood. There are two hotels—rough log shanties. Harris, a sort of Indian Agent, keeps one—Jean Lemon (the best one), the other. All out of supplies awaiting the arrival of the "Lady Franklin." Most of the settlers appear to be quite contented & determined to see it out while others are quite enthusiastic & sanguine.

The natives have much decreased, as indeed everywhere. The Catholic Priest has much influence. In talking of the fading away of the Indians, Bishop Demers told me that when he came to Oregon in 1838, the Chinooks were a very powerful tribe & their great chief Concomoly[9] was just dead. (His grandson Macdonald is one of our party.) The Cowlitz were also very powerful.[10] Now there are perhaps not one of the Chinooks. The Cowlitz are totally extinct. Once the chief of the Cayuse & his brother had 2000 horses.[11] The old man delights to tell the strange stories of his early work and still remembers the names of all the old chiefs & famous men.

In afternoon landed, and [purchased] supplies which had been omitted in our supplies & each man's individual kit. For instance the man with the longest hair had forgot his comb & the dirtiest faced his soap. I obtained from Harris: 1 Bar Soap, 2 Axes, 1 Cap Bag, Bullets for Indians—in all $ 5. for which I gave a bill on Mr. Franklin,[12] as I was anxious to save up the cash I had with me for more urgent occasions. Went along to Lemon's with Whymper. Took a tracing of Tomo's map of the Great Lake "Kaatsa" [Cowichan Lake]. Lieut. Verney with his boat's crew & my men in another boat with stores pulled ashore. I went ahead with Verney. Entered one of the many mouths by which the Cowichan River empties itself into the sea, & landed at M. Jean Campagnon's.[13] We were received by the venerable old gentleman, a great friend of Capt. Verney's. Saw through his garden. He had only been here two years and yet what had formerly been a wild desert was now in such a state of cultivation that it was difficult to suppose ourselves in one of the wildest of the wild districts of Vancouver Island. He had about 100 acres under cultivation & the soil was of the very richest quality—in fact he told us would grow anything. What surprised us most was Oregon grapes (*Berberis* <*Aquifolium*> Bulbonnana) in his garden & the vicinity sometimes 6, 8, and one 12 feet high with stems <averaging> varying 4 to 8 inches in diameter.[14] Beet roots he was growing for sugar & considered the climate & soil remarkably suitable for it. He presented us with some fine Cowichan grown tobacco & considered that the whole valley might be planted with it, with immense profit to the cultivator.[15] His garden was arranged into terraces & bowers with shady seats & all spick & clean. Everything seemed to have been in the same state for

4 Frederick Whymper, *Comiaken—from M. Jean Compagnon's Garden* (Yale Collection of Western Americana, Beinecke Rare Book and Manuscript Library). The wooden mission church on the hill was built in 1859. A decade later it was replaced by a stone church which recently has been restored and converted into a cultural centre.

years. We pitched our tents in a field adjoining his garden—& to our supper he added some trout, raddishes & onions, in which he joined. Scenery very fine—Mount Prevost in the distance with Indian village & Church on the Hill.[16] Behind lay the shores dotted with settlements.

[Thursday] June 9 [1864]. Up at 5 o'clock—& shortly afterwards visited by Capt Verney on his way on a fishing excursion to Quamichan lake. Saw a very old Indian Locha formerly Chief of the Comiaken village.[17] When Bishop Demers saw him first 24 years ago, he seemed as old as he is now. Is said to be 100 years old. Famous warrior. About 15 years ago the Northern Indians attacked his camp and committed much havock. He retaliated by stratagem, on their return afterwards. Hearing that they were about landing, he concealed about 200 Comiakens in the bush—& his son Sam wrapped

himself up like a squaw in a canoe on the shore. The Stickeens[18] immediately landed to capture him for a slave. He ran into the bush. The Stickeens fell into the trap and were killed to a man—150 in all. The Comiaken villages of which there are three now number about 100 people.[19] Nearly all are baptized.

The Indians are complaining of the conduct of the whites. They say "You came to our country. We did not resist you—you got our women with children & then left them upon us—or put them away when they could have no children to keep up our race (a fact or nearly amounting to as much). You brought diseases amongst us which are killing us. You took our lands and did not pay us for them. You drove away our deer & salmon & all this you did & now if we wish to buy a glass of firewater to keep our hearts up you will not allow us. What *do* you white men wish?" This is in part very true. The Indians have not been treated well by any means. There is continually an empty boast that they are British subjects, but yet have none of the privileges or the right of one. Their lands have never been paid for in these districts at least.[20] They are not taxed nor yet vote. They are confined in their villages to certain places. Nor are any means taken to protect their rights of fishing & hunting & yet if an Indian kills another in obedience to their laws of chivalry & right he is immediately taken up to Victoria. Witness the case of How-a-matcha in Victoria regarding whom the Indians are in a great state of excitement & doubtless if hung there will be a disturbance with the Indians.[21]

Had Compagnon at Breakfast, & the old man has been very kind to us indeed. After breakfast called with Whymper on the Rt. Revd. Bishop Demers about an Indian Hunter—one-armed Tomo an Iroquois whom we were recommended to engage in that capacity. Tomo was at Maple Bay but his Lordship advised me to engage no regular hunter as game was so plentiful that there would be no difficulty in our procuring all the game we wanted. Besides our Indian guides & packers would all hunt without expense to the Expedition. I therefore for this trip engaged no regular hunter. The worthy Bishop on departing blessed the Expedition and pressed on us a small present of some nice butter—the last we would get for a long time. Through his kindness I obtained an Indian Boy Baptiste "Lemon" who understood English very well, the son of the old Comiaken Chief "Locha" [and] cousin of the present chief, as general guide & canoe man. He had been at the great Lake (Kaatsa) in 1860.

Though the weather was very stormy I was anxious to make a start

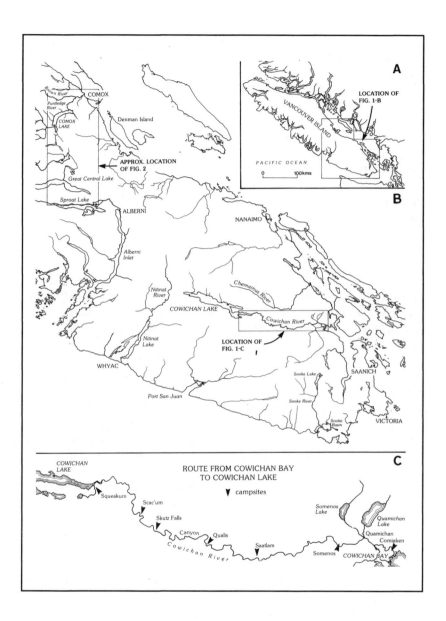

Map 2a Vancouver Island
2b South Vancouver Islandd
2c Route from Cowichan Bay to Cowichan Lake

so I engaged two Indians & a canoe to take our provisions &c up to the Somenaw (or as it is written on the maps but erroneously Somenos) village while we proposed to walk over the trail. But now commenced the tug of war about pay. I had been prepared to have to pay them high wages for several reasons. (1) Poling is very hard & dangerous work frequently resulting in the swamping of the canoe. (2) The Indians are few now & busily engaged in obtaining clams, gammass[22] & sea salmon. (3) Their natural inclination [not] to stir from home, wife & children. Besides at present they are all anxious to see the end of the How-a-matcha business. (4) The river is swift & there are many portages. We found as there was with us a prestige of coming in a man of war we had also to pay man of war price—& that the regular price was 2 dollars a day for each man[23]—& though I stuck out to the last & refused until I saw that I could not obtain them—I was forced to give it. Added to this a patriarchal savage threatened (from the other side of the River—it may be remarked en passant) to shoot, because I would not pay for the canoe, which he said was his—& even jumped into the River to effect his threat—but finding his bravado had no effect on me he quietly sneaked off to his lodge & when we landed was nowhere to be seen. Accordingly put Mr. Foley in charge—with the two Indians—in the canoe with baggage up the river [and] started with Mr Lemon over the Nanaimo trail[24] for Somenos. The old Frenchman ferried us over the river in two parties and as we ascended the bank we gave him a deafening cheer.

The trail was very good, fit for the passage of a waggon. We passed one or two settlers' log-cabins & out of one of them the worthy Bishop protruded his jovial face—and gave us a God speed. We cheered him & passed on. The Settlers came running out to look at our long single file & shouted good luck to us. The soil in the woods very good—fine spars & a little cedar and hemlock. After about two miles we came to the Quamichan Indian Village upon the Cowichan River, consisting of twenty or thirty scattered lodges on each side of the river.[25] They gathered out to take a look at the white pioneers of those who are to drive them from their fathers' hunting grounds. They have now vastly decreased. An Indian [illegible] tells me that he does not think there are more than 1500 in the Cowichan Valley composing Clemenclats, Taikos, Chemin &c &c. Three years ago a census was made of all the Indians in the Nanaimo district & Cowichan Valley & the whole (men, women & children) was only 2500.[26] Now they would number much less. There is a quantity of good open land here. Capital soil. River very swift here and cannot be ascended without poling. We noticed Indians in front of village pushing their canoes ahead in front of them. About a mile from the village is a small prairie of 20 acres of open land surrounded by woods, soil good, dark loam.

About a mile further we came to the Indian camp of Somenos on the River,[27] situated in a lovely place embosomed among alders. The whole population with the exception of about a dozen old women & children were absent gathering clams to dry for winter use and gammass in the district round Victoria, particularly a place near Mr. Yale's on the Saanich Road called "Tummas."[28] The old Chief Kakalatza was at home & gave me this information. He is a queer looking old man with a tuft of hair on his chin & wears a "stove" pipe hat when dressed in state.[29] He is about the only hunter in his tribe. They are a very lazy set, only laboring to get a bare sufficiency of fish food, and only caring to work if they get high wages. (Camp No. 2.) The old chief goes regularly every Autumn to the great Lake to dry meat, & is thoroughly acquainted with the whole neighbouring country. Here again was the same sad tale of "fading away."

Alas for them their day is o'er
Their fires are out from shore to shore
No more for them the wild deer bounds
The plough is on their hunting grounds
The white man's sail is on their flood
The white man's axe is in their wood
Their pleasant springs are dry
Their children look by power oppressed
Beyond the mountains of the West
Their children look to die

5 Frederick Whymper, **Kakalatza and His Hat-Box** (Yale Collection of Western Americana, Beinecke Rare Book and Manuscript Library)

"But you have not all surely gone to the fishing at the salt water?" I
said. "You had once a great number of warriors in your village." "My
women," he said, "have gone to the salt water, my young men are
here—three are at the great lake hunting & fishing, two are in Victoria, but most are gone away. When they go there they never return
again." I felt sorry for the old man as he pointed amid the bushes to
some carved figures marking the last camping place of the warriors of
Somenaw!

I have mentioned Kakalatza as chief but since as in the Indian
tribes near the white settlements the old distinctions gained by prowess in war have ceased, it is difficult to say who are chiefs. It is now the
man who has most blankets. There are several other chiefs but the
principal one is Jean Baptiste (so baptised for they are all in name at
least Roman Catholics) but is in Victoria.

The great Chief of the Cowichans used to be Thosieten[30] whose
prowess as warrior was sung along the sea board for many a long
league and still lives in the memory of the neighbouring tribes whose
terror he was. In "piping times of peace" he lived on an island <in one
of the many mouths of the Cowichan River> ("Indian Island") in a
village surrounded with pickets and bastions out of which there
peeped three large sized cannon. Blind & helpless, childless & power-
less, last of his name, he still lives in his ruined fort, with only the
dim recollection of his deeds of prowess! Sic transit gloria Mundi.

We selected as our camping place (Camp No. 2) an exposed place
near River. Put up the tent we had along [with] us and settled
ourselves down to wait the arrival of the canoe with the provisions, in
which we were kept company by the whole village. The members of
which squatted down in front of our camp chattering & making lazy
remarks upon everybody and everything while our boy Lemon gave
them an account of how we came in the little man of war, & all about
us what he knew, and what he did not know but only thought he did.
About 5 p.m. [the] canoe arrived with Foley; [he] describes River as
very swift & had to make one portage, poling the whole way. Found 5
colours to the pan on a bar below Somenos. Wrote short note to
Cruickshanks[31] (V I Exploration Committee) by return Indians.

Later in the evening "One armed Tomo" (his name is "Toma Antoine" or "Thomas Anthony") of mixed Iroquois & Chinook origin
but undistinguishable from a half breed, & noted as a linguist &
hunter, arrived at our camp. He had heard that Ranald Macdonald—
whom he had known in early days at Fort Langley—was in our party

& posted in haste after him. He is now rather a notorious character and from report mingled with feelings of a personal animosity to him from causes which it is unnecessary to speak here, I had resolved not to take him on the Expedition, in any capacity. He was at one [time] high in favour with Governor Douglas whose constant factotum he was on every expedition. He served for some time in the H B Company in several capacities, as guide, hunter, and interpreter in all of which capacities he stands unrivalled. Of late months he has got into disrepute & suffers by the reputation. Last summer he was employed as interpreter by the Expedition against the Lamalcha murderers[32] and shortly after his return his wife was found dead in the cottage on a farm in Saanich which Govr. Douglas gave him (promising to pension him off). Tomo was hauled up for it but acquitted for want of evidence & since then he has been in bad repute, for excepting this stain on his character coupled with the rather venial offence of being somewhat obstreperous in his cups, no one can bring any serious offence against him. Give a dog a bad name & you may as well hang him at once, unless indeed he may be a remarkably good dog hereafter which he has very little chance of accomplishing—& so with Tomo. I have stated the above particulars in defence of what follows for I know there is a strong prejudice against [him] & some whose feelings like my own go against him may think it might have been better to have left him behind. He had just returned from the great Lake & appeared to be well acquainted with the surrounding country & as our journey promised to be an intricate and difficult one, with the best assistance, I did not think I would be performing my duty to the people, if I allowed my private feelings to stand in the way of engaging one who promised to be of such use to [us]. Moreover I found that Indians could not be had below $2 a day & with difficulty at that. Besides, few understood any Chinook or English while Tomo spoke English without an accent, besides understanding nearly every Indian language on the Island. At his own request I entered into negotiations agreeing to take him as hunter, guide and canoe man, at $1.50 per day—for such time as I might choose to take him. Besides let his character be as bad as possible (though it is only such under the influence of whiskey & we have none) we are not a reformer founding Expedition & if we investigated by as close a standard the character of any of our Indians as we have Tomo's I am afraid it would be a long time before the VIEE would reach the coast & a few very namby pamby priest-ridden scoundrels we would get. Through his assistance

I managed after a long talk with his people to engage, for such time as I choose, bounded by the country he was acquainted with, Kakalatza the chief at $2 per diem—and the promise of a cultus potlatch[33] if he behaved very well—& $1 per day for the use of his large canoe until we got to the Lake after which we reserved the right of striking a new Bargain. At the same time I engaged the boy Lemon who had also been at the Lake, & was accounted a good poler for the same time at $1. after heavy talking & bargaining. The other Indians (always great nuisances the making bargains with other Indians for if they do not go themselves they are sorry to see their neighbours get anything & accordingly take these means to prevent them going) told him not to be a slave to work for $1.00 a day, that nobody but Stickeens would take that. We were chiefs of King George[34] they said & if cultus men did pay as much surely we ought, an argument somewhat lost on me. When I shut them up by telling them that the Bishop told that they wrought for him for $1/2 per day—they answered me that when they wrought for the Bishop or Priest they did not wish for pay—the old policy of the Catholic Missions. This with Tomo made our number 12 men. I found that some Whites who had wished to ascend the River before had to camp three days here before they could get any Indians to go for less than $2 per Day & had finally to return, though the canoe was their own.

Friday June 10th [1864]. Sent the canoe with Tomo, Kakalatza, Lemon, in charge of Mr. Buttle, up the River with the provisions, appointing an Indian fishing village called Saatlaam as the rendezvous, the exact situation of which had been described to me by Tomo & said to be reached by tolerably good Indian trail. To lighten the canoe each of us took our personal [belongings] though this was somewhat compensated by the amount of personal baggage Kakalatza took—amongst others his hat and incredible to say a hat case to hold it which he had got from some young Englishman who had "gone through the mill" in Cowichan since the <banyan> halcyon days of Regent Street. His villagers gathered out to see him off. He wished to take one of his young men with me but I declined.

With the rest of the party I started off, taking with us an Indian boy Selachten to put us on the trail. Part of our road was on the Nanaimo trail through shady woods: timber good—pine, cedar, hemlock & maple. Crossing a stream where coal is said to be found we passed the Drinkwaters' ranch—the last tangible trace of Civilization. It is at the base of Mt. Prevost ("Smaent Swuchas") (Smaent a

Mountain). He has perhaps 30 or 40 acres cleared, but upon the whole it is a somewhat forlorn looking place. I believe he has horses.[35] On a creek a little further up, <coal> gold has been found in paying quantity it was said by Mr Jas. Langley who prospected it in company with Harris & Durham in 1860,[36] but we now know better what pay [is] in placer diggings & I am assured by Harris that it would not pay. It yielded according to our washing about 8 colours to the pan, but I have no doubt but that more could be got.

At the corner of the ranch the trail struck out to the left into the woods, then along elevated ridge—trail good, soil stony until trail forked, right hand branch going to the "mowitch illale" (Chinook— "deer trail"), left our trail. The boy described it to me minutely & returned with a present of tobacco. After losing the trail frequently and tearing our hands & feet through thick undergrowth of crabapple & raspberries (*Rubus spectabilis*)[37] growing in swamp and sides of creek, we emerged in an open prairie thickly covered with fern and dotted with clumps of trees. The grouse flew up in every direction. A Creek flows through middle of it. In one corner was the commencement of a log house which had apparently been given up. The trail had been blazed until the middle of the prairie plain. Here we lost it & after many vain attempts to find it again which nearly exhausted the patience of the boys, I ordered a break to be made for the river by the East end of the Prairie, thinking that it would take us nearest to the River & soon we struck the trail. Crossed several creeks, passed two small lakes on the left overgrown with water lillies, and after about 1/4 hours travel heard crack of rifle, and soon emerged into a fine open space surrounded by green trees—poplars, cottonwood (*Balsam Salicaceae*), alder, and pine (*Abies Douglasii*) [Douglas Fir]—with a couple of deserted Indian lodges. Our canoe had arrived & our fire blazing cheerfully, Mr Buttle baking bread & Tomo skinning a fine deer he had just killed—a good look out for that indispensable of travel "grub." Saatlam meaning the place of green leaves is inhabited by one or two of Kakalatza's people in winter for hook nosed salmon fishing,[38] and a few graves near showed it to be occasionally a resting place also.

Mr. Buttle reports river still very swift. A creek on left hand side with coal. It crops out on banks in a thin scalelike cropping & is continually lost again, about 1/2 inch in thickness. Perhaps a continuation of Harris Mine on the Koksala River (which does not flow out of the Shawnigan Lake). One house, a fishing station called Isaam on

left hand side a little below Saatlaam. (Isaam means the place where
something has been torn off, as in skinning an animal. What is the
meaning we could not learn, as it was named in days long gone by, by
the old people from something they could not understand, just like
places in our own country.) No portages—no opportunity of making
intended observations as much too busy; if they missed their hold
once, down went the canoe.

Moonlight night—late to rest—stood round the camp fire listening
to Tomo's description of Indian astronomy and was struck with it as
similar to the Arabian in the similitudes they draw between constella-
tions and known objects. The handles of the plow are two men in a
canoe, the pleiades are a collection of fishes, Four stars (The Plow?)
are an elk. The Moon they think travels and has a frog inside of it (Is
this worse than our Man in the Moon?) The stars are little people.[39]
A strange people are these Indians. The more you know of them the
more can you appreciate their shrewdness—the curious store of lore
and traditions they possess; to judge them as you see them "loafing"
about the white settlements is like judging a man by the coat on his
back. Few ever take the trouble to learn about them and still fewer
know anything bad about them tho' loudest in their general dogmatic
denunciation of them.

Saturday June 11th [1864]. Up at 6 a.m. What! think ye Victorians of
our camp fare, Roast Shoulder of Venison, Rump Steaks, grouse stew
with bacon and grouse eggs & hot cakes and coffee with a little of the
worthy Bishop's butter. We could have added trout from the stream,
gammas and wild onions from the woods, and a crane[40] that went
screeching or rather creaking over our heads but they are unblessedly
tough. I take all a traveller's pleasure in relating our "square" meal to
contrast with the banyon days of *Sans bread, sans Bacon, sans beans,
sans everything* but a stomach [is] very easily dispensable to a
traveller.

As we required to make several halts to cross the river and assist at
portages I took Tomo with us & put Barnston & Foley in the canoe
with the two Indians. After leaving camp No. 3 we passed for nearly a
mile through a fine natural park dotted with clumps of pine tree, soil
in general good, in other places rather stony, but fit for pasturage—
enclosed by pine woods & separated by a small strip from the river.
We then passed by beaten trail (Indian) into pine woods—bad travelling—soil poor & pine occasionally tall but thin. This is backed by a
rising ground on which there is a plateau—soil good & very thinly

covered with ([*pinus*]*monticola*) white pine. In the course of the day our route lay for the most part by the river side—very bad travelling—very nearly all the time through the bush & having to cross the River frequently up to the knees. The River is one continual series of bends to cut off which under Tomo's guidance we made many short cuts, made two portages over rafts of logs, which stem up the River in many places. Passed on right hand side a curious mountain known by the Indians as Shella—a name which will not bear translation.[41] It is called so from its form. This is the commencement of a range of hills about 2000 ft. high; which with few breaks encompass North side of great lake. At the base of it at North side are two log shanties of the same name, one of the fishing stations of Kakalatza whose people are the only ones of all those in the Cowichan valley who fish either on the Lake or River.

After making the last portage we came to *Qualis* a fine open space of ground, backed by pines through the vista of which you could see a beautiful natural park. Here once a strange incident of Indian Life occurred. Kakalatza on coming up one season to fish found a Eucatlaw woman cowering in the lodge. She & another woman had escaped from the Scallams at Cape Flattery where they were slaves to Port San Juan. Took to the Mountains. The other woman broke her leg and was left. Kakalatza sold her for a slave to the Lummis. Such is savage life.

Tomo went out hunting while we were pitching the tents. (The work of a few minutes—as I have [made] camp orders to the following effect. All the stores [are] put in the middle tent (the large one). In this Buttle, Lewis & I sleep. In the other, Whymper, Barnston & Macdonald. In the third Leech, Meade & Foley. In each tent every man's private effects, with his arms & a small hatchet. The sleepers in each put it up—if all present. Articles for present use in big bag. This has the effect of our getting tents up & supper ready in about half an hour.) Before the tents were up, the crack of Tomo's rifle [was] heard & he came in and reported killing a fine fat Buck. After supper sent Meade & Lewis to help him to bring it in. With ravenous camp appetites the last is nearly finished. He reports many deer & bears, with marks of wolves. Several cranes flew overhead. Saw a Cottonwood about 200 ft high & about 20 ft. in circumference in damp soil.

Foley reports poling very bad—river shallow in many places—canoes had to be pushed ahead. Foley (a very experienced Miner) prospected a bar & found about 1/2 cent to the pan & thinks pay might run ahead of the prospect and that Chinamen might by using Blankets and quicksilver[42] make $ 1. to $ 1.50 per diem which would be a great thing for the country. On every creek and bar yet we have found the colour of gold and plenty of black sand but too fine. Hitherto the River has been bordered by flats (more or less wooded) & it is not likely that good prospects can be got on bars in their vicinity. What gold comes down the hills lands on the flat where an equally good prospect can be got. When the hills come down to the water that is the time for prospects.

Sunday June 12th [1864]. Qualis means the warm place & according to the wise regulation of ordering a resting on Sunday whenever practicable, I ordered last night the tents to be pitched until Monday & all hands hailed tomorrow as a holiday. Having ordered men to wash any dirty shirts, grease boots with fat of deer, clean arms & do any odd jobs. For myself I wrote up the last days journal. Talked with Tomo and Kakalatza about the Lake &c. Macdonald caught a young

6 Frederick Whymper, *Qualis (The Warm Place). Cowitchan River* (Scott Polar Research Institute No. 75/5/1, CN64)

deer. Some were fishing & got a few trout. In the evening Tomo put
on his moccasins & went hunting bear. As the coolness of evening
came on, the valley resounded with many sweet voices joining in
"God Save the Queen"—first time it was ever heard in that lone place.

Lieut. Leech made some observations and carefully determined the
latitude absolutely, but could not reduce his observations for Longitude until he had obtained a rate for the Chronometer—the one
obtained by Dr. Walker[43] being found to be erroneous.

Latitude observed at Qualis Camp 4
48 45′ 37″ N
Longitude 2. 54. 58″ W of Victoria
corner of Humboldt St.
approximate var 23

Monday June 13th [1864]. Up at 6 a.m. Off at 8 a.m. Put Barnston and
Foley in canoe and took Tomo with the land Party. Course at first
W.S.W. Passed through fine parklike piece of country. Soil in general
stony but suited very well for pasturage, then through thick Pine
underbrush to River. Crossed the river in the Canoe and as the Cañon
of the River now commenced, unloaded the canoe to make portage
(this place is called Kuck-saess or commencement of the rapids or
swift places) each of us carrying from 70 to 100 pounds each, over a
good beaten Indian trail which they used in the Autumn and Winter
to pack their Salmon from the falls past the cañon of the River to
where they leave their canoes. Our course lay through very open flat
woods—soil sandy. From high banks we could see the River several
hundred feet below us rushing through a narrow cañon—too deep to
allow of poling. Accordingly the canoe had to be towed along by the
two on shore while two remain[ed] in the canoe to stave it off from
the rocks. Canoes are frequently split in passing through this cañon.
Harris canoe was split here in 1860.[44]

Rain commencing to fall very heavily & there being no prospect of
its [stopping] for the day, & the travelling through the wet bush
being so disagreeable, on arriving at the last fall where we found two
Indian lodges I determined to Camp here for the night & it [was] well
we did for the Canoe did not arrive until 4 o'clock & the rain continued to fall in torrents all afternoon. These lodges were empty just
now. Three young men & two women having gone (so old Kakalatza
said) to hunt elk at the great Lake. We accordingly took possession of

7 Frederick Whymper, *Squitz [Skutz]. Falls of the Cowitchan River* (Yale Collection of Western Americana, Beinecke Rare Book and Manuscript Library). The drawing indicates Indian fishing practices. In the foreground, the platform projecting into the river was used for dipnetting, the net itself being attached to a wooden frame at the end of a pole. Beyond this is a further device for catching salmon—a fence-like structure that served as a trap.

the best lodges—& as our trousers were very wet, we took them off & fastened our blankets round our legs Indian fashion & stretched our length upon mats belonging to the "three hunters of Kaatsa" in which position Mr. Whymper took a rough sketch of the party. I noticed one of the planks of the lodge—hewn out of a solid piece of cedar (*Thuja gigantea*) 3 ft. 4 in. in breadth & 10 ft. in length. The falls are merely a series of rapids—about 12 to 18 ft. high. The Indian name is Squitz [Skutz] which means in the Cowichan language the fall or the end of the swift places though in the Chinook jargon it comes under the same category as *Shella* untranslatable to ears polite.[45] On the opposite side of the River—in a line with the fall—about 2 miles from it—Direction S.S.W. from the Fall—Height about 1200 feet above the level of the surrounding country—is a Hill called *Smalumuch* from which the surrounding country derives its name.

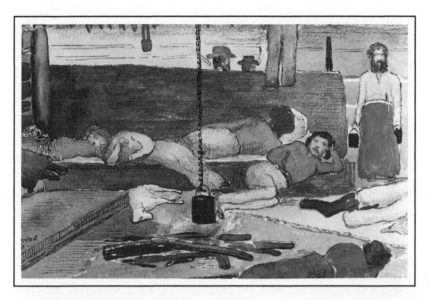

8 Frederick Whymper, *Squitz (Skutz). Camp in Deserted Ran-*
cherie (Yale Collection of Western Americana, Beinecke Rare
Book and Manuscript Library). In his journal for 13 June, 1864,
Whymper wrote: "Camped at Squitz—(the falls) and took possession of a deserted rancherie—divesting ourselves of our wet
nether garments and donning our blankets a la Siwash."

This is the commencement of a range of hills. Keeping in general
about the same distance from the river, but at the concavity of some of
the bends approaching the river, right on, & with a few breaks round
the south side of the lake.

A dismantled weed overgrown village once of considerable extent
exactly opposite the lodges on the left hand side (descending) was
pointed out to us [as] at one time the autumn fishing village of the
Masolomo's[46] & we were told that this country is divided between
them and the Samenaws—and moreover though their village has
been long abandoned that still they come to plant potatoes here, &
that half of a few miserable weed choked potato patches near the
lodge we had taken possession of belonged to them. The lodges here
being the property of the [Samenaws]. Here then we began to get the
first tangible intelligence of this inland [illegible] tribe whose name

& history had been repeated to us all the way up the Cowichan Valley
each time increasing in credibility until now we have arrived at the
borders of their country. It may be useful to shortly review what we
have now gained regarding the history of this people whose history
was treated previous to our departure from Victoria either as a fabled
Indian story or on the other hand was believed by the more credulous
with such exaggerations as to lead the generality of the coast whites
to treat the whole affair as a mere yarn & myself as something of a
wild goose hunter to ever entertain the idea of establishing or dis-
proving the fact of their existence. They may be shortly summarised
as follows, premising that my authorities are: [i] Kakalatza the chief
of the Somenaws who annually hunts on the great lake who is inti-
mately acquainted with the whole surrounding country & who has
frequently passed through the lake & down to Nitinat where his son
is at present. His wife is a Masolomo, & most of his tribe are half
Somenos, half Masolomo; [ii] Lemon who speaks English very well;
& [iii] Tomo our hunter who has frequently met members of the tribe
& was well acquainted with the chief who died last winter. (Chehenuk
is his name. He died on the lake & is buried on one of the islands.)
(1) They are not a distinct tribe peculiar to this lake but certain
members of some tribe or tribes on the sea board who visit this lake
for fishing and hunting, perhaps from Nitinat. (2) They come to the
lake during the fall with their women & children, stay generally all
winter, or until such time as they can procure a sufficient quantity of
salmon & dried deers meat—generally elk which inhabit the borders
of the lake in great herds. Their method of procuring their supply of
flesh is something like this. Starting into the mountains or wherever
the elk are plentiful they kill & dry the meat until they have obtained
a supply. They then make baskets and pack basket after basket to
where they think a convenient place & so on until they get to their
Camp. (3) Their language is different from the Cowichan. They are
however good friends—and intermarry with the Somenos, & come
down in the autumn to plant potatoes near the Somenaw Village
undistinguished by the whites from their home Indians (vide also
Harris' report).[47]

Tuesday June 14th [1864]. Very wet. Started at 10 a.m. though still
raining. Made a portage of the canoe over the rapids. (Above the
rapids we found a good canoe hid in the bush. I would immediately
have pressed [it] into service of the Colony but the old Chief told me
that it belonged to the young chief of the Masolomo who was in

Victoria & that he would be returning soon, so I left it alone.) Sent
Barnston & Foley with Lemon & Kakalatza in canoe. Land party
struck through woods—W. a little S. of W.—level river bottom—soil
very good near river—further back not so good. For three or four
miles a well marked Indian trail—then through woods—level bottom—very fine spars, cedar, hemlock & maple with a few pines—soil
clayey with gravelly undersoil. Here it was rather better further back
from River. On both sides of the River, flats stretch right on to the
Lake back to the range of mountains of which Shella is the commencement on the right (ascending) & Smalamuch on the left. These
flats are watered by many creeks flowing into the river, up which the
salmon ascend, & the waters getting so shallow often leave their backs
bare when the bears & otter reap a harvest. By the side of one Creek
we observed many beaver & otter traps, made on much the same
principle as the fox traps in Greenland. We struck the river at one of
the bends, to wait the canoe. Wet to the skin. Lit fire & as we had no
food, Tomo went out & brought in a slight refection of the hind
quarters of a fine fat buck—which we roasted on sticks. He saw many
deer with fawns &c. Getting dark & rain incessant, no canoe, which
caused me much anxiety lest some accident [had happened]. Got
dark, so we "seven poor travellers" made the best of the bad job &
made ourselves as comfortable as possible round the fire & slept
soundly all night amid the pouring rain dreaming of the quondam
comfort of our Indian camp of the night previous. Now we appreciate
our waterproof sheets. It seemed true as Macdonald declared that "the
devil was whipping his wife" &, if we may judge from his frequent
allusions to that gentleman, he appears to be on terms of considerable intimacy. This bend of the River is known as Scac'um—Camp
No. 6.

Wednesday June 15th [1864]. Up at 6 a.m. No canoe, still raining.
Sent Tomo to ascertain its fate. Glad to see it coming round the point
at 10 a.m. Found that the Canoe had stove the night before. They had
camped & started as soon as the canoe could be mended. The river
was described as very bad. Had to make three portages, very swift.
Foley prospected an old bar & found 1 cent to the pan, fit to pay a
good miner with a rocker $2.50 to $3.00 per day. It is on the old bars
of the river that we have found the best prospects & hence the best
gold. The present was obtained about one mile below the Camp No. 6.
These are good "Chinamen's Diggings" & I doubt not but that there
will be a rush up here presently. Such a rush I would not encourage by

any means but I would certainly recommend men who have the means & the inclination with appliances superior to ours, & more time at their disposal, to test further a river which we have proved to yield more gold than any other place yet tested in Vancouver Island. Foley is a very experienced Californian & British Columbian Miner & may be relied on. I particularly cautioned him against the slightest approach to exaggeration, telling him that I was not at all anxious to swell out my report with reports of gold but only want the naked— even underestimated—statement of the truth. He assured me that he had gone under rather than over, when he stated the prospect at from 3/4 to 1 cent the pan. A very experienced miner can wash out 300 pans a day. Call it $2.00 a day. I saw many Chinese on Fraser River last autumn between Lillooet & Yale—particularly about the far famed Boston Bar weighing out their day's earnings, and dividing from 55 cents to $2.50 to each—& yet they were contented, notwith- standing the privations of these out of the way places, & the high rate of provisions.[48] Here provisions could be brought up at very little expense in canoe or flat bottomed boats, & the country abounds with salmon & game, while the finest description of timber is all around. Very different from Fraser River. So exciting is gold hunting that men are willing to leave the certainty of good wages to take the uncertainty of poor ones, led away by the hopes of striking large ones. Nothing but this could ever make them endure the hardships & disappointments of their work.

The Canoe party saw many bear and otter traps along banks of River—also some Abies Menziesii [Douglas Fir—*Pseudotsuga men- ziesii*] in addition to other timber. Ship loads of knees,[49] now very valuable & which here only require to be cut out & floated down the River yielding a very handsome profit to those who go into it with capital sufficient to purchase an axe. Orders frequently come from France & other Continental Governments for cargoes of knees & the orders are very difficult to be filled up.

Had breakfast and started off. Canoe party as before. Land party, through bush by River's side, cutting off bends; then through burnt timber; travelling very bad, brush wet, so that soon we were soaked but we had now resolved to encourage Mark Tapley (a "being jolly")[50] under every difficulty & resolved to trudge on as jolly as possible notwithstanding the rain which now commenced to rain in torrents only relieved now and then by a shower of hail. Bush composed of salmon berries (*Rubus Spectabilis*) & the terrible pest of *Panax hor-*

ridum well deserving its scientific name as well as its more general undertow one of the "Devil's walking stick." Then over a more undulating piece of country intersected by ravines through which brawling <streams> brooks swollen with the stream went gushing down to the river. The timber was however of the most magnificent description. Within an area comprehended by our eye was an easy fortune for any man of the most moderate means. Spars of Douglas pine & hemlock (*A. Bridgei Kels.*) 100 to 150 feet in height & even higher, & from 2 to 3 feet in diameter, without a twig for 80 or 100 feet were shady in every direction, and the difficulty would not be in getting good ones, but in selecting among so many magnificent sticks, all standing within a few yards of the River's banks. I remember just before starting from Victoria that the "Granada" gave £30 for a spar roughly hewn and not one whit superior to any one we saw around us and indeed had seen for the last few days. Vancouver Island has now got into repute for spars & the supply cannot equal the demand & ships come to Alberni to load & after being long delayed have to go over to Puget's Sound before completing their cargoes. Here cargoes could be hewn down by the hundreds of idle men about Victoria in the fall & winter when the River is at its height & floated down in cribs with the utmost ease. The river would require to be cleared of the rafts of fallen trees. This however would only be the work of a few days. To speak of the facilities which the river affords for the establishment of mills of every description would be only a jest to those acquainted with it, such description being considered a mere waste of words— the whole river from beginning to end being perfectly fitted for such purposes. The timber alone would be a certain fortune. The gold bars would be best wrought on in & after July when the river is at its lowest.

Struggling through bush or tramping through noble open forest all day until late in the afternoon. The river begins to get slower & we were told that the lake was now commencing. Emerging into an open space we found on a cedar tree divested of a piece of the bark, written in pencil fresh as the hour its being written "Harris, Langley & Durham Augt 1st/60" marking the limits of their exploration. We added our autographs to this memorial tree. A little further on we found the canoe waiting for us with Kakalatza & Lemon, the rest having encamped. We embarked & for the time being our weary brush journey was ended, & one of the objects of our journey accomplished. Here we lost Buttle's dog. It had gone after a deer & not being forthcoming we had to leave it behind. It was a useless cur, good only for eating. Its first experience was allowing our supper to be stolen by some two legged or four legged animal or animals unknown. Its last to eat itself the four or five pounds of venison intended for the breakfast of the "seven poor travellers of Scac-tun." The river began to widen—& the bends less until we came to an island in middle where the water became so deep—& the current so little that poling was now no longer of use. Here the Indians pitched their poles ashore. The Island is called Sweem-kun, & has been used for the purpose mentioned for time immemorial. Here the lake is generally understood to terminate and the river to begin. The water is known as Squakun the still place.

About a mile further came into the lake proper & encamped in a snug cove. We found Barnston & Foley busy cooking supper before a blazing fire which we soon encircled to dry & warm ourselves, until the heat made us retreat to a respectable distance from it. The Indians say

9 Frederick Whymper, ***Cowitchan Lake. 8th Camp*** (Yale Collection of Western Americana, Beinecke Rare Book and Manuscript Library)

"You White Men are fools. You build a fire to warm yourselves but you make it so big that you cannot get round it," & I daresay they are quite correct. A White man's camp you can know for years. He cuts down trees, he heaps on logs, & altogether he makes a very "tall" fire, but the Indian manages things better, & saves himself a great deal of trouble. He gathers a few sticks, saves his axe, makes a small fire & crowds round it, warming without burning themselves.

The time we have taken to arrive at Kaatsa is to be no criterion of the time required to reach it, as our work requires numerous delays, & the canoe being heavily loaded with inexperienced hands our progress has been comparatively slow. The Indians usually ascend it in two or three days & descend it in one or one and a half. They can travel overland by base of Mount Shella & Prevost across country in one winter's day with loads of salmon. A Dog started from this lake about noon & was at Samenaw before night.

Thursday June 16th [1864]. Devoted the day to drying our clothes & provisions which had got wet during our last two days' travel. The party cleaned & oiled their arms & as the party was out of fresh meat Tomo went out hunting. I examined some of the men's journals. Dried the towing cords & tents. Greased our boots. It is an axiom among N.W. travellers—"Grease your boots & keep your powder dry." During the last nine days I had been testing how much provisions on unlimited allowance men required & now began to find that at the present rates our flour &c would barely last out our time, & we had fully as much as it was possible to carry, so I issued regulations to the cook for the week beginning anent the amount of bread to be exhibited at each meal, beans to be cooked &c, & as the old Indian Chief used to go round his lodges on a morning crying "Eat the little potatoes. Keep the big ones for seed" so now the cry went through camp—"Eat plenty of venison—save the flour & Bacon for hard time. No bread when there are beans, & bread to be baked a day before hand" & saving the mark it was —— tough but men eat the less of it. Heard shots along the lake. Was told it was Masolomo hunters. The first camp of the Masolomo was opposite. It was dismantled at present until the body of them arrive here for the winter, from the coast.

Friday June 17th [1864]. Last night troubled with Martins with which the lake abounds. Tomo unsuccessful last night. Sent him at 5 of a.m. to hunt, & Indians to find the other canoe. Both returned unsuccessful, Tomo having seen nothing and the Indians reporting canoe gone. Sent half our party & the provisions to a more central

Camp. Remained myself with Whymper, Barnston & Macdonald. Whymper took sketch of lake. Went back about mile & a half on the proposed route of Leech's party to San Juan (Pachena of Indians). Found a small shallow round Lake [Beaver Lake?] at base of hills emptied by a creek flowing into River. In fact the creek forms the lake, by being dammed up by Beaver dams. The lake is full of them, & Kakalatza tells me that his father used to hunt them long ago when the King Georges wore beaver hat & [beaver] skin was worth trading at Fort Langley to Mr. Yale[51]—a very old story indeed.

In evening canoe returned for us—paddled eight miles. (For description of Lake vid. Mr. Leech's report[52] [and] Mr. Whymper's sketches & after summary.) Found the party encamped at the mouth of a large creek on North side, shaded by gigantic cottonwoods & backed by fine fertile flats covered with Maples (*Acer Macrophyllum*) pines & cedar but so thin in places that you could run anywhere through the woods among *Polystichum aleuticum*, *Athyrium filix*

10 Frederick Whymper, *"Quoitquot" or Foley's Creek. Cowitchan Lake N. Side* (Yale Collection of Western Americana, Beinecke Rare Book and Manuscript Library)

femina & other beautiful ferns. Further back—mountains & some snow peaks—the haunt of herds of elk & deer. In front the summer lake merry with the leaping trout & salmon, & undulating wooded hills, & the music of the Brook ever on our ears. It would be a beautiful site for a quiet summer retreat—a magnificent shooting box far from the haunts of man—a sort of "lodge in some vast wilderness." The Creek is called Why-e-coot by the Samenaws.[53]

Great News!!!

Foley & Barnston returned with prospect from about a mile up creek—one scale about three times the size of a pin's head—the gold in general very fine. Had got as high as three & four cents to the pan—frequently as much as 1 1/2 cents. Brought to me from one pan of dirt 2 cents—& lots of black sand. I think with proper appliances could make here from 5 to 8 dollars a day, but without proper tools he could not sufficiently test it. All the party elated & to show my approval of Foley's labours which in every department had been most unremitting & useful, I named it by universal consent "Foley's Creek."

Latitude 48 51′ 56″ N
Longitude 3′ 28.22″ W of Vic

The rate of the chronometer 2.767 gaining daily. Corresponding with Pemberton's rate. Dr. Walker's was ridiculous (losing 16″ daily).

There is a quantity of level good land along its banks, with fine maple, generally considered an index of good soil: fine cedar for rockers &c—& pine for houses and sluices. A scow could be built with the utmost ease upon the lake & if necessary either this or any of the other streams would drive a sawmill. A Farm could be very easily cleared out here. When coming up the river we saw no granite or rather syenite Boulders—now quantities of them. Along creek very fine Knees for ships. Magnificent spars & on the whole the timber (particularly cedar) very much superior to that on coast. A few weeks before we came here 3 white men had come up with Tomo but had made no observation & returned. They were in search of gold & on a stump we found penned the following:

The following persons
'a prospecting party' from Victoria encamped

> *at this place May 18th 1864—destination*
> *The Mountains of the North West*
> *G L Boswell*
> *Josiah Lawrie*
> *J W Donnel*
> *Thomas Anthony*
> *Thickallassa Indian Chief*
> *"N B." Found in river bed adjacent some scales*
> *of gold, plenty of black sand*
> *GLB*

Thomas Anthony is our "Tomo," "Thickallassa" is Kakalatza. Tomo tells me they did little or no prospecting & never went further than this.[54]

Saturday June 18th [1864]. Sent Foley, Barnston & Lewis to prospect Foley's Creek & report upon it. The general bearing of it is S.E. (as the waters flow) as far as they explored it for about three miles. Two & a half miles up is a cañon on a small scale, for nearly a mile. The Creek is said by the Indians who hunt along its banks to flow out of the same mountain as the Chemainus River (called in Cowichan language Sail-ac-wus). Prospects much the same as yesterday. This must be a furious stream in winter. Confirmed yesterday's report. [Foley] considers at the lowest estimate that $2.00 per day could be made. Sent Tomo to hunt. He tracked elk but shot nothing & feeling very bad thereat. Lewis shot a deer & brought in hind quarters. Leech & Meade took observation for rate, latitude & longitude. Examined some of the journals & find an awful mess of the Indian names. This requires experience & shows the use of their keeping a journal. Meade's, Foley's and Barnston's are the best. They differ in the distances traversed. That was one of the reasons I wished to examine, so that such differences could be settled as long as we were on the spot.

Two young Masolomo hunters visited the camp today. They were camped on some Islands, with a squaw and a little girl, who however did not do us the honour of a visit. As a piece of Kaatsa gossip I may mention (not necessary for publication but as a guarantee of my good faith with the Committee in communicating everything I hear & see) that the lady in question bears a somewhat notorious character & is known by the Indians as "moos-moos" (the beast). I told our Indians to give their friends sweet coffee and bread which they relished with a vengeance. They had a few trout which I tried to bargain for but could not come to terms, so I preferred to want them rather than allow them to suppose we were the least dependent on them or would submit to any extortion. Whymper sketching—Macdonald fishing—Lovely moonlight.

Sunday June 19th [1864]. Though this was Sunday & we had been recommended as far as possible to make this a day of rest[55] yet as we had been in camp several days this week & the Indians were anxious to return, the young man wishing to marry, the old man to get food for his children, for the salmon had not yet ascended to his village. Accordingly organized two parties for exploration as follows: Lieut. Leech, John Meade, John Buttle, Kakalatza, with provisions for three days to make a careful exploration of the lake, its feeders & borders, & to make astronomical observations to determine its absolute position as a station for the Southern district of the island. I at the same [time] directed them to mark as near as possible the site of any Indian Encampments so as to form reserves for them, in the position they have chosen for their camps, & I gave him [Leech] presents (such as ribbons, tobacco &c) to present to their head people enjoining upon him the utmost caution in dealing with them, & directed Kakalatza to enquire from them, promising rewards if successful, for any copper or other minerals they were acquainted with or open lands of any description. Also I ordered the party particularly to ascertain if any river flowed out of it as it was supposed that both Sombrio & Jordan flowing into De Fuca's Straits, took their rise in this lake. I took another party under my own command to look for minerals in the surrounding Mountains, taking the same amount of provisions, being as much as we could carry in climbing these hills. If however we killed anything I proposed to stay out longer. The following were members of it: Commander, J M Foley, F W Whymper Artist, Tomo, Lemon. I left in case of Indians visiting Camp on Marauding tour, Barnston & Lewis as Camp Keepers & directed Macdonald to hunt as it was his week for cooking. Started both parties at 8 a.m. (vid. Leech's Report).

Weather yet lowering, we started out from behind the camp through fine open woods—fine spars—flat—crossed creek N.N.W.—Open woods—fine timber—little undergrowth—no longer *Pteridium aquilinum* (bracken) or very rarely but *Polystichum* & *polypodium* with *Athyrium* [different forms of fern]—timber, hemlock, (*A Bridgea*), cedar (*Thuja gigantea*), *Abies Bridgei*—soil rather sandy & so for about 1 1/2 or 2 miles. Then changed course to N. 2° W. through very beautiful, very open woods—flat bottom, loamy land—gently rising ground intersected by streams & Indian hunting trails. The trees (hemlock, cedar & maple) twenty to thirty feet (on an average) between each so that land would be very easily cleared. Close by Creek much maple, alder (*Alnus Oregana*) & cottonwood (*Salix Scouleriana*). On drier ground magnificent white pine (*Pinus Strobus*) [*Pinus monticola*] rather rare on the Island but worth $100 per M. in the Chinese market. Many of the trees were from 80, 100 to 120 feet in height & 3 to 4 in diameter & unbranched 50 to 60 ft. from the base. There is immense wealth in the timber alone. The smallest of these "sticks" are good for masts of schooners, bow spits, bows, yards, sail booms &c. Mouth of the Cowichan River good for ship-building. Tomo tells me there is a quantity of good white pine in the Sanich Inlet, down from Sayward's Mill[56] which no-body knows of. This style of country continued for 3/4 of a mile. Then crossed the creek. Course N. 1° pt. E. soil loamy, banks of creek above cañon with brush. Ascended hill. Course N.E. Country much the same. Signs of Bear, Deer & Elk. We now travelled along the face of the mountain ridge about 100 feet above the creek. The whole style of the back country back from the lake is a succession of wooded hills, intersected by valley or ravines through which numerous creeks flow, falling either as independent creeks into the creek or as tributaries of Foley's or other Creeks. Sides of hills covered with magnificent timber (pine & hemlock, principally latter)—little undergrowth.

Here Foley's creek branches—main stream running 22 1/2° N. of W.—other E. & so on subdividing into innumerable streamlets taking their rise in the snow. All along ridge Indian trail & marks of hunting camps for drying meat—principally used by Kakalatza, who brings his family here in autumn & waits until the snow begins to fall. Saw several boulders of green stone full of pretty garnets. A few weeks before we left Victoria my old friend M. Lemon of Cowichan came to Victoria with rock containing garnets & reported a perfect Mountain of them.[57] Tomo tells me that it was he who gave them to him & that he got them from such a boulder as this.

Travelled along the ridge for two [miles]—crossing numerous ravines—good Indian trail—sign of deer, bear, & elk. Fine hemlock. Camped by side of Kakalatza's meat drying station. Tomo went out to hunt but unsuccessful. Came in cursing English shoes which frighten all the deer by the noise they make in breaking through the woods. After Supper (bread & tea & that a modicum) sent Lemon out—also unsuccessful. Discovered a mineral spring—very alkaline—flows into creek—very useful as a watering place for the fashionable inhabitants of the city of Foley (!!!) (Perhaps first on Island.)

Foley found hill of quartz which he is certain contains gold. Highly elated. Wished he had only six months provisions, three men with tools to sink a shaft. Vein of Iron stone also. Decomposed quartz exactly like Cariboo—(vid. *Foley's report on Metallurgy of this Expedition*.) Found no sign of gold in stream but every indication of deep diggings.

Monday June 20th [1864]. Passed a very comfortable night among the fir branches—the sweetest of all beds. Tomo out at Daybreak to hunt. Came back at 7 a.m. unsuccessful & in high dudgeon thereat. He thinks he is bewitched. After going over a few miles of country before

11 Frederick Whymper, *Camp with "Blaze," or Camp-Mark*, in Whymper, *Travel and Adventure in the Territory of Alaska* (1868). In his journal for 20 June, Whymper wrote: "Proceeded to the head waters of the Chemanos River—camped and sketched the same." However, he was mistaken in supposing that this lake was the source of the Chemainus River. Of this tailpiece to a chapter, he wrote: "The future explorer will have no trouble in finding our tracks, for at each camp the trees were 'blazed,' i.e. marked with an axe, and an inscription affixed . . . the artistic part of the work being performed by the writer-painter, but not glazier, to the expedition."

the sun was over the hills & seeing plenty of tracks of deer & elk—but saw nothing of the animals themselves.

Started at 8 a.m. through a similar country to yesterday. Through some huckleberry (*vaccinum ovatum*) bushes—haunt of deer & elk: layers & tracks everywhere. Kakalatza marks knotted twigs same as Barclay Sound Indians—trail marks &c. The Masolomos hunt deer here in the winter & autumn. In the summer they go to the mountains to escape the heat & concomitant flies. On the top of a snow covered mountain here, the old Chief tells me the deer are so thick that you only require to go behind a bush—sound their hunting whistle, and take your pick of the fattest and the best. If you kill a lean one by chance let it go. In the summer, the Bucks; in the autumn & winter, the does. In the fall they come down to rut and remain in the low lands all winter. On this track when the huckleberries prevail— very poor timber. When Tomo was here last (May 20th) the snow was on the ground in some places a foot in depth. The travelling for 3 miles further very good—beautiful shady woods silent as the grave. In early dawn and evening the deer feed on the huckleberry foliage by the side of the creek, during day all quiet—as they sleep in the bush. Never visited by a human being save once a year by a solitary Indian hunter, Kakalatza Chief of the Somenaws. If a man sees a deer and goes behind a tree—the deer run, and if he stops and waves his hand, or makes some motion to attract attention, he stands still attracted by curiosity when the wily hunter gets a shot.

Came into an awful yet beautiful gorge through which the Chemainus River near its head water took its rise. Snow a foot deep summer & winter together. Here encamped and sent Tomo and Foley to bring back and report on specimens of Copper which was said to exist here—said to be about 3 miles into Mountain.[58] I was anxious to accompany them but someone had to get Camp in order and it was as well as I was no judge of copper and our extra walk would have told on our appetites and in a direct ratio on our now remarkably limited supply of bread.

Whymper took a sketch while I prepared the Camp. Towards evening Tomo and Foley returned, but very successful, having discovered a perfect Mountain of Copper ore & Iron stone, specimens of which they brought with them (vid. report on it by Foley). Ate all we had and lay down to sleep, within a foot of snow, with the pleasant feeling that our breakfast was still on 4 legs, somewhere in the woods. Very cold.

Tuesday June 21st [1864]. To make the longest day a little longer we started at 5 a.m. Tomo had started ahead to see if he could knock over a breakfast for us. Found him a mile off—no deer. Took a cup of tea and reached old camp by former track in 3 hours. Mr. Whymper dropped behind on the way and got lost. Reached camp No. 5 voracious, and in about a couple of hours Whymper came in having followed the course of Foley's Creek. Found the Camp Keepers very tired of their berth. Leech and party had returned this morning and had started off again. In the evening returned with report on Lake.

Wednesday June 22 [1864]. Occupied all day in making preparations for a start to the salt water tomorrow. Made up provisions &c into parcels. The two parties wrote up Journals. Wrote out formal instructions for Leech (Order No. 2).[59] Wrote to VI Exploration Committee (Dispatch No. 2)[60] and enclosed for postage the following: Mrs. Brown, Professor Balfour (British Col. Bot. Ass. No 8),[61] Mrs. Buttle, Mr Soar (Leech). Mr. Whymper requested permission of me to add a little nonsense for Chronicle & Colonist;[62] these I enclosed to Cruickshanks and according to my orders about express messenger (in this case return Indians) requested them to be left open which was done with the exception of my two letters for England, not being necessary in that case—the reason of the orders being to prevent members communicating private information.[63] Organized parties as follows:

FOR PORT SAN JUAN
Lieut Leech, J M Foley, John Meade, Tomo Antoine
FOR FALSE NITINAT
Commander Macdonald, Barnston, Buttle, Whymper, Lewis

In addition to provisions gave Leech letter to trader, instructions, a few trading articles and $ 10 in cash & the pick of the men which he took as above. All parties highly elated at prospect of a start. Heaped up a high fire and late in the night sung many a merry song & spun many a ludicrous story of their experiences in many a land. Sand flies very troublesome at night.

Thursday June 23rd [1864]. Up at day break. Breakfast and got Leech's party first dispatched from near camp No. 7 East end of lake which was considered the best place to strike Port San Juan to the South. Boiled naked bulb thermometer for height of lake. Average 209° Far.—making lake above sea, 513 feet. At 10 o'clock canoe returned and took us to West end of lake. On the way up met two Canoes loaded with berries on their way to the sea, by the Cowichan

River—"the 3 hunters of Samenaw." Paid the Indians & gave them
flour enough to get down, and as I found that after supplying ourselves we had still some lead which it was inconvenient to carry I
made them a present of it with all the empty Coffee Canisters, a pipe,
a little tobacco and a piece of ribbon to fasten to their caps. Their job
and gratitude knew no bounds especially in Lemon. He told me that
when he saw me in Victoria (he would know my whiskers) he would
give me some grouse, as I was his very good friend, and turning to one
of our party, whom he supposed had cast certain sly glances at some
damsel of his acquaintance "Nika wawa Mary copa mika" ("I will speak
to Mary for you") & turning to another "Spose Mary halo tiki yaka nika,
hiyu wawa copa mika" ("I hope Mary want him. I want will speak
plenty for you") a most liberal arrangement certainly. In addition at
their own request I gave each of them a "hyas paper" or memorial of
their character as I found it on the expedition (these papers when true
are very useful, but you find them scattered all over the coast full of the
most absurd nonsense and untruths) and recommending to the other
white men for similar employment. This I could do conscientiously as
they behaved to my satisfaction. The old Chief (who expressed his
gratitude in a much less demonstrative form) contenting himself with a
"Klosh, Klosh" [Thank you] which nearly exhausted his Chinook, gave
me directions about the trail and when it strikes the Nitinat River and
all party [parted?] very well pleased with each other.

Packs very heavy; trail good, general direction S.W. for 1/4 mile by
side of a dry swamp-ground blazed by Leech's party for exploration of
the lake. Open woods—fine spruce (*Ab. Menzeii*) [Douglas Fir—
Pseudotsuga menziesii] & hemlock. About 2 miles on, the trail takes
through a swamp, and here we lost it. After reaching a little Creek we
camped for the night & for the first time mosquitoes very bad.

Friday June 24th 1864. For the first 2 miles today the Indian trail
pretty good over a flat country, blazed by Barnston last night (who
went ahead to follow it) with occasional Indian blazes and trees cut
down. Then through a considerable amount of fallen timber where it
led along logs for a considerable way. For some way through open
country and thickets of *Panax horridum* [Devil's Club] with swamp
on right hand. Timber—hemlock with a little cedar, rather mixed
quality. It then led over rising ground and once over the bed of a dry
creek. On right, hill about 800 ft. which I took for Mt. Gooch of
Pemberton[64]—only one in this portage. We came about 2 o'clock to a
large creek with remains of Indian camping ground. Here stopped for

12 Frederick Whymper, *Mount Gooch and Nitinat River* (Yale Collection of Western Americana, Beinecke Rare Book and Manuscript Library)

a cup of tea after crossing creek. The trail now took through a well defined Valley alongside the creek. Trail excellent, soil of a mixed quality—when good, very good, but mostly inferior. Timber in general poor, principally hemlock, some of which are very large, but, for the most part very scrubby. Then further on still by banks of creek, soil stony, good in some places, with boulders, with some uneven ground & much fallen timber. On the left hand side of Creek, flats with hemlock, cedar and maple, very open, soil sandy and clayey. After going for about 2 miles from resting place struck Nitinat River at a place where the creek empties into it. In all about 8 miles from Great Cowichan Lake. The Nitinat here is tolerably swift—Course S.E.—about as large as the Cowichan with a greater body of water in it. Camped here (No. 10). Prospected Creek and found color of gold of much the same quality as in the river with a little black sand.

13 Frederick Whymper, **Descent of the Nitinat and Ascent of the Puntledge** (Yale Collection of Western Americana, Beinecke Rare Book and Manuscript Library). These vignettes illustrate the different forms of navigation that were called for at different times on the expedition. *Descent* displays Whymper and Macdonald on a raft, and *Ascent* illustrates the difficulty encountered in using a sizeable canoe.

Saturday June 25th 1864. Sent out parties to look for a place to construct a raft, found a suitable place about 1/4 mile down just below a Cañon. Constructed it of dry cedar, a task which occupied all day. Whymper took sketch of the river a little way up, with supposed Mount Goode [Gooch] in the foreground.

Item! Eat the last of our beans! (I find this in the Journal of one of the Members of the Party always particular in this respect.)

Sunday June 26th 1864. Up at 5 a.m. Food getting low & no game forced to make a start today though Sunday. Made up our packs and travelled down on the raft. Mode of construction of the raft. It required a few finishing touches before starting. Measured a Douglas pine 48 ft. round the butt & 20 ft. in circumference—20 ft. higher up. Started, all on raft: had frequently to get out to shove it off bars and over shallows and rapids. For first mile country flat, timber straight but in general poor (spruce & hemlock predominating)—much dead standing timber. The river consists pretty much of shallow riffles and calm deep reaches—& though it may contain more water than the Cowichan River yet certainly so much cannot flow out as out of the Cowichan, the latter being of a very uniform depth while a great body of the Nitinat is in deep lake-like calm places—general breadth about 50 yards.

We were going gaily along thinking that at this rate our journey would soon be at an end when we heard the roar of water: the current became stronger and before we were fully alive to the fact, our clumsy machine was being rapidly sucked into the current, and if Buttle and Barnston had not instantly sprang out, the probability is that we, certainly the raft with all on board, would have gone over the rapids and all been dashed to pieces.

We drew into a quiet eddy beside an Island in the river, climbed a height and found the River rushing beyond through a roaring Cañon—apparently more than a mile in length. Took a little refreshment and as there was nothing for it shouldered our packs and took the land for it. We had made about 4 miles by water. Found about 200 yards off two Indian Canoes which we should have liked to have pressed into the service of the expedition if we had known when the Cañon was to end. Found an Indian trail, followed it for 2 miles nearly in the course of the river, cutting off the bends as these trails invariably do. Country open woodlands, magnificent spars of hemlock & spruce. Country elevated above river. At termination of Cañon came to an old Indian hut, where we found a canoe near it and as the trail here terminated and the sun was setting, camped. Here a flat backed by higher ground, scattered with noble trees ran along right bank of River. On left also a flat, soil good—maple, &c, sometimes measured 27 and 50 ft. in circumference (Spruce). A warm pleasant night, made miserable by mosquitoes, ended this pleasant summer's day—far from the haunts of man.

Monday June 27th [1864]. Up at 4 a.m. Last night had sent Buttle & Lewis ahead to blaze the commencement of trail. They had reported the trail to take back from the river, cross a small creek with Salmon weirs. They had followed it no further but were of opinion that it was only a fishing trail and that the trail to Nitinat ended at our camp. (No. 11 marked like all others: "V I Exp Exped camp No 11 June 27/ 64.") Considered it better as the country appears very rough & our provisions getting to a close, to prevent any accident to follow the course of the river—this leading us through the heart of an unknown country by a much easier route than the land & one much safer. Accordingly caulked up the little canoe we had found, as well as possible with flour bags and pine resin (melted in the frying pan) and agreed that Barnston and I should go ahead in her to prepare the way and settle with any Indians we might meet so as not to delay the expedition, while the others should make a light raft with some large boards lying loose at the lodge—for which I would pay the owners if necessary (and if ever there is a possibility of getting anything out of you it is always a *necessity* with the Vancouver Island aborigines) & follow us with all possible expedition. We gave food to them to last for that day (and so certain were we that the river could not be more than six or seven miles long—that it was only when I commanded it that they could be induced to take anything) while we took all the bulk of our traps in the canoe.

The morning was dull—but off we started with a cheer, sweeping down the river at a fine rate, Barnston steering while I stood in the bows & staved her off logs & rocks which threatened every moment to destroy our frail craft.

The river was the same succession of shallow riffles with remains of salmon weirs & calm deep lake-like reaches through which we had to propel it with paddles. The river was remarkably clear of trees &c, there not being more than one or two stoppages from that cause. On one occasion we ran over a rapid in the middle of which was a tree forming a bridge with the lower branches depending in the water, between two of which we ran with great rapidity. We managed however to do so without touching but it was a very close shave—a regular "spitting through a keyhole without touching the ward." The river winding very much & at every bend it seemed to end, but again as we swept round some wooded point, again were we disappointed.

We passed many Indian lodges on either bank (principally on right) but now all deserted, though in the autumn they will be inhabited by salmon fishers when the quiet river will be busy with shoals of fish. In all we passed before reaching the mouth 11 lodges all separately located, inhabited by many families; each of these were surrounded by more or less open land, or shaded with mossy Maples; all embossed with Salmon berry bushes, bearing from the rich deposits of manure great loads of juicy fruit, and the entrances choked up as in all deserted lodges with rank nettles. These nettles always affect the vicinity of Indian Villages. They were backed by forests of magnificent hemlock, spruce and cedar though as a rule as we approached the coast the timber was of a less gigantic character & the forest denser with undergrowth of Sal-al (*Gaultheria Shallon*) &c &c. These lodges being indispensible to the Indians, they are located in the best situations (and an Indian lodge is always so located according to his ideas of salubrity—though I have often thought that they show great taste even viewing their "location" from an aesthetic point of view) & the land being cleared would soon be taken possession of by any whites who might choose to establish logging camps or farms on this river, it will be necessary to form reserves for them, not necessarily more than one acre, such being sufficient for their house & if necessary for their potato patches, though none will be cultivated I believe. (The regulation is that an area of 3/4 of a mile round every Indian village shall be a reserve.[65] This is too much.) Contour of the land along the banks was flat—open woodland with pine and maple, very open in many places & soil loamy. Farms could be cleared with very little trouble. Several well defined hills a few miles back lent variety to the scene.

All day long we shot along or paddled with only one halt, & the sun began to set and there seemed no end of the river though I calculated we had followed its windings for more than 2 miles (geographical miles always understood, not nautical even on water). The canoe leaked abominably, I was nearly up to my middle in water, and every now and then we had to get out and ease it over some shallow bar. We were about giving up the hope of seeing the end, when the current decreased & a strong sea-like breeze began to blow, and the down-

ward current was stemmed by a slight upward one—& we sighted
with thankful hearts a lake-like sea of grand expanse with large trees
which the winter freshets had brought down. We drew ashore and lit
a fire and as night closed in we got anxious for the safety of the other
party, who we were afraid at best would not arrive before tomorrow
night. Just as we were rolling ourselves up in our blankets we were
roused by shouting on the river, and we could scarcely credit our eyes
when Whymper and Macdonald landed from the raft all safe but
drenched to the skin. The raft being found too small, Buttle and Lewis
had started over trail agreeing to return to our old camp, if they found
that the trail stopped at the fishing station on the creek. So far well,
but we wished we had had Buttle and Lewis with us. I passed a
sleepless night anxious for my hungry associates.

Tuesday June 28th 1864. Up at 4 a.m. Barnston and I went off in little
canoe to seek Indians, to go after Buttle and Lewis and take us all to
the Nitinat village. Rounded the first point on right side in face of a
heavy sea and adverse wind, and found an Indian [village] or *Rancheria*[66] of 4 or 5 large lodges. As our canoe was leaking badly, [we] drew
in to see if we could get another. The whole rancheria was deserted
until the salmon season but in a chief's house (known by a ring in the
wall) we found a tolerably good canoe which we took possession of
according to the free and easy style of the North West. (What would a
member of the Exploration Committee say if we were to take the loan
of his horse!) Returned (about 1/4 mile) to camp No. 12 and sent
Macdonald and Barnston up the River after Lewis and Buttle. Returned in about 3 hours with them much to my satisfaction. Buttle
reported that he and Lewis had started over the trail they had found,
[and] discovered that it ended at the fishing station on the creek.
Returned to camp No. 11. Made a rude raft with two boards and the
rope round their blankets, holes being made with pistol bullets. Had a
tolerably hard time of it. Slept in wet blankets last night, supped and
breakfasted on salmon berries. They found the progress in calm
reaches so slow that, in despair they had taken to the land. Brush
travelling very bad: resting by shore when they saw the canoe. The
country back of camp No. 11 very bad with gigantic trees.

So once more all anxiety was off my mind on that score, and we
gladly dined on a modicum of bread and tea (without sugar) eked out
in the woods with salmon berries. Spent rest of the day in tinkering
up the canoe for tomorrow's start.

Wednesday June 29th 1864. Up at 3 a.m. and started off before the

THE RAMPANT RAFT.

14 Frederick Whymper, *The Rampant Raft*, in Whymper, *Travel and Adventure in the Territory of Alaska* (1868). Whymper and Macdonald descend the Nitinat River.

15 Frederick Whymper, **Head of Nitinat Inlet and Mouth of River** (Yale Collection of Western Americana, Beinecke Rare Book and Manuscript Library)

wind got up on the Inlet (or rather what the Scotch would call a "loch" or lake-like sheet of water communicating with the sea) as it generally does on such sheets after sun rise. Passed village on right, and a little further, on each side of a creek with salmon weirs, another stockaded in front, but, at present deserted; here landed and as the breeze had fortunately got up in a favorable direction, erected a blanket on each canoe for sail and went gaily along. At mouth of the River the salt taste of the water was not perceptible from the large body of fresh water pouring in, & though the tide seemed slightly to affect it yet I had supposed that this sheet of water was possibly a lake, as on Richard's Admiralty Chart no Inlet is marked,[67] but, the supposed existence of a lake behind slightly indicated; but now it could not be doubted that it communicated with the salt water as the water was perceptibly salt. The shores of the Inlet were in general on

both sides rocky and high. In one place found great cliffs of limestone. Coal is said to exist but I saw none. The timber very scrubby on
the shore. Then some Algae appeared on the rocks and that the
stunted *Fucus Vessiculosus*: an unmistakable sign of the sea.[68]
Crossed over to the other side and the wind being now in our teeth
camped for a couple of hours.

Started off again & crossed in high swell to the other side. Round a
point & found another Village also deserted (with a good creek of
water). Here the Inlet began to narrow, sea grass floated on the
surface, and the sea was alive with innumerable Medusa [jelly fish],
and the rocks clustered with mussels. A short calm paddle brought us
to a narrow entrance through which the tide was rushing with fearful
force (a perfect *race*). We could hear, though we could not see, the
glad sound of the sea.

Soon we sighted a village in a rocky cliff and through a narrow
opening the waves of the Pacific breaking on the beach—and all our

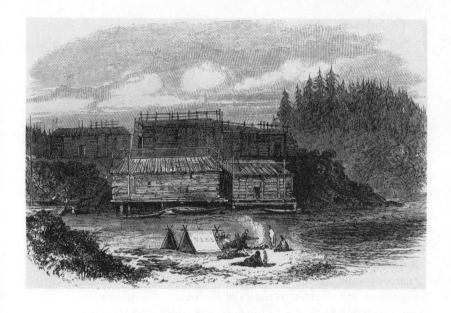

16 Frederick Whymper, ***Whyack Village***, in *Illustrated London
News*, 24 November 1866

fears and forebodings were over, for the moment, at the joyful sound
of that sounding sea we had so longed to look upon. (The native name
of Nitinat Inlet is *Etlo*. Their Village at entrance is Wye-yack
[Whyac].) With strong paddling we drew into a cove out of sight of
the Village, and we had scarcely drawn them up on the beach, before
we were sighted and in five minutes were surrounded by a crowd of
painted savages: some of their faces smeared with blood, others
blackened, but not the war black which is darker round the eyes than
the rest of the face and nearly all with shell (pieces of Haliota) in the
ears and nostrils;[69] all professing great joy at the arrival of white men
at their Village. Moquella the Chief was from home but a small chief
was excessive in his friendship and offers of assistance. I professed of
course to believe them all, though he assured me all his Indians were
of the most virtuous and honest description. I ordered all our stuff to
be got under cover as soon as possible and a sharp look out to be kept
on them, but notwithstanding all our Vigilance we discovered some

17 Frederick Whymper, **Aht Native**,
in Whymper, *Travel and Adventure in the Territory of Alaska*
(1868). Whymper remarked
on this illustration: "The . . .
portrait of an *Aht* native is
no imaginative production, but
is taken from a photograph
made on the spot, and gives a
fair idea of the type of native
we met at this village [Wyack].
The unkempt hair, the wreath
of leaves put on much for the
same purpose as they are put on
the heads of cart-horses—to keep
off flies and mosquitoes, and also for
ornament—and the limited amount
of costume, are all characteristics of the west coast natives.
The pin stuck in one side of his nostril is simply put there for
convenience, when not required for fastening the blanket
across his manly bosom!"

hours after that they had managed to steal 2 tomahawks and an auger. Their blankets (the sole rig of most of them—some of the women in a blanket of bark of cedar or white pine) giving them every facility for making off with such desirable "iktas."[70] "Uphp-a" (the sitcum tyhee)[71] would not hear of his very good friend King George's great Chief camping outside of his village, and as I wanted some favours from him yet (& we were whites in the power of himself and his athletic warriors for he knew we must leave his village, and if he chose to be nasty he might make our departure a very long and very expensive story), I had to agree to it with as good a grace as may be. Accordingly we camped in the middle of the village square, & until late at night our camp was [a] queer scene of trading for food, begging, talking, smoking and watching them. As the Nitinats bear a very bad name I thought it only prudent for the first time, to use the necessary precaution against theft or treachery. Accordingly set watches until daylight, Lewis from 10 to 12, Macdonald from 12 to 2 am when daylight would be dawning and to rouse me then. At 12 I was roused by Lewis to tell me that a large stone had been thrown down on him from above—but there had been no disturbance.

Thursday June 30th 1864. Very early this morning the Indians began to assemble, but at the sound of the first voices I was up and roused the rest of the party. While breakfast was preparing, and before any great number had assembled, Buttle and I climbed the Cliff on which the village is built to look on the Pacific ocean. The breakers were breaking with tremendous force on the beach and it was not possible for a ship to approach the shore by several hundred yards. The tide was rushing through the narrow entrance. The village is almost impregnable and stockaded facing the sea. (In winter canoes can very seldom land here at all.)

The Nitinahts (or as they pronounce it *Nittīnaas*) were at one time a very powerful tribe, the terror of the coast but they have shared in the universal decay, & do not number more than 400 fighting men. They are still great bullies—it being impossible to take their village. They have not been at war now for four years when they took 22 heads and many prisoners from the *Elwhas* nearly exterminating that tribe (a sub tribe of the Scallams or Scallam Bay ‹Cape Flattery› Indians).[72] They have been often at war with the Clay-o-quots & Kai-o-quots [Kyuquot?] on West Coast of this Island & accordingly carry it with a high hand. They are noted whale-fishers—& were at present in the stir of the halibut season. In another month the dog-fish oil season will commence when the shore will be heaped with carcases giving out an abominable stench.

After a great talk in which every argument was used to extort money from me I succeeded in engaging a large war Canoe & three good pilots to take our party to Pachena (Port San Juan) (not the Pachena of the charts—the latter is distinguished by the traders as Klootis or Kloochmans Pachena) for $16 which I daresay was more than enough but I thought myself well let off at that;[73] being as I have said wholly in their power; but Indian pay is not looked upon on this Coast as a reward for their services but as a bribe to induce them to work; the Indians not being compelled as in Victoria to face such opposition from the Northern Indians (who are universally looked upon by the Indians of Victoria as the Ultima Thule of "Siwash-dom")[74] to work for a living, having plenty of food, & unless a bribe large enough to tempt them to throw off their habitual laziness is offered they do not care to exert themselves. Before leaving Nitinat I took the precaution of laying in a stock of dried halibut and Elks meat & a few beans and rice as we were almost out of food.

Though the breakers were high, with admirable skill they watched the exact moment and buoyantly went through them. A very heavy swell was on; but under eight paddles it darted along swiftly to Pachena which I had appointed as the rendezvous for the two parties, and a place for our provisions being sent to, not later than 30 June (to-day). About 2 miles down we passed Kloos, a large village of the Nitinats situate in a sandy bay,[75] & further on Quamadooa (marked Carmanah on Richards Chart.) Then came *Echwates*, a small vil-lage—a short way—a little brook flows in where the Indians say there is a "hyou clayl-stone" (plenty coal!) a short way up. A fresh breeze was blowing & from the circumstances related I had unwillingly to pass without examination at present, though if nobody does so be-fore, I will try and visit this spot again. Further on is another village called *Karliet*, if indeed one house built after the white fashion can be dignified with that name. Further on we passed *Wawa-hades*—about a dozen lodges. This is the eastern boundary of the Nitinat territory. It extends west to *Klootis* (Pachena Bay of Charts) and right down to Squitz on the Cowichan River and with some allowances and restric-tions even to Somenaw, so that they have the largest boundary of any tribe on Vancouver Island.

Near here I had the misfortune to burst my valuable fowling piece, from some cause or other unexplained, though I am glad that with the exception of a cut on the finger nobody was hurt. It was certainly vexatious to lose it, especially at this time, but I had got accustomed in a varied and rough travel over the out of the way places of the world to such misfortunes—unavoidable concomitants of travel which can neither be avoided nor repaired.

Soon we entered Pachena or Port San Juan—Camp (Main) No. 13—a deep bight—rounded the point by the Indian village on the right up Coopers Inlet (the mouth of one of the Rivers) where we saw no Gunboat or sign of life. The village on the left being deserted & our hearts sunk within us at the prospect of an empty larder & certainly we had good reason to think that after all our exertions and hardships on the poorest rations & the smallest quantity—the very simple task of supplying us with a little food would not have been neglected by the Committee especially after their own injunctions warning of the exact destination of the rendezvous, where provisions were to be deposited not later than the 30th June and it would only have been reasonable to have deposited them with the trader a few days before. As it was, such neglect did not raise the enthusiasm of the members of the expedition & though I tried by every means to excuse the Committee still it would be wrong to expect subordinates who share all the toil and but little of the honour of such expeditions to take as lenient a view of every thing as their leader. A half <breed> civilized looking Indian boy paddling about showed at least that we were on the borders of civilization, and a neat set of block shanties assured us that the trader was here as I expected but no person was about, but soon the familiar face of Mr. Laughton who received us with numerous witticisms on the bank raised our spirits—& a warm welcome we received from him. A party of prospectors had visited him a few days before who told him that the Gunboat would be down in a couple of days (2 July) with our provisions. The Schooner connected with the trading post had gone with his partner to Victoria[76] but he had enough flour to spare us so that we were freed of fears of starvation (a more difficult matter than people would suppose). Mr. Leech's party had not arrived but I did not entertain much fear for his safety as his journey to the coast was only a matter of time. He had picked men with him and I did not doubt but that Tomo would keep them in food. As it was I would have liked to have seen them here in safety, but as he was only performing the duty for which we had been sent there was no use fretting that he had not performed his so quickly as I had done mine.

Soon a meal was on the table and we hungry demi-savages sat down to the plenty: we thought we had got into Utopia, and old Tom Laughton was the Sir Thomas Moore who had created it: & late at night we sat round his neat "fire room" relating stories or romances. Laughton I had known ever since my arrival in the Colony. He was originally a naval <man> officer and served on the antarctic Expedition and was at one time a midshipman on board Sir John Franklin's Yacht when Gov. of Van Diemen's Land.[77] His ruin was his inability to pass a public house. He had traded here many years, as a free trader of the HBC, and those were the palmy days of dog-fish oils, when he could take out 8000 galls of oil in four or five months work for which he got $1 or $1.50 a gallon.[78] He still finds it profitable, however, though oil is cheap and trade dear. We did not pitch our tents at night but slept all over his floor.

[Friday] July 1st 1864. We did not get up very early this morning as it was an idle day. Spent it in pitching tents, grinding axes, washing clothes and minding boots &c. Visited by many of the natives trading fish &c. I ordered the men to trade nothing themselves as they asked extravagant prices from us but allow Laughton to do it, as it was only fair to him after all his kindness to us that we should not destroy his tariff, by giving extravagant prices which would hurt his trade afterwards. Accordingly he bought for us some fish, berries &c, & as our men were in want of some little things such as soap, tobacco (an ultra qua non of bush men—Fred Walker the leader of the Victoria Colony Exp & Expedn. had to return when they lost their tobacco),[79] so I opened an account with him & bought some sugar and flour &c.

Curious method of felling trees as seen at San Juan Harbour. A Horizontal auger hole is bored in the trunk of a sloping one to meet it from above—a fire is lit with touch wood in the horizontal one, the slanting one [acting] exactly as a chimney, when the trunk takes fire and burns through.[80] The log is cut into lengths by the same method. The open space here was cleared by this method.

Saturday 2nd. July /64. The San Juan or Pachena Indians were once a principal tribe but what with war and disease (last winter many died of dysentery) they are now so thinned that they have amalgamated with the Nitinats. The Thongees [Songhees] from Victoria decimated them a few years ago.[81] Their head chief is Quistach—but he with the great body of his followers has gone to a great Potlach at Chowitzan (which accounts for the empty [village]) or Beechy [Beecher] Bay. They number about 60 fighting men. Their borders are

18 Frederick Whymper, *Patchinah [Pacheenaht] Indians* (Yale Collection of Western Americana, Beinecke Rare Book and Manuscript Library)

the Jordan River on the east and Karliet on the West. They ascend the San Juan & Onesmah Rivers for two or three miles to fish & hunt.

The Gun-boat has not come yet.

Two rivers flow into this bay separated by the Peninsula on which the Station is situated. The East may be called the Coopers' River (as is Coopers Inlet on Chart) [San Juan River], while the west is the Gordon—the distance between two as measured [account breaks off].

It was near sun-set when a canoe came down the river with an Indian and a squaw in it and a figure in the stern wrapped up in blankets. We gathered out to look at him and sure enough who should it be but Foley, one of the long absent Leech party. He was torn, dirty and bleeding—but soon a warm supper, and a long pipe put him in fine spirits and we sat round him like a second Marco Polo while he related his adventures. Since parting with us they had had hard times.

Last night he had parted by accident from the rest of the party until he again struck Coopers River [San Juan River] a few miles lower (they had followed it from first to last about 20 miles), heard a shot and found this Indian and his Squaw. The Indian had his gun pointed at him thinking he was a bear. He went up with him to see if he could find any more of the party, but failed. They told him that six King George Men with a Tyhee with long red hair had come and he was now contented.

They had not suffered from want of food, having killed many ducks and pigeons, also two Elk of which they saw great herds.[82] The Country was thickly wooded and mountainous but he saw some fine green prairies of 2 or 3000 acres.[83]

He had found quantities of plumbago and some ore like silver (specimens of both of which he brought in)—also copper, iron, gold and coal.[84] I ordered him to present a detailed account of the metallurgy of the Expedition from Cowichan Lake to here with a short account of the circumstance which befell him since parting from Leech.

I told the Indians to come back early tomorrow to go back with Foley to find Leech's party if a little way up the river, and convey food, and fire shots for them: promising to pay them well. Rainy to night the first time for more than ten days, during which we have had magnificent weather. Had it been otherwise our troubles would have been doubled.

Sunday July 3rd /64. Today a sloop beat into port and anchored in a cove. Laughton and I went off to her & found her to be the "Random" of Victoria with stores for us. A Plunger had been sent previously and when within five miles of the Port had to turn back, and even this sloop had put back twice to Sooke. My letters were dated 27 June & had only time to acknowledge receipt of letters from Cowichan lake, as the Master was afraid to come into Coopers Inlet having got so often ashore at various places. I engaged Quis-tach the Chief (who had just come into the Village from the Chowitzan Potlach & of whom more anon.) to take the provisions. They were all right, but I might hint to the Committee that a barrel of sugar is not a very handy thing to pack in bulk, and that there are lighter and more efficacious drills than four crow-bars & tea carelessly rolled up in a single sheet of paper, & when we got it, loose among Vermillion, tobacco, and matches. [This] does not conduce to the health or abstinence of swearing & bad language. There was enough of paper & envelopes in all conscience, but no ink or pens & so on, but the bacon was in splendid order, the coffee of Mr. Fell preeminently good, the beans were better than the last (from H B Co. full of dirt) & the flour bags not so rotten as Nesbitts.[85] The biscuit excellent and the tobacco fair, but the Indian tobacco ought to have been in plugs. Roll does not go much on this coast—further north they will take nothing else. Distributed 1 lb of tobacco to each man and charged it to his a/c, & bought a blanket for Tomo from Laughton. By the Bye the tobacco was rather too good for Indians as the sugar was rather too bad for packing about; we wish to pack sugar, not sand & water mixed.

Just as the Sloop entered, the canoe which I had sent up this morning returned with Leech's party. To-day Quistach the Chief arrived in his large war Canoe with his four Wives and other household Gods [goods?]. He is a man about 30, a good friend of the Whites but a terrible Jew at a bargain, having been "bilked" in a shameful manner by white men. He bears a good reputation as a warrior.

[Monday] July 4th, 1864. Very wet. Set all hands to make up bags & put up provisions in convenient parcels. Leech is very bad with dysentery and altogether worn out. Bought several trout & other fish from the Indians. The dog-fish season is just commencing. Laughton calculates that from Pachena to Woody Point [Cape Cook] there is about 15,000 gallons of Dog-fish oil traded every year, comprehending the only district where it is manufactured. This does not include what is taken over to the other side and traded by the Indians to the Americans, who can afford to pay a good price for it, having no duty to pay on it. For instance the Chief of Clay-o quot's son is married to the Chief of Clallam's daughter. The Clay-o quot Chief is a great trader & collects oil of the neighbouring tribes; he then goes over to Cape Flattery and sells it for American goods, and perhaps a little "fire water." I met him last year in Port Angeles in Washington Territory on a visit for that purpose. This 15,000 gallons does not also include what is used by themselves for toilet or culinary purposes. The Dog-fish is found in immense shoals all along the East side of the Island—but no oil is made. If the whites [worked] with improved apparatus (the Indian [apparatus] is merely a box of water into which hot-stones are thrown and the oil skimmed off) it might prove a source of great wealth; as it is already with its very limited manufacture a means of more than a livelihood to a considerable number of traders. I need not speak of the fishery if we only think of the enor-

mous number of all kinds consumed alone by the Indians every year.

Buttle and Leech drawing map of our Explorations. Still a little wet. Engaged Indians tonight to take me up the river to a lake, said to exist there. Engaged Indians and canoe to go in search of coal to Quamadooa [Carmanah Point] said to exist there by Indian report, as could get no canoe here to take us to Sooke & the Sloop not having arrived, we are regularly boxed in without the power to move out; and to take to the mountains with our provisions is out of our power, even if it would serve any purpose, the country having been already explored by Leech's party.

[Tuesday] July 5th 1864. Sent off Foley's party at day-break with provisions and written instructions (Orders No. 3).[86] Colbacks domestic tale of woe.[87] After breakfast started off with two young Indians in a canoe to a lake [Fairy Lake?] supposed to exist & communicating with Coopers River. Left orders with Leech (who is recovering) to have everything packed up for starting and Buttle and Meade to work at Maps &c. Up River with the Indians—mouth alternately shallow & deep. Lake turns off in creek on left—2 miles only in circumference. Descended in evening.

Strange Story of Eucletaw women fleeing from bondage: and endurance.[88] Uses of Indian pointed paddle. "Lord Nelson." Laughton's Tariff in old times. Women's customs in Menses. Quistach's description of Laughton's coming to trade. (Give in full as pictures of Indian life.) Vide Miscell notes on Indian Ethnography Vol I.

[Wednesday] July 6th. 1864. Started to day at 7 a.m. for the other River [Gordon River] flowing into bay—very shallow, water has fallen 2 feet within a few days. Some good land on water, good Hay meadows.

[Thursday] July 7th 1864. Very hot to-day. It is a very strange peculiarity of the barometer in this country—that it will fall for several days & yet beautiful weather, but as soon as it begins to rise rain falls.

Foley returned to day having found the coal, but unfortunately found himself forestalled by a party from Victoria under Mr. Green C[ivil] E[ngineer], [the latter] having heard about it from some traders. He has a very poor opinion of it. I was glad however I had sent a party as it may prevent the forming a swindling Company to work mines which can never pay: even if the coal was of use.[89] He brought back specimens of fossils. The following is his report. [Omitted.]

[Friday] July 8th. 1864. Lat. of Pachena 48°. 33'. 33". Long. [of

Pachena] 124°. 22'. 10" W. Leech getting rate for chronometer—present rate is for 2 days gaining daily 7" 488.

Tried to bargain for a canoe or canoes to take us to Sooke. Now as at first none could be got. Nearly all the Indians here have gone to Karliet to fish & buy halibut & have taken all their large canoes along with them.

Story of the Elwha war and Moquilla chief of Nittinat allaying his sick "Tum-tum" for his dead brother.[90]

[Saturday] July 9th. 1864. Succeed this morning in engaging two canoes and two old men, 2 women and 2 young men to take us to Sooke for $ 10 each canoe. This after very hard bargaining. Sailed with fair wind. Coast [of] low cliffs—dead and scrubby timber with undergrowth of Salal (*Gaultheria shallon*). Then the coast got higher and greener with a background of bare rolling hills like round Victoria, & sloping peaks down to the water's edge. After passing Sheringham Point about 100 yards on east side in a quiet bay found a seam of coal concealed by the foliage—Dip 35°—in the country behind of a thickness from 6 inches to a foot in the cliff—too high up to get good specimens but managed to knock down some indifferent ones with a stick. It promises well as it will probably be thrown up behind in the hills of a great thickness. Apparently continuation of Clallam Bay seams.[91]

Wind blowing too hard to round Otter head. Camped on grassy meadow (good Hay place) by side of a little Inlet where Creek flows in (marked on chart as an unfollowed up Inlet) [Muir Creek]. Found there a party of Sheshaat Indians camped, waiting for the storm to blow over. This place would make a good boat harbor and fishing station. Followed up creek a little way & found fossils in Sandstone & on a creek a little further East beside deserted Indian lodges a piece of coal in the creek, apparently washed by Creek out of seam. Very Wild night.

[Monday] July 11th. 1864. Lieut. Leech took his canoe on to Sooke, while I returned about a mile to inspect anew the coal lead at Sheringham Point. Found nothing new, except that we found outcroppings in hill beyond; Everything promises well for this coal. It does not dip into the sea like the Quamadoa Coal [Carmanah Point] & it is much thicker. Unfortunately there is no good [harbour] but the bay [Orveas Bay] is tolerably sheltered and a breakwater could easily be constructed. Started & beyond anything worthy of note as now entered the Sooke district. Went up Sooke River for about 1 1/2 miles

where found Leech camped on meadow by side of river opposite a settler of the name of Broullé. Got some information from him.[92]

[Tuesday] July 12th. 1864. Occupied all day in making preparations for a start. Gave Leech exact written instructions.[93] Engaged Indians (4 at $2 to pack up) at village. There were only 5 in village—rest gone fishing and to a Potlatch. Divided party as follows: eight to go to head waters of Sooke River. There, divide into two—one to go to Qualis & a second to Somenos. Thus opening up whole Southern section of the Island. While a third goes with me to meet them by way of Victoria, getting some things we are wholly out of. Make some arrangements with the Committee &c.[94] I calculate the first party may reach Somenos by Thursday or Friday [July 21 or 22] when I will be there. Having now arranged everything and as my presence could only avail as one of the party & after mature consideration, I thought I could better serve the interests of the Expedition by taking the course I have done than any other.

[Wednesday] July 13th 1864. Got Indians up—gave last directions. Saw all under way: and then started with Barnston for Sooke Rancheria. Got canoe to go to head of Sooke Basin. Got Half-breed boy to put us on the trail and after hard day's travel arrived at Judge Cameron's.[95] Crossed Harbour & came up to Victoria at 9 p.m.

[Thursday] July 14th 1864. Reported myself to Mr. Cruickshanks. I think I can complete all arrangements by Monday or Tuesday—quite early enough to meet party.

Friday July 22nd [1864]. Our business in Victoria being completed; left this morning at 10 a.m. for Saanich en route for Cowichan to meet our parties overland. The stage brought us at 4 p.m. to Fry's beautiful farm of Arlington at N. Saanich, a series of beautiful oak glades, fertile soil with indications of coal. The wind was adverse to crossing the bay, so remained there all night. Fry's is the best country Hotel I have seen since leaving England & it is certainly a beautiful spot.[96] On the way out are several pretty farms such as Yale's, Harris, Lind's &c.[97]

I heard of a most important branch of manufacture there: viz the gathering of resin to make turpentine from the Douglas and the common pines of the Country. Messrs. Donaldson & Dawson (coloured men I believe who are well acquainted with the manufacture in the great turpentine country of the Carolinas) made in six weeks 100 galls. of pure & very strong turpentine pronounced by painters and others to whom it was shown to be of as good quality as they had ever seen.[98] They are convinced that this Island presents a good field for the business. The turpentine is obtained by boring with an auger—only those trees supposed to contain cavities, "blisters" or "wind-shakes" are bored, and these when tapped yield from 10 to 20 galls. of liquid gum. This is then distilled in the ordinary way, the residue forming rosin. The best gum trees are found on rolling land with good soil—some little skill being required in selecting the trees containing the cavities where the fluid lodges. It is only found in healthy trees—& never in those badly scorched by fire as the gum in that case exudes through the bark. They say that a man can readily make from $2 to $4 per day collecting the gum. The price of turpentine during the last four years has risen 300 per cent. An American firm in Oregon commenced with 50 dollars (not as usual when Americans are making their rise in the world "without a *red* cent"—particular, mark you, as to the color, the most curious part being that cents are *not red*) and have now made $20,000 & have four Manufactories going—all within the last 2 years. This is better than gold digging. The present retail price for spirits of Turpentine is $3. per gall.

Saturday 23rd. July [1864]. Started this morning at 9 a.m. with Barnston, Skinner, & Hamway in Fry's regular Ferry Plunger ($1.50) for Cowichan. Arrived at John Lemon's at 1 p.m. Harris was from home much to our gratification. Found no news of my party. All the settlers busy hay making this year. This is the only year which would pay to take it to Victoria—hay selling at $45 per ton or 3 cents per lb retail. Last summer it was only $16 per ton. It takes $8 dollars to stack & cut it and $7 a ton to take it to Victoria. If you have a compressing machine you can freight it for $5 per ton.

Sunday 24 July [1864]. Went to church this morning. Service a mumble of bad Latin and worse English—a few Indians, French Canadians, and their half-breed families. Afterwards the priest addressed the Indians. Sometimes the little Log Church is crowded. Just now most of the Indians have gone away fishing so that just now it is pretty much deserted. After service talked with Father Rondeault & Frere Antoine his assistant. Found them simple, good natured men with great influence over the Indians. Asked in to stay to dinner but went over to my friend M. Jean Compagnon who was kindness itself in his mild amiable way. His garden if possible looked prettier than ever—a perfect pleasure ground. Walked over part of the Indian Reserve afterwards. I saw Mr. Marriner's house which forms a local bone of contention.[99] He has cultivated part of the Indians' land which was not however under cultivation by them. Most of the Indians cultivate potatoes and they have certainly plenty of land for that purpose; possessing 3 or 4000 acres of land reserved for them.[100] This is certainly too much [and] very inconvenient, being distant from their villages in many cases. For instance most part of the Comiaken village is built on private land. An Indian if he can help it will never remove the site of his village. The reserves ought properly to have been round each village, in all perhaps 500 acres with the sites of all their fishing villages which would amply have satisfied them. As it is the whites are deprived of a large extent of the most valuable land in the colony without its being of the slightest value except in one or two isolated patches to the people for whom it was reserved from pre-emption or sale. If a reserve is to be for the Indian let it be strictly reserved and not as in the case of the reserve at Victoria allowed (height of absurdity) to be leased out in building lots.[101] Here in Cowichan the same thing is being done. An Irishman has built & fenced in a farm on part of Indian Reserve & carries things with a high hand.[102] The best landing place is at his house and he refuses to carry any one across except at high figures beyond reach of the settlers' means. His pigs run out among the Indian potato patches and if they remonstrate they get nothing but abuse and ill usage & the other day he shot poor little Lemon's (The Indian Boy) dog because he thought Lemon had killed one of his pigs. The ball passed between two squaws. The men were much excited and begged of the priest (who has unbounded influence over them) to be allowed to kill him. This man ought certainly to be punished. The whole of the whites speak of him as the Black sheep in their midst and the Indians hate and despise him to a man.

Saw Sem-el-ton, Chief of Quamichan, a noble looking savage dressed in a soldier's coat. He came up and shook hands with me; he had heard of me from Kakalatza and was glad to see me back again. I must have as stout a heart as he had heard to go so far & yet return safe, so he said.

Saw also Jean Baptiste, joint chief of Samena. He has a paper from Bishop Demers saying that he is the only chief and ought to be recognized as such. He is certainly the hereditary chief but Kakalatza being a man of great weight & judgment & cousin of Baptiste is generally looked up to as joint-chief and the acts of one are not to be vetoed by the other & vice-versa. In the evening went over to Lemon's.

Monday July 25th 1864. Writing all day. Obtained a *Berberis*—a congenor of the Oregon grape but growing 10 to 14 ft. in height & 4 to 8 inches in diameter.

Tuesday July 26th 1864. This morning at 6 a.m. Jean Compagnon came and told me according to the directions which I gave yesterday, that the Chief of the Somenaw had heard firing about the River & that he thought it must be my men, as there were no Indians up there. I had been afraid to travel up the River as I had told them not to wait for me, and if they struck the River anywhere intermediate I would altogether miss them and give my labor for nothing. Besides little good would be obtained by adopting so laborious and expensive a course.

Started at 8 a.m. & reached Samena Village at 1/2 past 9 a.m. Found only one family living there. Kakalatza had gone to the Lake, Jean Baptiste to the mouth of the River. They all knew about my men but gave me the discouraging intelligence that it was a false alarm. By request I sat down in the place of honour in the lodge and answered their numerous questions about Govr. Kennedy—his appearance, his character, & policy to the Indians. I answered them as shortly, & as intelligibly as I could; as I considered it a good opportunity to impress upon them the true ideas which his Excellency had given me, rather than allow it to be done later & perhaps not so truthfully. The first impressions are always the strongest and as they now looked upon me from the representation of their chief Kakalatza who had been with us to the lake, as a great Chief "who always spoke straight," & as a good friend to the Indians—I told shortly and clearly: (1) That Mr. Kennedy was one of King George's soldier Chiefs. (2) That he was a very tall, strong man. (3) That he had a strong heart & always spoke straight. Suppose he said "I will do it," he does it. Suppose he says "I will punish you," you will *be* punished. His tongue never lies. (4) He was as good a friend to the Indians as Mr. Douglas; though perhaps he might think it was not good to do some of the things to Indians he had done & might do other things that Mr. Douglas (who had gone to see King George) did not do. However he & Mr. Douglas were great friends. (It was no use telling them that their great head was a woman, I once told them (some Snoqualimi) that our great Chieftaness was a woman, and showed them her portrait on an English shilling; & that the Chief of the Bostons was Mr. Lincoln; after being amused at our having a woman over us, they asked me if they were good friends. I said that they were very good friends. Had Queen

Victoria a husband? He was dead I replied. "Then," said they, as they
dug their paddles into the water for another spell, "Mr. Lincoln ought
to take Queen Victoria for his Kloochman"!) (5) That the White man
and the Indian would be protected and punished the same. (6) That
they would be protected in their Village & as much land as would
grow potatoes [account breaks off].

They were very well pleased but growled sadly at not being paid for
their lands. My business being finished I gave the head man a letter to
give Leech's party should they come down. Obtained an Indian and a
canoe and swept down the River to Comiaken and then to John
Lemon's. The Indian showed me a Copper lead cropping out on some
of Jean Compagnon's land (near Village at mouth of River) where he
found copper, & the Comiakin Cos. Claim. Cowichan Harbour is very
shallow (it can be crossed on horseback at Low Water) but at high
water a schooner of 25 tons can anchor in the river opposite Compagnon's. In passing over, the Indian told me a curious tradition. Pointing
to a row of sticks fixed in the mud and apparently crossing the
Harbour, he told me that this was the remains of a great salmon weir
which long ago extended right across the Harbour, when the Indians
were numerous and the salmon innumerable. At one time he said the
Indians had no canoes but lived by Hunting or catching what fish they
could without canoes; but long, long ago a man arrived from a far
country and taught them how to make a canoe. He burnt down a tree,
hollowed it with fire, and taught them to make an axe out of bones of
an Elk. Then they had little or no war except near home; now they
travelled far in their canoes, warred with each other, and from that
date began to decrease. At that time they never thought of splitting
boards to build houses, but when they made an axe they left their
holes in the ground, where they lived like some Indians on Fraser
River not long ago—and built board houses such as they now lived in.
Tuesday July 26 [1864]. In the evening Mr. Leech and the whole party
at Harris's house. He had not separated into two parties, considering,
from what he had seen from the tops of the mountains that the
country was not worth that trouble and having been delayed some
time by a brilliant discovery they had made: viz. the discovery of rich
placer diggings upon Sooke River, and its branch "Leech River."
They were wild with excitement and certainly the coarse scale gold
was enough to excite anyone. The whole particulars will be found
hereafter. That night I gave them a "blow out" at Harris's and wrote
an account of it to the Committee. Leech had written me previously

but he had subsequently found these much richer prospects. Encamped near Lemon's that night.

Wednesday July 27th [1864]. Up at 6 a.m. and desirous that such a discovery which promised to be of such value to the Colony should not be delayed one hour I dispatched Corporal Buttle with dispatches to the committee.[103] Gave him $20 to pay expenses & gave him the parcel of gold.

I found now on regaining the Expedition that there had been dissensions in the camp and that quarrels among the men, petty at first, had grown into importance. Before myself there had never been any word but I saw plainly that unless there was something done, there would be some deserting. I tried what I could, spoke to one, reasoned with a second and so on, and finally all was getting quieted down, until in a quarrel at dinner Mr. Foley drew a knife on Macdonald. I found it was high time to do something, so I told Foley he had better ask his discharge, & though I ought perhaps under the

19 Frederick Whymper, *Sooke Lake* (Yale Collection of Western Americana, Beinecke Rare Book and Manuscript Library)

circumstances not only to have dismissed him in disgrace & without
pay but as he had performed his duty so well hitherto I considered for
our sakes it was better to quiet the matter over & discharge him in
full. I did so—gave him money to pay his expenses and parted in
peace.[104]

Mr. Leech was much incensed against him and refused to stay
under the same roof with him. There had not been good blood between them since an occurrence on his party to Port San Juan & had
been increased lately. Foley was a very double faced fellow—a Yankee
at the bone, and he only entered the expedition for what he could
make of it & finally the gold discoveries upset him. The full particulars I have entered in my private despatches to the Secretary so that it
is unnecessary to repeat them here.[105]

Removed in the afternoon to a camp (No. 25) opposite Jean Compagnon's. Leech's foot had got burned so I left him at Lemon's.
Thursday July 28 [1864]. Writing all day. Then employed variously.
Visited by several of the settlers: viz. by the Lady Superior & two Sisters
of Mercy who have come to inspect the erection of a school here.[106]
Leech had brought over with him from Sooke a half breed Iroquois &
Sooke boy, a capital hunter & packer, called Lazare la Baggay; who was
anxious to travel with us as a packer and as I found it difficult to obtain
such when required, I engaged him at $25 per month. Received a
present of Potatoes, Butter and Milk from Father Rondeault the Priest
with a characteristic letter which I preserve here:

Dear Sir
I think it my duty by presenting you with what my limited
means allow me, to evince how sincerely, I deal in the general
sympathy that is felt for your Expg Exped. Although my
present is very slight indeed yet I hope you will be so kind as
to accept it together with the expression of my general con-
sideration, because it springs forth from a disposition to fur-
nish more, if more were in my power.

                                                      July 28/64

Cowichan Valley

                                                      P Rondeault

Sat for some time in Jean Baptiste's Lodge. He is co-joint Chief of
Somenos with Kakalatza. Told me of coal near Chemanus & his son in

law a Chief of Chemanus promised to go with me to show me it. Sent off dispatches to Committee of Mr. O'Brien.

Friday July 29th [1864]. Writing. Visited again en-passant by the Sisters of Mercy. We are out of bacon. Bought a pig for $ 10 from Jack Humphreys. Nasty people say he stole it! & on further belief do not doubt it.[107]

Saturday July 30th [1864]. Went down to Harris. Bought some sugar & tea from him. Gave the a/c to Committee as hitherto I have been paying for provisions and Indians out of my money for travelling expenses.

Sunday July 31st [1864]. At Church. Sent off despatch No. 7 to the Committee.[108] Great excitement about Sooke diggings here & I hear that [in] Victoria [it] is greater. Buttle returned from Victoria with letters & $ 100 from Committee. Told all hands to prepare for a start tomorrow. Went over to Lemon's and told Leech to get ready to start.

Monday August 1st [1864]. Tomo Antoine the Indian hunter got drunk but as Buttle returned yesterday determined to get off. It is impossible to keep the men from drink when they are inclined to get it and Tomo is the one I am most afraid of as he is a madman in liquor. As it is, the men complain that they are not allowed their full swing, but if so there is no end. In the afternoon anxious to get clear of the Harbour so as to make a clear start in the morning. Arranged two parties—one under Leech in Canoe as he was unable to walk: (1) Leech's party: Leech, Whymper, Meade, Barnston, Tomo, Jean Baptiste and his canoe. (2) Commander, Rest of Party. Willing to give Tomo a chance, I told Leech to camp for the night & if not sober next morning to discharge him.

Discharged all accounts and returned to Camp No. 25 that night.

Tuesday August 2nd [1864]. Yesterday I had engaged two Quamichan Indians to assist our men to pack to Nanaimo overland but they did not come this morning. Waited until 1/2 past 11 a.m. then started for the Quamichan district with the Chief of Chemanus and his wife.[109] On arriving at the Village sought out one of the Indians who excused himself upon the plea that the other Indian had changed his mind, and agreed with him for $ 1. a day, and finding I could dispense with the other Indian started with him. Through a wooded country until we arrived at Drinkwaters Farm—a good prairie formed into fields with some under cultivation. Travelled until 4 o'clock until we came to a creek beyond Drinkwaters, generally known to the Settlers as "Bannermans" from the first settler[110] and fearing that water was scarce

we camped (No. 26). A pleasant situation at base of Mt. Prevost—
glen slope with prairies dotted or encircled with clumps of Trees.
Visited by Smithe.[111] Sent Lazar out to hunt—got nothing.
Wednesday August 3rd [1864]. Up at 6 a.m. Started off travelling
through a succession of prairies for 3 miles, then thinly wooded
country, then thickly wooded with occasional swamps in hollows until
we entered the Chemanus Valley. Passed through fine Prairie once
settled on by Major Begg J.P. an old East Indian Company Officer.[112]
(Begg has gone to England intending to bring out his wife.) Another
man has jumped his "Claim" declaring that the improvements for
which Begg obtained his certificate are not on the farm: since dead.
Here we struck off the Nanaimo trail on to the Indian trail until we
struck the Chemanus or Salwaenth River flowing N & S (Mag-
netic)—very shallow at this season, many cattle grazing about. Soon
visited by a well educated young gentleman Mr. Mangey [Minguay]
who settled here a few months ago. (Here we pitched our tents, the
afternoon being advanced & the Indians travelling so very slowly.)
With him I visited Mr. Holbert [Habart] the principal settler. He is
the son of a French prisoner in England who married an Englishwoman. Holbert has gone into farming heavily: besides quantities of
pigs he has 70 head of Cattle grazing in the woods and salt marshes.
He came from Australia and has a partner.[113] The Settlers are loud in
their grievance against some ridiculous regulations which the Superintendent of Police wished to inforce. These I have noticed under the
head of *Indians.*

The Indians told me that the coal was still distant at the salt water
and as it looked wet, remained. Called on Manguy [Minguay] in the
Evening, and had a long talk with him about the Indians.[114] (Vid. my
"Notes on Indians of the North West Coast.")
Thursday August 4th [1864]. Very wet all day, remained in camp.
Poured with scarcely an interval from morning to night. I spoke
yesterday of the complaints of the Settlers. They are as follows: A
Half-breed Negro & Oneida to ingratiate himself with the Indians
had been putting them up to all manner of grievances—among others that the whites' Cattle &c were over-running their Potato patches.
Accordingly the Superintendent of Police wishes them to fence in
their farms and Cattle-runs to protect the little patches of the Indians. They fence in *their* crops & would it not be easier for the Indians
to fence in their patches than for the whites to fence in their cattle? If

the regulation is enforced the whites who have cattle will be forced to leave the valley.

Another [complaint] is to the reserves. A Reserve has been made for the Chemanus tribe proper which they do not desire as they only come there for a short period each year for fishing and all they wish or require is the site of their village (a few lodges) but, to form this reserve, land was taken from a Settler which at great labour he had cleared & as yet he has received no recompense. Instead of cultivating it the Indians are allowing it to get overgrown with bush again.

As we had killed no game and were now out of Bacon, I bought a deer and pork ham from Mangey [Minguay]. Awoke at night by a fight between the dog and a raccoon close to the tent. Too dark to see the sport.

Friday August 5th [1864]. The rain last night had rendered the trail almost impassable & as our food was getting low and no good purpose to be served in scrambling over fallen logs for the next three or 4 days as the strip of coast was passably well known & the coal was further down the river I determined to take to the sea for it—crossed the River to a few lodges called "Hap-hap-ye." There engaged an old man and his large Canoe to take us to Nanaimo; he insisted on taking his two squaws and a brood of children with him & as they would supply dunnage I consented. A little lower down the Indian showed me the place where he had taken out the coal but we could see none, but the rocks were the same as those of Nanaimo & I do not doubt from the whole conformation of the country that coal exists in the valley. The old squaw told me that once when she was gathering berries, she had seen coal—but as I had no time to waste here I had to content myself with recommending search to be made in the district for that important object and I have no doubt that to properly equipped parties it would yield good results.

The timber on the river is *A. Douglasii, Juniperus* [*scopulorum*—red cedar], *Thugei* [*plicata*—western red cedar], Arbutus, and a few oaks (*Quercus Garryana*). Sailed down the river for 1/4 mile (not before having to haul the canoe over a raft of logs). Came to mouth of the River—Helelt & Penclehut Islands [Shoal Islands], Island of [illegible] where lives Thoseatan [Tsosieten] Chief of Taitka, once a chief of Cowichans long ago. (His history.) Passed large village of Chemanus Indians. Saw Mills—men boring for coal[115]—party of White men taking sight for turpentine manufactory.

At 6 p.m. camped at a regular Indian Camping Place.[116] Found
Water where none but an Indian would have found it in a mossy pool
in the woods. After supper Lazar and a Quamichan (whom from his
red cap I had christened Ny-qua-Yusack "Red-cap") only returned
after firing shots long after dark. They carried a fawn with them.
Saturday August 6th [1864]. Up at 4 a.m. Saw a steamer in the
distance. On coming below Dodd's Narrows (The Rapids) we found
her to be the mail steamer—"Emily Harris." "What news," we
shouted. "Big news from Sooke—a seventy dollar nugget!"[117] and we
shot past thinking they were only joking us. They apparently suspected who we were. They were waiting the turning of the tide to get
through the narrows. A little further up we found a party of 3 Nanaimos on their way from Victoria, cooking breakfast. We went ashore
to get the news: but scarcely had we put foot on the beach before they
shouted "*Hyou gold copa Sooke—Konoway King George man clatawa
copa Sooke, Wake Siah halo man Midlight Victoria.*" ("Plenty of gold
at Sooke every Englishman goes to Sooke. In a short time nobody will
remain in Victoria.") The current was strong but the men dug in their
paddles with a will as the news lit them up. Curious honeycombed
cliffs on way up. Fresh breeze starting up—made Nanaimo by 10
o'clock. Landale.[118] Found Leech camped by the mill stream creek.
Fixed the camp & "Emily Harris" coming in shortly afterwards found
that the Committee had sent up two more men, Drew & Hooper,[119]
to join the party who reported themselves.

Reported myself to Captn. Franklyn J.P., Chairman of the branch
Committee at Nanaimo.[120] Received offers of every kindness and
assistance from him. Drew on him for $150. Injustice of having my
private journal being made accessible to the newspapers without cor-
rection or any supervision as I see by the papers. If so I shall be
obliged not to send anything but what I wish for publication as the
committee have broken faith with me in that matter, my Journal
being for the time being private & for their information only.[121]

Paid off all Indians—of course with usual growls. Agreed to meet
the Committee at Nanaimo. Leech's foot not better.
Sunday August 7th [1864]. Nanaimo is the Colville town of the
Hudson Bay Co. I notice a great change in it since I was last here.[122]
Description of Nanaimo and its Institutions. Excitement about gold
discoveries through town. Visits &c.
August 8th Monday [1864]. Writing all day. Met the sub-Committee
of Mr. Franklyn's in the evening. Gave them a resumé of our plans &

20 Frederick Whymper, *Nanaimo* (Yale Collection of Western
Americana, Beinecke Rare Book and Manuscript Library). In
Travel and Adventure in the Territory of Alaska, Whymper
wrote: "Nanaimo, seventy miles north of Victoria, is the second
town in point of size on the island; in fact, the list ends there;
there is not a third as yet. It owes its existence mainly to valuable
coal deposits . . . and it has had a steadier and more healthy
career than Victoria."

course. Agreed with me & determined to leave the whole matter in
my hands.[123]
August 9th Tuesday [1864]. Mr. Franklyn gave me an order on the
Company (V.I. Coal)[124] for provisions &c. Selected them and as the
men required some things put these also down to men's accounts.
Wrote to Victoria by Mr. Hollingsworth. Tried to obtain some Indians—found great difficulty as had heard of great strike for pay all
over the country.
Wednesday August 10 [1864]. To day the Indians refused to give an
answer. They are waiting to see what will turn up. The Colliers have
struck for pay and all the Indians that can be got all engaged by the
Coal Company. Went to the Indian Village but found none but old
men and women there. Great excitement in Nanaimo. Fear of my
men deserting.

Thursday August 11 [1864]. Today again I went to the Indian Village with no better success than yesterday. No men there.

[Friday] August 12th 1864. Tomo of Course drunk.[125] I was compelled to keep the men quiet to advance a little Money of their pay which pretty much used up all the Cash I had remaining over and of course we had to return our Hospitality slightly but this is essential especially in a Community like Nanaimo where it is important that the good will of the people should go with the Expedition. Went to Mr. Nicol's[126] (as Mr Franklyn was from home) to ask his assistance about the Indians. Sent for one of the chiefs who promised to try and get some but these Chiefs have little influence and do not like to interfere in making bargains with white men.

Steamer Arrived from Burrard Inlet—reported that nobody was there and no lumber—all had gone to Sooke. Consulted Mr Franklyn and finally succeeding in engaging three Indians and obtaining their Marks to a paper with the Govt Seal to it. Pay $1 per diem, a pair of boots and a premium of 12 1/2 cents for every Deer killed with the proviso that at least one Weeks Notice is to be given before leaving. [The] other two promised in the morning.

Saturday August 13th 1864. This morning got all ready for a Starting to Leech up the Nanaimo River or Swoelum. It is marked on some of the Maps as Quamquamqua which means the Swift River, and then via Cowichan Lake for Barclay Sound. Three Indians came—the other two would not come. Somebody had told them that I would not be back until the snow was on the ground so they got frightened. Called on Mr Franklyn who sent the policeman round and succeeded in obtaining one more, and adding to them the boy Lazar I made up Leech's complement much to my satisfaction. The labour and vexation I have had during the week cannot scarcely be conceived & all the brunt had to be born by myself alone as none could help. With cultus men they would not strike bargains and those who ought to have assisted me preferred to give me all the labour and take the Honour if all went well and who never were amiss to lay the blame and responsibility on my back. It was not too late to start. Concert in Nanaimo in the evening. I am now fretting to be off—not only to go on with our work but to keep the men out of the way of excitement and desertion.

Sunday August 14th 1864. Thanks to Brother Crosbie[127] the Indians were too pious to work on Sunday. They had solemnly declared that they would not fail to come tomorrow (Sunday) but they were engaged from yesterday (Sunday included) and made their petty excuses for their idleness. So another day was lost which might have been employed for though I keep Sunday when practicable, still when a week has been Idle, I think especially considering the circumstances that I am justified in starting them. Walked out with Mr Landale C.E. to visit the Harewood Coal Company's claim.[128] Described it in Report.

Monday August 15 1864. Up at 5 a.m. this morning. All the Indians came. Got Leech off—each Indian with 100 lb on his back!! Troubles with Leech—Vanity &c &c. I trust that he will perform his duty as he has every advantage—a river to guide him as we know to the Cowichan Lake ranges (the Kennedy range) and then the Cowichan Lake to within a day's journey of Barclay sound. Gold is known to exist on the river.[129] He has the pick of the men and the part of the country he wished to explore. Besides he has got good packing—every thing forethought for him, but the gold fever sometimes turns men's heads. *Verb. sap.* As my funds were nearly expended and as I had to pay my Indians &c, I drew on Mr. Nichol as Manager of the Branch Bank of British Columbia for $250 and gave a bill on Committee for it. At the same time I wrote to the Committee full particulars about the whole transactions & left specimens of the Coal which according to the directions I gave Leech & which I had received from an Indian he had found on an Island of the De Courcy group which I named after the quantity of Arbutus on it "Arbutus Island." On the cliff above, Whymper painted V.I.E.E. & the date. There is a good cove for Steamers there.

Engaged an Indian and his canoe (Eyees) and his squaw to take our party to Comox or properly ("Comoucs" country) for $16. I found it was impossible to haggle about engaging Indians here though several Comoucs applied to me—but I knew that the prices asked were exorbitant (one fellow when I refused his demands shouted "All gold Chief"—the name by which they had begun to distinguish me— "soon money will become so common that it will be given as a cultus potlatch") and it was quite possible that after giving them a passage to their own country they would desert—besides I did not know how long I would require them, and there were plenty at Nanaimo.

Met tonight Captn. Hugh McKay of the "Surprise" a famous Indian trader of this coast.[130] He gave me much useful information & much which had I met him sooner would have been of much use to me.

Tuesday August 16 [1864]. Got everything ready. Signed the a/c for stores &c and endorsed an order for $25 dollars from Macdonald's pay in payment of a/c at "Nanaimo Coal Cº." Got the canoe round and put the provisions on board. The Revd. Mr. Good requested to be allowed to accompany us to Comox; which of course I immediately granted.[131] Embarked at 10 a.m. Messrs. Franklyn, Turner &c saw us off and we cheered, and re-cheered by them and the crew of H.M.S. "Forward" which was lying in the Harbour. Passed the old works of Hudson's Bay Company & the Town of Newcastle [Island] the voters on the town lots of which can turn the tide of an election at Nanaimo. On getting outside found the wind ahead. Camped at Blunden Point (Admiralty Chart: St Georgia in sheet 2).[132]

Wednesday August 17 [1864]. Magnificent morning. Slept in the open air last night, but heavy dews are now falling and for the first time this summer I have felt chills at night. Visited by a Portuguese and his squaw on their way to Nanaimo. The Portuguese told me that he had a ranch in Nanoose Bay and begged us to make free with all he had. Wind still ahead which increased to a gale, so put into Nanoose harbour. Scenery round Nanoose Harbour rocky with open glades (only patches) and a few scattered oaks, maples &c. Found in Portuguese's garden pumpkins, potatoes like marbles and a few provisions—helped ourselves to what we wanted—sailed up to near the head of Bay and there camped. Notched Hill on the right—snow peaks in the distance. Nanoose Harbor was once the headquarters of the Nanoose Indians but they have nearly all [been] killed off by disease or war and stay with the Nanaimos and only visit here for clamming or fishing. We noticed a grave or two on the other side of the Harbor, and heard the shots of a few Indians shooting, for Nanoose is a great game country. They now number only 12 and all their Chiefs are dead. Sent Drew and Macdonald to prospect the stream flowing into Nanoose Harbour. Sent Tomo to hunt, Whymper to sketch, & Meade to cook dinner. After a cup of coffee all started out.

Mr. Good and I went to the head of the Bay—previously discovered some nice patches of Indian's potatoes to which in the name of Queen Victoria and her faithful Deputy His Excellency Arthur Edward Kennedy &c &c, I commanded the cook to help himself and excellent potatoes they proved to be. Macdonald proposed to leave our note for the amount, leaving it on the nearest tree, but his proposition was vetoed in favor of the time honoured policy of "God helping those who help themselves." The mouth of the River is surrounded by fine meadows permeated by mouth of River. Leaving the flats we struck into the woods & were rather (it must be frankly confessed) disappointed to find a log shanty showing us that we could not describe the land as a discovery though I do not suppose 99 in 100 know such lands exists. Returned. An hour afterwards Macdonald and Drew returned—had penetrated back until they struck the Victoria & Comox trail (a clear loss to the Colony of $50,000 [sic]—nobody wants it) now almost useless—covered with fallen trees, and requiring to be cut out again.[133] It is a regular Contractor's road, a fearful imposition upon the Government. They had found the creek quite dry and of course no gold. Found some cleared patches with potatoes.

August 18th 1864. Tomo went out hunting early this morning, but had no luck. Crossed over the neck between Nanoose Bay and North West Bay. Found the woods open & in some places soil rocky. Flat lands. Started off at 9 a.m. previously helping ourselves to some more potatoes under the approval of the Church, so we took the buckets with a clear conscience! Still a head wind—hailed some Nanoose Indians fishing. Bought a splendid rock cod from them. Hitherto the forest had come down almost to the water's edge, or green rock had frowned above you. Now all was changed. Beautiful grassy meadows or what in the North of Scotland are called "Links" skirted the coast for a quarter of a mile in breadth. In some cases intersected with "slues" or Inlets of the sea & in some cases overflows at high water but in some cases intersected by Creeks wending their way to the sea—and in some cases scattered with rural, lovely looking clumps of pines and quite dry. Wild pasturage of various species grow thickly all [over] these flats, and when hay is at $29 a ton and the howl is everywhere for pasture land I have no sympathy with men who have not the enterprize enough to occupy these flats with the thousands of cattle they are capable of supporting. The worst of them are as good as the famed Essex flats on the Thames. Through the middle of one of these flats flowed a river, and as night was drawing on and the ground formed a good camping place we sailed up for 1/4 mile & there camped in a beautiful place.

This river is not marked on the latter Survey, or at least not named, but I like it to be the Rio de Grullas of Eliza Survey[134] & it is so marked on the reduced Survey of this part of the island which is Spanish though on the recent enlarged Survey (not yet reduced) it is not marked.

Friday August 19th 1864. Up at 6 a.m. Fresh breeze and heavy surf on the beach. Erected a cross at mouth of Rio de Grullas opposite one of

Captn. Richards with names and date of visit. Heavy surf on the beach. Accordingly shipped some water which did not improve our sugar &c. Flats extend all along the coast to past Point Leonardo of the Spanish Charts, (from which this part of the coast on the reduced scale is copied—the large survey has not yet been reduced)[135] and with intervals to past Qualicum. All of the same nature as those seen yesterday. Breeze continuing fair—rain past Qualicum or Quallecham (so named from the large Salmon which are found) spanned by a pretty bridge, about the last of "Malcolm Munro's Contract trail" bridges standing. A little previously we had passed Saatlaam "the place of green leaves." (It may be remembered there is a place of the same name on the Cowichan River meaning the same thing as they all speak the same language.) Once the village of the Qualicom Indians but now desolate except at chance times. Still the same old story of passing away! What with war and small-pox the Qualicoms have ceased to exist as a separate tribe. They only number 3 and have united with the Comoucs for mutual protection. Mahoy ahoy, a Qualicom, is a notorious scoundrel but withal a very clever fellow as most scoundrels are. (Mahoy ahoy in the Cowichan language means "basket." What reference it has to his patronymic I cannot tell.) He will have the honor of appearing at more length in these pages.

Qualicom River flows out of Hornes Lake from [where] a well known Indian trail takes to Alberni.[136] It is much travelled by runaway sailors and mill men from the Alberni saw mills. It can be travelled in from 1/3 to 3 days according to the facilities for finding Canoes. There were several on Hornes Lake but they were so convenient for running away of sailors, that Capt. Stamp J.P. ordered them to be destroyed. I believe there is still one on it. M^r. Cave the Missionary[137] is in possession of a very pretty drawing of the lake by Lieut. Bedwell R.N. who visited it in 1859.[138] Passed on the right Denman & Hornbys Islands, which with the main land go to form Baynes Sound of the Admiralty Charts last Survey.

Judging that we could not make Comoucs before dark, camped on village point of Denman Island, on the deserted Village of the Comoucs. It still retained traces of its former grandeur—pickets, carved images, &c, & massive hewn cedar frames. These carvings are all much of the same nature, some of them very obscene, their women and children being represented *in partis Naturalibes*. Others of their figures refer to their Mythology & the figure of the owl occurs frequently, the bird of Athens among the Indians as among the Greeks being a bird of superstition. It is they say the spirit of the dead and they will crowd closer round their camp fire as they hear the solemn hoot in the gloomy pine forest & wonder if they have offended the dead by talking about any one in the land of spirits. Among Indians it is a great breach of etiquette to mention the dead. "The Dramatic Raven" "that croaked from Duncan's battlements" or nodded over the chamber door of the poet[139] was not more a bird of ill-omen than the matter of fact one which devours the offal round the Indian villages or sit in long solemn rows on a salmon-drying frame—this "gallows swan" as the Norse poets call it. There is a story of its original transformation from an inhospitable Indian who refused Helse (the great Spirit who taught the Indian everything) food, into the Raven. Its croak foretells battle, and old patriarchs will be pointed out to you who have long foretold disaster & ruin to the tribe. Its croaking as among the weather-wise of all countries also bodes rain, and altogether it is an important element in Indian Mythology. We are apt to despise the "poor Indian" in his rudeness, & those who know least about his ways & feelings & ideas about things are loudest in their abuse. They treat him as they treat a man loafing about with a ragged coat on his back—and the Vancouverites are only too apt to judge the whole race, as they see them lounging about the towns—at once the most civilized and most degraded of his race. Civilization spoils a savage. His whole ways are changed. He is not fitted to take the polish of the whites and his barbarism sits but rudely on him. He is a parody on the white man. "He is neither Flesh nor fish nor yet good red herring." The writer of this (possibly dogmatic) assertion has seen much of the savage, the semi-savage, and the "pious-Indian" and states it advisedly and if necessary can substantiate it by a thousand instances. He knows there are exceptions, but the rule is too common to be pardoned—by exceptions. In this place I cannot go into it. In another place and at a more convenient season, I will write more at full on this point, unpleasant though it be to those well meaning people who subscribe to the Society for "the propogation of the gospel in foreign parts" in general and "British Columbia" in especial.

Their own Theology is what Mr. [Joseph] Addison would call a very pretty piece of Divinity. There are Pans & Driads—Gods of the woods & the groves, the running streams and the fountains. I have seen the women sitting for hours listening to the God of the Waterfalls! With all their rudeness I wonder if our fore-fathers were one wit

more civilized than these Indians. I do not think that the Ancient
Briton's Chariot showed a degree of more skill than the Indian canoe
or that woad was any better than Vermillion. I suppose that it bore
much the same relation to vermillion as "Wool" to "Haar" [Hair] for
a profound authority has declared the latter to be as good as the
former. But I am away from my subject.

The Village where we camped (No.33) must once have been very
extensive but is now quite deserted & nothing but the frames stand.
After a long search found their water in a wood where none but an
Indian could have found it. This village has a history. Once upon a
time (my informant is Eyees, a Nanaimo, and his eyes glisten as he
tells it) the Eucletaws threatened the total annihilation of the Comoucs, who then lived nearly wholly at this Village.[140] An old Seer
foretold this. So the Comoucs fortified their Village and asked the
help of their quondam enemies the Nanaimos, who, however they
bitterly disliked, the Comoucs happened just hated the Eucletaws, the
terror of the coast (as they are yet), still worse. So they came in force
& lay as a reserve in the woods. The Eucletaws' Canoes hove in sight
but suspecting strategem they considered prudence the better part of
valor and concluded to retire. So the Camp of the Comoucs was safe
and a great "Potlach" was given to the Nanaimos. The site of the old
Village from the quantity of manure was covered with rich grass.

Saturday August 20 [1864]. Up at 6 a.m.—cold & chilly with heavy
dew on the ground. The heavy dews commence about this time. This
day last year I was sleeping on a gravel bar on the banks of the
Snoqualami in Washington territory—& then for the first time I
began to think it too late in the year to sleep in the open. I think so
now too. Still, fair wind through Baynes Sound. Beautiful scenery on
North—the snow peaks of the Beaufort range (5431 feet, 4861 ft.,
4903 ft. 4829 ft. & 4426 ft.)—on the right the little sound dotted with
canoes & the shore all along merry with smoking fish [and] "clamming" camps of Comoucs.

We entered Port Augusta (Comox Harbor) about 11 a.m. with a
large convoy of canoes returning from fishing. On being told of my
mission one of them, a wrinkled old woman, remarked "Ah Sir, you
will see a fair country for white men, but the better for the whites, the
poorer for the Indians." Several canoes were fastened together & over
them was a gangway of boards on which were placed their household
Gods [goods]. This is the method of removing their lodges from one
fishing station to another. They pressed upon us many "cultus Pot-

laches" of berries which of course according to etiquette we must accept, though every one knows that an Indian "Cultus Potlach" is a small gift repaid by a large one, & if you are not acute enough to take the hint you will be reminded of it in still plainer terms. As we entered Port Augusta we loyally and dutifully sang "God save the Queen" much to the astonishment of the Indian convoy, who doubt-less but for the presence of the parson would have considered it as one of the King-George profane songs, but, I believe had not a very high opinion of it. One remarked "These Englishmen do not sing, they only speak," a very natural remark, as their songs are merely one long chorus with a word here and there for variety & are mostly extempo-rized. Some of them celebrate the beauty of their lady-loves, others of the mountains, their country &c, such as the "Mountains are beauti-ful."

> 'Chorus' *He - ne - e - neli* (and so on)
> *I love to look on them*
> ('Chorus') *He - ne - e - neli* &c &c &c

"Comox" (or as it should be written "Comoucs" or the country of the Comouc Indians—it is marking the plural with an x instead of an "s") of course as every-body knows is a great agricultural region.[141] The prairies are up the river but the Town site of course is on the Har-bour: unfortunately it is very shallow until near Goose-spit where there is good anchorage in 11 fathoms.

Here a Mr. Robb with a laudable faith in the country has preemp-ted land though the site is principally bush: when he could have got good prairie as he came among the first about 2 years ago. We landed at his house as he is land recorder of the district & generally ac-counted a person of some importance among the settlers.[142] His three fair daughters were from home, but we were kindly received by him-self and his good lady & offered the run of his garden and all that he had. The old lady apologized to me for having nothing better to offer. "Mowich" (deer), she said, was scarce just now. Formerly there was "hyou" (plenty) but now the "Siwashes" (Indians) brought in little and wanted for that little *hyou chickaman* (plenty money). Mrs. Robb is an Englishwoman and of course with all a Britisher's contempt for savages, but like all others out here mixed in her conversation Indian Jargon. His garden is on the site of an Indian Village which must have at one time extended from here to where Mitchell's Farm house now stands.[143] His onions were magnificent. Beans he found succeeded but poorly: his oats were full eared and yellow while his parsnips we can pronounce with authority to be excellent.

The tide running out fast we said good bye to our new made friends and prepared to push up the River which flows into the Bay. On a flat further up a little past the Indian Village are Burrage's (licensed) and Mr. Hart's stores between whom there exists a lively competition principally in the Indian trade which is very considerable indeed. During the Winter they will sometimes trade tons of deers hides alone and Burrage is said on one occasion to have sold 3 tons of flour to the Indians in as many days. Mr. Hart is a gentlemen of the persuasion which the "Hebrews were before they knew Christ" and was one of Walker's Filibusters in Nicaragua.[144] Some time after this (Dec 1864) he got into trouble about having his store on the Indians' land & contrary to law, allowing whiskey to be landed and drunk there. Mr. Franklyn mulcted him in $500 & $250 expenses & default payment [and] sent him to durance vile.[145]

While struggling up the mouth of the River a flag with "Explorer" on it was run up in honour of our arrival.

Passed Mitchell's farm. Beautiful field of oats in sheaf. Passed Ford's on left hand.[146] Excellent place for spearing salmon. Ford catches them with the net. It is the site of a former Indian Fishing Village—Kus-kus-sum. The River is about 40 yards wide and at high water fit to float a stern wheel steamer for about 2 miles. It is bordered on each side with a strip of gloomy spruce and gay maple in their Autumn leaf. In many of the trees were the "Grave-Boxes" from the top of one of which we shot a raccoon (Proceon Vison-Baird)— terrible pest of poultry. It was on entering Comox Country that I first noticed the custom of burying the dead in boxes (into which the body is squeezed) & placed high in trees. It prevails all along the W. Coast.

After paddling up about 2 miles we left the main river (going off Southerly) and entered a branch more like a slough (which indeed it is) known by the Indians as "Tsalum" and by the Settlers as the "Slue" & in a short time arrived at a little log shanty on the right— the present parsonage of Comox where resides Mr. Cave, a young gentleman officiating as Missionary Catechist. He has been here about one month and we brought up a man to build a log church. The Mission is on a pretty prairie of 100 acres sloping down to the waters edge & bordered with belts and clumps of trees. Here we pitched our camp, finding this the most convenient spot for that purpose as we intended to make this our headquarters while examining the neighbouring country.

After Supper (We ungenteel Explorers dine when we dine at all at 12 o'clock noon, but in travelling our Supper is our mainstay & this is consumed after Camping—I mention this lest some highly respectable people might suppose that my excursion *ut infra* was taken by moon light) Messrs. Good, Cave & I walked over the prairie calling on a Norwegian settler of the name of Gunderson but better known by his Christian name of "Oliver."[147] He has a very neat house and some crops, was busy hay making. Talked with him for a few minutes— then on over a beautiful rolling prairie through which a stream slowly crawled along (called Nein-wa-quam—Nanaimo Language) & an offshoot through Blakely, & Funlys (called Pil Choose)[148] and dotted with belts of trees. A group of merry girls were gathering berries on the prairie & we stopped and spoke to them. They courtsied politely on being told who I was. On turning away I was amused to hear one of them say: "Is *that* Mr Brown they are all talking about!!" The little girl was apparently disappointed & expected to see instead of a rough looking fellow with a leather hunting shirt & a yankee bowie knife, a Bayard at least 8 ft. high with a long sword, cocked hat, silk stockings and a velvet waistcoat!

Then to Harmston's, another Settler who has a very neat place with an avenue of trees planted & each tree railed in—among the utilitarian Settlers known as "Harmston's Folly."[149] It is rather a specimen of his good taste. We walked on, still over miles of beautiful prairie land visiting several settlers all well pleased with the country but complaining and justly too of the want of a market. The non-tariff on American produce from Puget sound more than competes with them. On the way back we passed a neat log-shanty and barn, the property or claim of a Yankee at present in Cariboo. I am told that on going away he placed a bowl of sugar & arsenic on his table as the Indians were in the habit of descending the chimney for predatory purposes.

Returned after dark—walked home by moonlight—highly delighted with Comox, and all Settlers were pleased to see our party in hopes they would do something for Comox. I really do believe the good people would have thought I had a spite against them, & refused to give them the benefit of the "Philosophers Stone" which I possessed. As events so happened we did do something for Comox.

Sunday 21st August [1864]. Attended service down at the bay with

Good & Cave in Burrages store. Very fair, though smell of Deer hides
rather high. Afterwards went into the Chief's (Wacas) house & had
service with the Indians. All came to the number of 30 & listened
most attentively. I have some remarks to make on this service and the
mode of converting Indians but I will reserve this.

When coming out, an Indian from Nanaimo who was present told
E-yes that the Comoucs knew of gold in a stream flowing into the
great lake out of which the river takes its rise. He had seen some in
their possession but that they wanted to keep it among themselves.
Though willing to believe it true I can scarcely credit the story, that
they know any thing about gold mining, or that they could keep it
secret even if they knew of it. Mahoy a Qualicom repeated the story to
Tomo. I suspect they mean copper.

While sailing down the Courtenay River—one of the Indians killed
a fine sturgeon 6 ft in length—the first instance to my knowledge of
the Royal fish being caught in Vancouver [Island] Waters though it is
common enough in Frazer River and Harrison River where the Indian have a tradition of its appearance.

After service Mr. Good made a speech to them & introduced me to
the assembled crowd of rude looking customers, as a great chief, who
had a very strong heart & was not afraid to go any where. He had
come a long way and had now come to their land with some of his
men to look for gold, coal, good land and every thing of that sort. "If
you know of these he will pay you and give you a good name" and
finally he told them that I wanted two of them to go away with me for
one day and after a while some more to go up the River with me.
There was immediately a great commotion among them & the Chief
pointed out to me two young men who would go with me. I told them
to come to Mr. Cave's tomorrow when the sun was small & I would
talk with them. They agreed and I left the throng amid a surge of
"good byes." Wacc-aas their chief is a bold looking middle aged
man—dispensing with (as most of the old men do) European Customs and sporting only a blanket. (Today in honor of our visit he had
donned a hyou robe of Marten Skins.) He appears to have considerable influence with the tribe. I noticed the great number of old men in
the tribe and the small number of Children. This must soon make the
tribe very small. Most of them were present as the salmon season is
at hand and all are on the *qui vive* for the grand "Potlach" or (feast)
at Cape Mudge—to be given by the Eucletaws.

Monday August 22nd [1864]. Indians did not come according to promise. I waited all day for them, not wishing to go cap in hand to them, & as I suspected something must be wrong I descended the river to the Village & went into Waacaas lodge. I told the old fellow in very plain terms that he had not spoken straight to me about the Indians. He told me that one of them had refused, being afraid that he would not be in time for the "Potlach" at Eucletaws & according to wont the other had refused also; he however pointed out to me another who was willing to go and in his turn sought a tillicum[150] who would go with him. These Indians like all others have only a few places where they have gone for years & the slightest deviation from the beaten track fills them with fear. At first these two fellows were suspicious of being paid, having I suppose been "done" before. I told them angrily that I was a chief and never lied—so without another word they jumped into a canoe and paddled up the river to our camp.

Sent Macdonald, Meade, & Tomo (Meade in charge) across country until they struck the main River (the Puntledge) to ascertain the extent of Prairie-land if any & make whatever observations may be practicable. With the rest of the party (Drew & Whymper) I proceeded to sea for the same purpose. After passing Baily's Farm[151] we travelled for about 2 miles in a Westerly direction through open prairies, some of which had been preempted but as yet had no houses. After passing through the explored district it began to rain heavily and the afternoon being far advanced & there was a likelihood of not meeting with water for some time I camped.

Most of the prairies were covered with deep fern (*Pteris-aquilina*)—in other places with blackberries (*Vaccinium*). Most of the prairies are cut up or surrounded with branches of the Slue formerly mentioned & this in general forms the only watering place. Some have dug wells for family use. Took the opportunity before dark of sending Drew back for a frying pan, which he had omitted to bring. Returned just at Dusk.

Wednesday [actually, Tuesday] August 23rd [1864]. Started at 6 a.m. Prairie and Woods very wet; we first travelled nearly W. then Easting a little, finally due North where we struck the sea towards the afternoon. The character of the country travelled over is flat open woodlands good for cattle runs. Undergrowth mostly fern with no extensive wide spaces. Here and there however we found patches without timber. Timber in general good: cedar, hemlock &c. A little fallen timber. One creek on the way. Travelled along the coast towards Comox for about 1 1/2 [miles] until we found water—a little spring

trickling over a rock. Indians thought we would never reach the sea—
they were out of their track & frightened as they always are when
they lose sight of the "salt-chuck." "You run and run back and forward just like a deer," they said "and you never will reach the sea" &
much astonished were they when I pointed to the compass and told
them I would reach the sea though I never was here before & knew
nothing of their country.

Thursday August 25th [1864]. Aroused early this morning by shouting. Started up but found the cries to proceed from several canoes of
Coguels [Kwawkewlth] or Fort Rupert Indians on their way up from
Victoria. They were all drunk and drew close in shore to bandy com-
pliments with our men. The Indians told me that these Coguels
always have whiskey when they go North and this is the principal
reason of their going to Victoria.[152] It had poured all night. Started
off at 10 a.m. keeping a Southerly direction. Flat open woodlands
much the same as yesterday. Struck the prairie about 3 p.m. Returned
to Cave's.

Friday [August] 26th. 1864. Went down to Burrages to see the newspapers. Whilst there Meade's party returned and reported themselves to me. They were in great exultation. Had found a splendid
seam of coal on a tributary of the Puntledge which they insisted on
calling "Brown's River"[153] & indications of coarse gold on the River
(Puntledge) apparently washed down from above as there was no
black sand accompanying it. Presented the party with a few creature
comforts to make merry over the discovery which as far as my party
goes redeems this month—& all enjoyed themselves without the least
unpleasantness.

Saturday 27th August. [1864]. Writing all day to the Exploration
Committee describing our discoveries. Tomo hunting. In the evening
a messenger arrived to tell me Lieut. E.H. Verney R.N. of H.M.S.
Grappler was in the harbour and would be glad to see me & shortly
afterwards I was visited by Mr. Howell, one of the Lieut's. guests & a
fellow passenger with us to Cowichan. Independent of other motives
I was bound to see Mr Verney as chairman of the sub-committee of
Exp. Expd. in Victoria. I accordingly descended the river to the Gunboat's Anchorage.

Previous to this however a disagreeable "accident" (shall I call it?)
occurred. I had written my [letter] & closed it leaving it among others
on Mr. Cave's table beside a bag of specimens of coal addressed to the
Committee, care of Lieut. Verney R.N. & had gone to the tent to

21 Frederick Whymper, *Junction of Brown's River with the Puntledge* in Robert Brown, *Countries of the World*

change my moccasins. When I got back my letter was gone. It must have been stolen by some outsider and as there was only one person who could have gone in, I accordingly had my grave suspicions. After in vain searching for it I visited Mr. Verney & received from him all kindness & offers of every thing for self and party. While on board the letter was brought on board by Mr. Howell & from the description of the person who brought it to him to deliver it to me and other accounts and circumstances I can have no doubt of the perpetrator of this mean and clumsy theft; he is one of the Settlers on the upper Prairie and no doubt did it with a view to learn the whereabouts of any discoveries, so that he might pounce upon them for his own benefit.

Left the *Grappler* at 9 p.m. much to the discomfort of Messrs. Meade & Macdonald who were making particular jolly in the forecastle and astonishing the simple Tars—as the grog let loose their imaginations with wonderful tales as having happened to the Expedition in general & they two unworthy members of it. A dense fog had set in and afraid to risk the mouth of the River we concluded to pass the night at Mitchell's Hay-Stack. But fortunately Mr. Burrage was knocked up & we were made comfortable among the everlasting deer skins & late we slept on Sunday morning: after, breakfasting on the inevitable "clams" of the Coast lying Settlements.

Sunday Aug 28th [1864]. Service by Cave in Burrage's store. Half a dozen people with two females. Nothing of consequence unless it be an incident likely to be remembered in the annals of the Settlement: viz. that our general jester Mark Tapley (Macdonald) probably overpowered by the unaccustomed homily of Mr. Cave, quietly fell asleep on the sack of flour which he used [as] a pew much to the scandal of the parson but delectation of all the Congregation & snored most audibly until he was aroused by a vigorous kick from the nearest Colonist when he had the impudence to look around most unconcernedly and proceed apparently to make notes of the heads of Mr. Cave's discourse; but in reality to post up his diary for the last 24 hours. This is one of the anecdotes of the expedition and the grave reader will pardon the record of it.

Found nearly all the Indians, especially the young fellows whom we require, had gone off to the merry-making at the Eucletaw "Potlach" at Cape Mudge. One or two grave old bucks had not gone and on asking the reason were not backward in telling me that the Eucletaws had been to Victoria & bought lots of Whiskey & that when they got drunk (a matter of course) old quarrels would be raked up and broken heads would be certain & I suppose on the principle of everyone knowing his own business best these old fellows had been content to forgo the chance of "pessisses" (blankets) sapalil & lum (food and rum) when pitted against the intention of somebody taking it into his head to do a little "hair lifting" on their enemies of a few months ago.

Spent the evening with Davis, a grim Indian fighter in the Oregon Indian war, & added somewhat extensive stock of illustrations of men, manners and things in the North West.[154]

Monday August 29th [1864]. Wrote to the Committee to day by Indians going to Nanaimo. Spoke to Mahoy about going up with us to the head waters of the Puntledge. After a deal of haggling about the pay, he told me he was willing to go providing he could get some more Indians but all those who would go were at the Eucletaw Potlach. He was rather afraid of the Ses haas [and] Op is chinats [She-shahts and Opetchesahts], his old enemies at Somass—but the fact of his being thought a big man among his tribe weighed with him. He had heard all about us and told Tomo that all the Indians thought that I must get a great deal of money from King George for discovering so much gold, but was astonished when told I got nothing. Then, said he, "he must be a great Chief." He is rather an intelligent fellow and gave me much information on various subjects.

Tuesday August 30th [1864]. Went down with Macdonald, Meade and Tomo to harbour & bought some sugar &c to replace a few articles spoilt by sea water on coming up to Comox & lb 30 of Bacon as we were getting out of meat, having killed no game for a very long time—the game being very scarce and Tomo having had a run of very bad luck. Found the Indians had not returned from the "Potlach" & could get nobody to go up the river with us: only one or two had ever been to the head of it and these were from home.

Wednesday August 31st [1864]. This morning Mahoy sent me a message saying he would not go with me. A settler named Baily having cheated about payment for some work: his heart was very sore: he was not going to work for any White men for a long time. In the mean time he was going to have a good long sleep and then going salmon fishing. Poor fellows, they scarcely know their minds for an hour at a time! At the same time I learnt that the salmon were beginning to ascend the river, and all prospects of obtaining Indians except at ruinous prices would be at an end. The salmon season is all round the Coast a season of joy and merriment. All the wanderers come back to the tribe. Plenty reigns and such is the fascination of the sport that they prefer it to any other employment even if they could get higher pay. At the same time I was certain they would not go higher than the lake at the River source, the old fear of getting outside their circle being dominant. Tired now of waiting any longer I considered the cost and found that if I took Indians I would require them for at least 10 days: during a portion of that time they would be Idle, but it would be necessary to retain them for the sake of the canoe and then their pay would run on. Altogether I calculated it would cost at least $30 before I was done with them, and even then very unsatisfactory, so I broached the subject to the men and all agreed that I had better buy a canoe as suggested & try to get it up ourselves for use on the Lake and it would be more convenient than packing. Accordingly I looked round among the canoes on the beach and selected a good new

one, long and shallow so as to draw little draw, strongly built and
thick at Bottom. I found that it was owned by a Clahoose Indian
(Desolation S[ound]) on a visit & after some haggling bought it for
$20, accounted according to the rate on this coast a very good bargain.
(I suspect the Comoucs came originally from Clahoose as they speak
the same language.) The knowing in these matters pronounced it a
splendid craft, and all were pleased with the new arrangement and
once more we were our own Masters and ready to start—for when
with Indians you are anything but your own master—continually
vexed with them, shirking and idling besides eating up provisions: so
I felt easier in mind. May be we had [many days] of hard-work and
water before us and not knowing how much or where but we were
used to such littler matters. We named her the "Twelve Spies," our
number & mission—I daresay our nationalities—exactly corresponding to the Twelve chosen men whom Moses sent to spy out the land—
certainly the first exploring party on Record.

Got all on board, gave and received 3 cheers and paddled off up the
River to our camp—to prepare for the morning's start. Occupied rest
of afternoon in this work.

Before leaving Comoucs district I may be allowed to preserve here a
few memoranda concerning it:–

COMOUCS COUNTRY SETTLERS & INDIANS

Comoucs country was commenced to be settled about 2 years ago with
the aid of Gov. Douglas. The area settled comprises the prairies—a
place or two on the Courtenay, & 3 or 4 Settlers and 2 store-keepers
on the Harbour. The soil is rich and the surrounding country beautiful. There is none of these extremes of bad soil as in the Cowichan
District. Timber belts are convenient—the river is lined with Douglas Spruce and other pines. Cedar is very scarce—accordingly shingles
fetch a good price. There are good sites for saw-mills a mile or two up
the Puntledge. The Number of actual Settlers are about 40 and the
whole population about 50.[155] Several Claims are unrepresented and
there are still good prairie claims for about 30 settlers independent of
the bush land capable of supporting a large farming population &
very easily cleared—good runs for cattle through the whole Valley of
the Country. Brown & Puntledge up to the lake is flat & good soil,
thinly wooded & worthy of cultivation.

Monster potatoes, onions as large as Spanish ones, parsnips, wheat
and oats full headed, and sound turnips, splendid butter & milk are

productions of this most beautiful Valley. During our visit hay was being cut in the meadows at the river's mouth for the Victoria market & the farms are capable of producing everything a farm can. I have rarely or ever, even in England, seen more lovely situations for homes to men willing to go into their work with heart and spirit—believing in the Country and its prosperity—a subject not now requiring a great amount of faith. Beans are said not to prosper so well. Mule breeding might become very profitable, as well as cattle. Pigs and Bacon curing might prove a fortune to the man of Enterprize enough—& a "hen ranch" with eggs at $1.50 per dozen during the Winter & 50 cents at least during the rest of the year. The thrifty wives of some of the Victoria farmers, I remember telling me last spring, that they sold many Goose & Turkey eggs at 50 & 75 cents & in one or two cases at $1 each! Turkeys, Geese, & Chickens command high rates. One of the settlers went heavily into the business but I regret to say met with misfortune, 40 of his fowls being killed within a day or two by Ravens and Raccoons. Perhaps this was owing to carelessness, but it cannot be denied that "coons" are sad pests to fowls, clearing a hen-house in a night. Sheep none of the Settlers have attempted to keep, the wolves in this as in other outlying districts rendering this a very precarious business. The Settlers of Comoucs are in general a more enterprizing set than the Cowichan or Chemanus farmers, but still I notice the same apathy and fear of going into things too heavily. The same fear of the Country "caving in" and all alike afflicted with the "fearful crime" of poverty.

Most of them have raised more or less grain crops, all [have raised] potatoes & other vegetables. All have neat log houses, most of them [have] barns: and have fenced in their farms. Three or four are married and several cohabit with native women who, it ought to be said to their credit, look closely to the interests of their "husbands" & in more than one instance which I could mention have been the best Counsellors of their unworthy mates. Most of the native Comoucs women, however, are given to drunkenness. The Settlers are English, Irish, Scotch, Canadian, 1 Norwegian, 1 Portuguese and 1 Jew & are generally speaking a quiet steady set of men.[156] They complain sadly of the want of a market for their produce, the non-tariff on imported produce working most disastrously to the interests of the island farmers—the farmer having all uphill work, having to compete with our neighbours in Puget Sound, California & the already cleared and settled up farms, the cheaper rate of most necessaries of life, & the better access to a market—there being constant communication with Puget Sound whilst the freight is an item scarcely worth taking into consideration, while it is heavy on the Comoucs Settlers and Communication seldom. A Road through the Settlement is much desired but this could be effected by enforcement of Statute labor. The Settlers are willing to make it provided the Govt. lays it out according to route decided on by the majority of the Settlers.

I may note here that it would be well to have a change in the mode of acquiring lands in Vancouver Island: 100 acres alike being allowed to be pre-empted without reference at all to the nature of the soil, character of the Country, and distance from Market. I believe that if these points were under certain well considered laws attended to, many more settlers would be attracted to the Island, and Districts now desert be settled up.

Though not a pleasant topic I cannot help noticing the want of confidence in the stability of the Colony manifested by most of the settlers and a "Waiting for something to turn up" Micawber sort of disposition.[157] This is more or less the way in all countries. (People with heads on their shoulders stemmed the Westward flood of Californian emigration with the cry of "The Country will never feed itself.") But though this is every day more & more decreasing owing to the recent discoveries of the expedition yet it is pre-eminently so among a large portion of the Cowichan, Chemanus, Salt Spring, and Comox Settlers whose only ambition (it is no use mincing matters by refined Language) seems to be "a log shanty, a pig, a potato patch, Kloochman (Indian woman) and a clam bed"! This is easily accounted for, most of the Settlers being either men with no business & totally unacquainted with farming: Men who came here attracted by the gold-fever & got their eyes jaundiced by their Cariboo failures, prodigal sons who are just waiting to get reconciled to their families, or to go home having mistaken their vocation. The few who have been really bred to farming are the men who are doing most, but the country is new and it is wrong to compare it with old established Colonies. On the whole have met less grumbling here than in any other Section. The Settlers are all in all well pleased with their district and with the above exceptions with their prospects.

INDIANS.[158] The Puntledges [Pentlatch] were the original inhabitants of the Comoucs Valley and their Village was about one mile up the river of the same name called [blank in transcript]—now deserted &

the site occupied by Potato patches. The Puntledges were very powerful, and lived in peace and plenty until the Comoucs speaking a
different language came from further north and settled at the mouth
of the river on their present site and on Denmans Island. War ensued
and many were killed on either side but it soon happened, to use the
simple but expressive language of my informant, an old Puntledge,
"The Great Chief above became angry with the Puntledge and killed
many, viz many of them by Small pox, until what with disease and
war, the Puntledge became very few indeed & sought the friendship
and alliance of their old Enemies the Comoucs for mutual protection
& defence: & from that day they lived together." The Comoucs had
broke or seceded from a tribe called the Ey-exen but God in time
became angry with the Ey-exen and joined camp with the Comoucs.
The Saatlaam or Qualicoms lived at Saatlam (the place of green
leaves) but they too became so thin by war and pestilence that they
were glad to ask to throw in their lots with their former enemies &
ever since they have been one people—composed of 4 tribes all under
the name of Comoucs & here allow me to observe that this is ridicu-
lously enough spelled "Comox" & "Comax Country." I am a Comouc
they will say & this is the country of the Comoucs. It should therefore
be written Comoc's or Comouc's and not Comax thus making the
plural with an x instead of an "s."[159] This is like the frontiersman
spelling Tennessee " 10 a,c" a quite unnecessary economy of the English Language. The proper name of the tribe is "Sae-luth." Comoucs
was originally a name of derision applied to them by the Eucletaws.
Pequodiem is the name for their name for the Comoucs' country. They
speak a different language from the other tribes of V.I. The Puntledges or Qualicoms spoke the widely spread Cowichan language. [An
Indian vocabulary at this point in Brown's journal seems to have been
rendered incoherent by the copyist. It has therefore been omitted.]
Waācaas, a bold looking elderly man, is Chief—he is commanding in
his voice & bearing and seems to have more influence with his tribe
than most of the Southern Chiefs. Nonmoncāas is a minor chief.
Their houses and persons differ little from other tribes. Carvings
predominate around in their dwellings. They are a very drunken
set—few hunters, mostly fishermen.
    In Victoria we continually hear of the disorderly character of the
Comoucs Indians, but they suffer by the reputation of the Eucletaws
who are often at Comoucs & continually drunk when quarrels are the
consequence. They [Comoucs Indians] are notorious thieves & sell the

settlers potatoes but here again, the Eucletaws get the lion's share. They had to be removed to their own Village this year by the Gunboat.[160] Whiskey is their ruin; every Canoe that enters the harbor has whiskey. I have heard some of the disreputable characters round the coast declare that they can just trade as much as they like by bribing the Police. They obtain any quantity from Victoria & Nanaimo—I believe little or none is traded in the settlement. A man named Bill Jones formerly in the police used to reside at Qualicom and sell them any quantity of whisky but he is now gone and they obtain most of their whisky from Victoria.[161] They say they get it from a white house between Victoria and Esquimalt. They leave their canoe in the bush, go a short way up on the road—and there get it in casks. Another place in James Bay supplies them. They paddle fast out of the harbour, but no sooner are they free of Victoria than they drink it like water, and a man who once came up with them described to me their condition as that of demons. They threw their women down on the bottom of the canoe, trampling on them and tearing out their hair by the handsful. In these furies no one is safe. They threw overboard bales of blankets and other things they had bought—careless of property in their madness. The settlers are loud in crying out for a magistrate & Indian Agent (in one office) to look to the enforcement of the law generally in the Settlement and to the management of Indian affairs between here and Fort Rupert. The Indians require to be removed from their present situation (between two Settlers) to another reserve and the law to be enforced about whiskey selling or otherwise. The most convenient reserve would be "grassy point" of the Admiralty Chart [Gartley Point]—"Trents Point" by the Settlers from a settler who at one time lived there but has now gone to Canada.

Here as everywhere else the Indians are growling about payment for their land. The deer are fewer, and the berries are also & I noticed them cutting down the crab apple trees to get easier to the fruit. They never would do that before but now they think they may as well get as much out of their land as possible, as soon they will be altogether deprived of it. When travelling or sitting round the camp fire with them they always appeal to me on that subject & I assure you that it is no easy matter to answer the question satisfactorily when an intelligent [Indian] looks up in your face and asks "Had you no good land of your own that you come and deprive us of ours"?

I tell them that once upon a time the great good chief above gave all the earth to the White man and Indian alike. The White man took one part and the Indian another, but the Indian instead of cultivating his land went to war & was very wicked; but the white man increased and multiplied and learned all things and filled all their Country: so the white man said to himself: see our land is full, we wish to grow corn and potatoes and rear Moos-Moos (Cattle) but our friend the Indian over the salt water does not care about corn and oxen but likes Salmon and Gummas [Camas]: he does not require all his land—so we will go and ask him to allow us to live in his land in peace and friendship. If we take any land he has need of, our chief good King George will pay for it. So if we have hurt and not benefited you by coming to live among you—send your Chiefs to have a talk with Mr. Kennedy & he will pay you if he thinks you speak straight—for he is a just man with a straight tongue that never lies. But my mind is you have got much good by us king Georges. When we came you were ragged in a skin blanket or a poor one that you made out of bark or dogs-hair. You have now shirt & hat, coat, trousers & boots. Who brought these among you? You would starve some winter if it was not for potatoes! Who gave you these? Was it not Mr. Yale at Fort Langley? and is he not a King George Man? Eh? Who gave you tea, tobacco, flour, & sugar & Molasses & Biscuits you are so fond of! Was it not King George man? Who taught you to shoot and gave you Muskets, powder and shot, axes and knives and all good things? Was it not King George man? What are you talking about? No wonder people say you are silly and know nothing!! Eh! You say the White-man gave you rum, but who makes you buy rum? Did not the White man's Chief pass a law that you should not get it! and don't you see every day White men punished for selling it to you? but yet you sneak at night into the bush to buy that "rum" that is killing you: to buy it from wicked men who are as bad as you! Why then complain of the King George man? I know some bad men have done bad to you but Mr. Kennedy or Mr. Douglas is not *Helse*, the great Spirit that can see or know everything, but you know that if you go and tell Mr. Franklyn or Mr. Pemberton[162] are not they punished? Did ever any one kill you without cause? Who killed the white men last year? Was it not Indians? Then you talk like a fool. I am a good friend to you but if I were to tell Mr. Kennedy what you say, though he wishes to be good to you! his heart would be angry at your talk.

An Indian is a shrewd fellow, reasoning acutely but not like a White man—& poor fellow he harps on his wrongs without ever thinking of any alleviating circumstances and it is the part of the white, to give him no reason to think of himself wronged always and in every case, not allowing him to think we are frightened into paying for our privileges.

Civilization sits badly on them & the miserable desire of making proselytes (I say in religion, science or politics) leads to a competition among missionaries often little suited for their work for the souls of the Indians—from the Roman Catholic Padre to the unctuous individual of the "Chadband" type—vid. Nanaimo.[163]

From talk I have had with both Whites and Indians it is my opinion that if a commission[164] or Commissioner was appointed to enquire into the state, number and lands claimed by the native tribes, ascertain the number of families & the feelings of the Indians, it would save much future trouble as well as facilitate future proceedings after settling what would be proper. Let the Chiefs be summoned to Victoria, matters all fully explained to them, their voice heard on the subject. And after all is settled, let each of them receive a sealed paper with the Govt. seal and a sketch of his reserve: Give them a feast and a speech & a reasonable "Potlach" for the rest of their lands. If this was done now it could be done tolerably cheaply. In a few years it will be difficult, they will have got too knowing and trouble will be the consequence. Then let an agent be introduced to them, one to so many tribes, who will remove them (if necessary), point out to the chiefs their limits and generally be the mediator & law-giver. He must be a man of great intelligence & one to whom the Indians can look up to as their head.

Such is the outline of what "put to rights" the whole of the Indian affairs [would be] here. For so long was this under Hudson's Bay Company misrule that it was never thought of, but now it becomes us to look to these things, but I do not consider it necessary to expend such a large sum upon the Indians (in proportion) as the United States and Canada does upon theirs. (Vid. Commission of Indian Affairs—Reports, San Francisco "Bulletin," Oct/64).[165] These meetings of the Chiefs would have the effect among other things of getting them acquainted with one another.

Thursday September 1st [1864]. Up at 5 a.m. Bade good bye to all our friends at the Mission and started with our canoe "The Twelve Spies Alone" and now I found it necessary in order to prevent confusion in description to more accurately define the nomenclature of the Rivers.

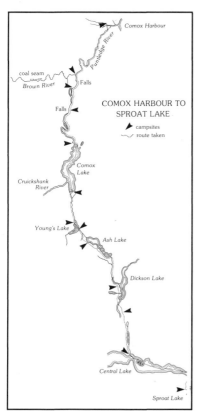

Comox Harbour

Puntledge River

coal seam
Brown River   Falls

Falls

**COMOX HARBOUR TO
SPROAT LAKE**

campsites
route taken

*Comox
Lake*

*Cruickshank
River*

Young's Lake

Ash Lake

Dickson Lake

Central Lake

Sproat Lake

Map 3
Route from
Comox Harbour
to
Sproat Lake

The general name of the River has hitherto been the "Comax-Courtenay" (Admiralty last Survey), Puntledge (from Indians), or Onymakqtam (native) River. On the right bank ascending is a slough (pronounced "Slue") threading through Mitchells Meadows & full at high water so that a schooner can go in about 3/4 of a mile. Further up is another of the same nature through the claim of a settler named Green. About 1/2 mile further up the River forks—the main branch taking off in a Southerly direction to the left—this has hitherto been known as the "Main River" but has been ascended to its head by no white man. To the right the [river] narrows into an almost still slough-looking river & it is navigable for canoes to Mr. Cave's "The Mission." This is the head of all navigation. The tide forces the fresh water up to this point & at high water Stern Wheel Steamers could easily ascend thus far. Then commences the "Slue" indeed. This may be said to commence at the forks, which divides into two branches of the size of a ditch & permeates through marshes, now dry now full, until lost among the prairie. It is not of the least consequence except as a drainage for the prairies and a supply of water for cattle. On the Admiralty Chart this is shown on a needlessly important scale: while the main stream is only shown by a supposed course by a dotted line going through the Bedford Valley. For the sake of description I propose the following names: which are in fact only a definition of those conferred by the Settlers. (1) The River as far as the forks to

be known by the name of the "Courteney" as placed on Captn. Richards chart. This & Port Augusta are a needless and egotistical geographical pleonasm to flatter some unknown personages but as they
are published it is better to keep them[166]—for independently of the
confusion caused the first published shall be the received. As the
Admiralty Survey is known to few of the settlers it will be generally
known by the old name of the "Comox river" but it will be more
familiarized when our map V[ancouver] I[sland] appears. The mouth
& left branch is known by the Indian, as Too-lain-a-moot: the right
branch Ca-pa-ji. (2) The 1st Slough known by the Settlers' name of
Mitchells Slough. 2nd by the Settler's name of Green's Slough. (3)
The Slough by that name or the Indian one of Tsalum. (4) The Main
River after it forks by the name of Puntledge (from the Indian tribe
who used to live on its banks).[167]

The River was very swift and our poles were soon in requisition.
About a mile up were some Indian Potato Patches, to which we
helped ourselves, expecting to see the Indians shortly fishing when I
would pay them. This is the site of one of the former Puntledge
Villages. Before long the River became too swift for poling and all
hands were out in the water hauling and shoving the canoe along.
Now we were up to the knee & the next step up to the shoulders:
some of the lighter weights were forced to hold on to the canoe—the
force of the Current taking them off their legs. We were lifting the
canoe over some rapids when 4 Indian canoes, 2 in each, shot round &
Poles raised at one time & the wild shouts drowned by the roar of the
waters was rather picturesque. They were seeking big salmon. Working this way we arrived at 3 p.m. at what Meade's party had named
"Browns River" & as the whole party were very wearied we joyfully
camped on its left bank (ascending)—a beautiful spot under the
shade of cedar trees, a perfect "vision of green leaves." Previous to
this a canoe had again descended the river and I bought a salmon or
two from them. I told them to tell Mr. Cave I was thus far. They
promised to do and faithfully performed this Mission, only adding
that the Canoe was split, we had lost all our provisions & blankets,
and that the [Tyee] (Chief) had broke his leg. Had it not been for a
mere chance this news would have gone to Victoria in a few days
affording excellent items for the papers—all the better because it was
not true.

The river all day was very swift & one succession of rapids. It is at
present about 20 yds. wide and rises about 3 ft. more in Winter. The

banks are low wooded flats with occasional earthy cliffs with coal shale and fossil. Timber indifferent—a few good cedars, hemlock & pine—plenty of maples & kalmias [swamp-laurel]—soil all good.

After supper while felling some maple for camp fire we came upon some human remains which told a strange story. There were the tibia, fibula, femur and one or two other remains but no remains of skull or teeth, the last thing to decay. It was doubtlessly one of a war party decapitated near here and the head according to custom carried off by the Victor. The Comoucs were formerly frequently at war with the Opischesal [Opetchesaht] & Seshaat [Sheshaht] Indians in Barclay Sound. In one night they came over and utterly destroyed a whole tribe nearly opposite where Stamps Mill [at Alberni] now stands, nearly exterminated the Opischsaats on the Somass river (they now number only 17 men) & thinned the Seshaats (who were fortunately however mostly at the fishing village down the sound [and] so escaped). They are yet a cry of terror in that country. Strange to say, I hailed the discovery of these bones with something akin to joy for it told me of a short land travel to Barclay Sound or rather Alberni Canal. Last July Quassoon an old Warrior of Opeschesaat[168] told me he had frequently been to Comax on hunting and War parties but I thought he had gone by the Alberni Canal-Qualicum trail [via Horne Lake]. Subsequently Mah-ay informed me that though he had never been by it himself, the others (Indians who had been) said, that after sailing to the head of the lake whence the Puntledge took its source: you passed over a Mountain and came to the Seshaats lakes. The source of the Seshaat-Comoucs war was this: A Comouc Indian used frequently to trade with the Opeschesaats for furs: and then pack them over the Alberni-Qualicum trail, & so for long he was on terms of great intimacy & had (if I recollect rightly) an Opischsaat wife— but it so happened that he went once too often, for some Opeschesaats followed him to his camp at Qualicum where they Killed and robbed him. War was the result. It was then that the Comoucs learned of this new path to Alberni.

Thursday [actually, Friday] September 2nd [1864]. By some unaccountable oversight of the person in charge of that department the bag containing part of our ammunition had been left behind at Cave's. Accordingly I dispatched Tomo overland for it. Took Meade, Whymper & Drew with me to examine the coal seams on Browns River. Left Macdonald in charge of camp in case of visits from marauding Indians or not less destructive Bears.

The scenery on Browns River is very pleasing. The River is 15 yds. wide & must be pretty full in the winter and spring seasons. For the first mile or so the right bank is a high cliff. The left, flats heavily wooded—then the river rushes through high cliffs on either side & thus opens out again into meadows and woodland as before. During its course it forms many pretty Water falls and the Sandstone bed rock is formed into many cavities and basins by the rush of waters. The bed of the stream is flat, firm sandstone—or for one stretch, boulders. We prospected but could not find a trace of gold. We examined the river for about 5 miles. The Coal seams are much as described by Meade.[169] They are two in number. The upper broken and about a foot—the lower one can be traced for far up the River dipping in the bed & doubtless the same as Fawcetts at Valdez Inlet.[170] After making a section of the seams and sketch of the river we camped at the coal. Drew mined out about 3 cwt. which we put on the fire in great blocks—it burnt splendidly all night and forms good coke. The

22 Frederick Whymper, ***Coal Seam, Brown's River. Comox*** (Royal Geographical Society). In his journal for 2 September 1864, Whymper wrote: "Went up the stream to the coal seams—one of which 8 ft. thick I sketched."

discovery is of inestimable value & it is certainly the best on the Pacific. (Vide. my Dispatch to the VIEE.) We marked the place and the trees as being the locality of the first coal fire in this quarter. Alarmed by Bears tumbling fallen timber down the cliff. Probably attracted by the unwonted fire.

Saturday 3rd September [1864]. Returned to main camp. Tomo had returned from the Mission & had hunted for several miles along the river without success. All the deer are in the mountains. Saw many trees cut through by beaver. He had made a map of the River as far as he had gone, showing the rapids &c. I resolved it would be necessary to make a portage of the goods for 3 miles in order to lighten the canoe over the falls. Fine weather. Whymper sketching.

Sunday September 4th [1864]. The day of rest. Meade, Macdonald, & Tomo volunteered to go ahead and blaze a trail for the portage. Returned in the evening—reported having seen the lake. Whymper sketching—myself writing. So much for a day of rest. Ordered all hands to prepare for a portage tomorrow.

Monday September 5th [1864]. Up at 5 a.m. Erected a memorial cross & left Brown's River. Made a portage above the first falls (or rather succession of rapids). Skei-ep (or "The laughing Waters")—1 1/2 miles—very hard work. Flat woods open—some good spars. Each packed from 90 to 100 lbs. We then camped and returned for the canoe, dragging it—all well tired for every one must put his shoulder to the wheel if the Expedn. is to be pushed forward: it is difficult enough overcoming the many obstacles in our way: but doubly so if there is any false modesty about dignity. While we are talking, opportunities are passing. If I had once allowed this in the least to creep into the camp, or listened for a moment to the suggestions of outsiders about Officers &c not working & that hard too, the Expedn would not have completed a week of existence and all its great success been a matter of some future day.[171]

Finished about 5 p.m. Whymper sketched the fall. Found here a tree for first time with large alder-looking leaves known by the French Canadians as *Pabina*. It is quite new to me. *Taxus Lindleyuna* Murr. [Taxus breviofolia—western yew], a nor[thern] spec[ies] in fruit, two species of yew, one a shrub. *Pyrus[fusca]* (crabapple), the *Powich* of the Flatheads. *Panax horridum*: the Devils walking stick—sad pest in travelling. Its little prickles I verily believe go through Buckskin breeches— at least they go horridly through the shot holes in the skin! Another tree with black *vaccinium*-looking fruit new to me.

23 Frederick Whymper, *Laughing Waters Rapids, on the Puntledge*, in *Illustrated London News*, 24 November 1866

Tuesday September 6th [1864]. Up at 6 a.m. Made rest of portage today through open woods. Can scarcely say what is the nature of the
soil, as the ground is a springy moss of decayed vegetables so that if a
fire is lit it will after an hour or so burst out in a miniature Volcano—
a considerable distance off—the fire having undermined. Many good
patches of pine—& Spars of Douglas and hemlock pines. Returned
for canoe. Whymper sketched one very pretty fall—several smaller.
Finished just before dark. River of the same uniform width as before.
Wednesday September 7th [1864]. Off this morning quite cheerily as
most of our hard work for some time was over. Paddled up. Beauti-
fully calm. Came to a colony of beaver and beaver houses (Describe
Natural History of Beaver hitherto a mass of fables.)[172] Just before we
entered the Lake [Comox Lake] we had to drag the Canoe over one
fall. Entered the lake and camped in a quiet bay. Climbed an eminence

and sighted a beaver lake with extensive swamps. The Indians at one time used to hunt here for beaver, but have ceased to travel so far for many years. The Lake is from 10 to 12 miles (taking the course of the river) from the sea, but I believe they used to travel overland, about 5 miles in a straight line. Wet day—spent it in tinkering our Canoe, strained with her labor in ascending the Puntledge—mended clothes and generally dried and recruited ourselves after the labours of the week. Travelling round the shore found again sandstone strata and a piece of inferior coal but failed to find the seam. Tomo hunting beaver—unsuccessful. Very wet all night.

Thursday September 8th [1864]. Miserable wet stormy day. Spent it as I spend most stormy days, in drawing from Tomo's extensive store of Indian lore and tradition and committing them to paper. A Savage's traditions are his history; his superstitions, his Metaphysics. "Give [me] a nation's ballads," says somebody, "& I will give you their history." "Give me their traditions & superstitions and I will give you their minds." The people who know these strange traditions, records & ideas are rapidly dying out & in a few years nobody will be able to tell their ideas of things. Now is the time to keep them from falling into decay. In the evening it cleared up and Tomo shot a fawn and goose. Beaver attracted by the light and splashed round the Lake sides of the camp until the camp fire died out.

Friday September 9th [1864]. Up at 6 a.m. Cleared up along the Lake. Sailed up the Lake—on right, high hills down to water's edge—on left, ditto, but not so high. Right about 2500 ft.—left 2000 ft. Timber indifferent. Saw some Nootka Cypress (*Cupressus Nutkanus*) [Yellow Cedar—*Chamaecyparis nootkatensis*]. Hitherto I have only found this rare Cypress on the banks of Lakes. Camped at end of Lake which I calculate at 8 miles in length & 1 to 1 1/2 miles wide. Here two Creeks flow, merely Beaver creeks. One is a perfect nest of Beaver & has 3 dams. In this low dry Valley at End, good timber—many traces of Wolves & Elk. Stormy night with rain.

Saturday 10th September [1864]. Unsettled day with wind and rain. Went up Lake and found on left side N. a River flowing in [Cruickshank River]. Meade, Drew & Foley [sic] followed it up for 4 miles— much larger than Cowichan. We missed it on coming up though I landed for that purpose on coming up. It was concealed by rafts of drift Timber. This is the River where Mah-ay said there was gold. Brought back the color and plenty of black sand. Wild stormy night.

Sunday 11th September [1864]. Again the day of rest which we spent

24 Frederick Whymper, *Cruickshank River. Puntledge Lake*
(Yale Collection of Western Americana, Beinecke Rare Book and
Manuscript Library)

in beaver hunting—breaking down their dams and watching by moonlight when they come to repair it as they find the water ebbing out. Killed a fat old patriarch in the act of cutting down a tree for that purpose. Anxious to give the River we had found a chance—organized a party to prospect it.

Monday 12th September [1864]. Pouring rain all day & night. Could not go up River. Set the men to look over their journals for there is a disagreeable proverb—something about the Devil finding &c &c &c. Working at my Vocabulary of the Cowichan & Thongeith [Songhees] Languages.

Tuesday September 13th [1864]. The day looking fine, despatched Meade, Drew & Whymper up the River (named in honour of Geo. Cruickshanks Hon. Sec. Exp. Com.) with 4 days provisions. Put Macdonald in charge as Meade had had last command & so prevented heart-burnings. Turned out a beautiful day. Writing &c. Sent Tomo hunting on mountain—returned unsuccessful. Sat round the fire till late telling me stories of Indian life & warfare. Fine Moon-light. *Wednesday 14th September [1864].* Up at 5 a.m. Had breakfast. Climbed the highest peak of the range on the North on the flat. At foot of Mountain—good spars; higher up—not so good—long and then good for poles. Travelled along the side gradually until reached the top—nearly 3000 ft. Several small ponds with *Nuphar* &c [water lilies] growing on them. Cascades rushing from top. Found a species of *Abies* new to me with great clusters of purple cones (Vid. catalogue of plants—private MSS.) The real and rare *Picea Amabilis* [*Abies amabilis*—Amabilis Fir]—& what I thought perhaps P. *lassocarpa* [*Abies Lasiocarpa*—Subalpine Fir]. These pines grew on the very top. Several species of *Vaccinium* with blackberries—one Le billouet de Montagnes of the French Voyageur, very pleasant to eat: also [blank in MS.] (with its clusters of red berries). Andromeda

25 Frederick Whymper, *Young's Lake* (Yale Collection of Western Americana, Beinecke Rare Book and Manuscript Library)

26 Frederick Whymper, *Central Lake* (Royal Geographical Society). Of Central Lake, Whymper wrote in his journal for 22 September 1864: "It is a fine expanse of water and although monotonous in character like every lake on the Island we have seen, makes rather a better subject for a sketch."

often called the heather which does not exist here. Heard the cry of the Siffleur (Marmot)—traces of deer & Elk. The view from the summit was magnificent. I took a birds-eye map from the summit; of the surrounding Country.[173] Among these ranges were many intermediate valleys & smaller clefts. I calculated this first cleft to be the Central Lake. The next cleft to be the North arm of Sproats Lake (named in honour of my friend Gilbert M. Sproat Esquire of Alberni & Victoria) and the jagged peaks the mountains on Taylor's River.

At this point, the holograph copy of Brown's journal breaks off. His group continued to Alberni, where it met Leech's group. After some exploration along the Alberni Canal, the expedition crossed Vancouver Island to Qualicum and subsequently sailed in mid-October from Nanaimo to Victoria on H.M.S. Grappler.

27 Frederick Whymper, *View Near Sproat's Lake* in G.M. Sproat, *Scenes and Studies of Savage Life* (1868)

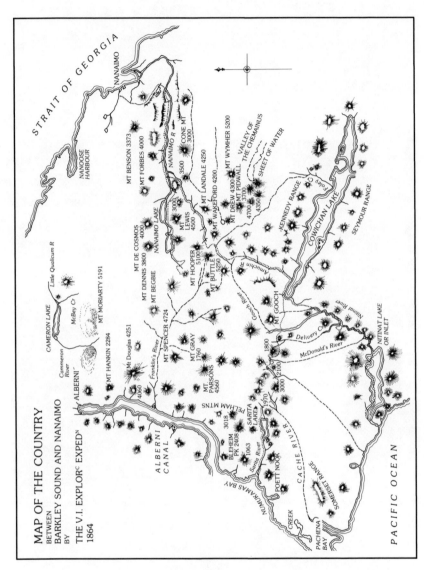

Map 4
Country between Barkley Sound and Nanaimo

NOTES

1 Sir Edmund Hope Verney (1838–1910) commanded H.M.S. *Grappler* from 1862 to 1865. He was a member of the VIEE Committee, and the *British Colonist* [Victoria] noted on his departure from Victoria that he was "always the foremost in every good work" (5 June 1865). *Grappler* was a wooden gunboat built for battle against Russia and had been in service on the northwest coast since July 1860.

2 Sir Arthur Edward Kennedy (1809–83) had arrived in Victoria as governor on 25 Mar. 1864, following almost ten years as Governor of Western Australia. In Australia he had sponsored explorations for farm land and minerals, and he had proposed an exploration of Vancouver Island. (See p. 9 above.)

3 Samuel Harris (?–1877) settled at Cowichan in 1859. In a letter to the Colonial Secretary (10 Apr. 1862), he noted that in December 1859, "the Governor was pleased to give me a Commission as a Special Constable . . . for which I have never received any compensation" (Colonial Correspondence, F725/11, PABC). In addition, Harris remarked that he had "attended to the Indians as their Agent sometimes with a deal of trouble and expense." His venture into real estate, by the creation of Harrisburg at Cowichan, apparently had failed, and he was consequently in need of a "small remuneration." According to Harris, the House of Assembly approved the payment to him of £50 in 1862, but he received only £10. He therefore wrote to the Colonial Secretary (20 Feb. 1863) requesting the balance—"My necessities [being] very urgent" (F725/13, PABC). A month later, he made his complaint public in a letter in the *British Colonist* (21 Mar. 1863). Brown, a supporter of Governor Douglas, was not disposed to credit Harris's account.

4 Advertisements for John Lemon's hotel in the *British Colonist* date from 21 Feb. 1863. The advertisements note: "The best of Ales, Wines, Spirits, &c. . . . Steamboat landing within 50 yards of the Hotel."

5 In an article on Tomo in the *Victoria Daily Chronicle*, it is remarked that "he shines most in the character of a draughtsman and topographer. Dr. Brown has two sketches of the courses of rivers made on tracing cloth which have been . . . found to be remarkably correct, and show wonderful skill for a native. They are the unassisted work of this disorderly admirable crichton, except the calligraphy" (16 July 1864). Brown included the article in a scrapbook and attributed it to A.D. Bell, the editor of the *Chronicle* and a member of the VIEE Committee (Brown Collection, I, Scrapbook 2, 154, PABC). For Tomo, see p. 12 above.

6 W. Ladler had written to the Executive Council of Vancouver Island on 28 May 1864 concerning the discovery of copper in the area: see *Journals of the Colonial Legislature*, ed. James Hendrickson (Victoria: Provincial Archives of British Columbia 1980), 1, 132.

7 Bishop Modeste Demers (1809–71) was ordained a priest in 1836 and became a missionary in Oregon in 1838. In 1847, he was consecrated Bishop of Vancouver Island.

8 "Report of the Exploration Sub Committee" notes: "The general outfit to consist of maps and drawing materials, in a tin case, 2 large Axes, 2 geological hammers, Powder, Shot and Caps, 2 small tents, a 2 inch augr, 3 small hatchets for blazing, 2 Beaver Traps, 6 large strong canvas bags, 2 prospecting pans, 2 Fry pans, a shovel, Tobacco" (Brown Collection, I, 6, PABC).

9 In *Astoria* (1836), Washington Irving remarked that Concomly "possessed great sway not merely over his own tribe, but over the neighbourhood" (ed. E.W. Todd [Norman: University of Oklahoma Press 1964], 87). He died in 1830, about 66

years old (J.F. Santee, "Concomly and the Chinooks," *Oregon Historical Quarterly* 33 [1932]: 276).

10 The population of the Cowlitz in 1780 has been estimated as 1,000, whereas in 1853 the estimate was 165 (John Swanton, *The Indian Tribes of North America* [Washington: U.S. Government Printing Office 1953], 422–3).

11 In 1838 a mission was established among the Cayuse by Marcus Whitman. In 1847 the Indians blamed the missionaries for a smallpox epidemic and destroyed the mission. By the early 1850s, the population was much reduced (Swanton, *Indian Tribes*, 454–5).

12 Selim Franklin was Chairman of the VIEE Committee. He was also an auctioneer, real estate agent, and member of the Legislative Assembly.

13 Jean Compagnon settled at Cowichan on 29 January 1863. According to the Land Recorder's report, he had by 1 November 1863 made improvements of $240 and was "clearing & making gardens and pruning trees &c." In a subsequent report, dated 22 Oct. 1864, the Land Recorder noted improvements of $400 on an 85-acre property (Herald Street Collection, I, 223, PABC). Brown has added in the copy of his journal that Compagnon received the explorers "in a very friendly manner."

14 On revisiting this area, Brown referred to a plant of this size as a "congenor of the Oregon grape" (25 July 1864).

15 Whymper noted: "He raised last year 300 lbs of tobacco and disposed of a part of the same in Victoria" (Journal, 8 June). Under the heading "Home Grown Tobacco," the *British Colonist* had earlier reported "a very fine sample of tobacco grown by the Catholic Missionary in the Cowichan settlement" (2 Dec. 1862). In this report, the mission is said to have grown 500 lbs, while other settlers had grown about a further 1,000 lbs.

16 The wooden mission church was built in 1859, following Father Peter Rondeault's establishment of the mission the previous year. A decade later, a stone church replaced the original structure.

17 In *Illustrated Travels*, Brown wrote: "Old Locha is the chief of his tribe, an ancient now quite blind, but a dandy of the first water, for his nose and ear pendants of *Haliotis* shell must measure, each of them, more than an inch square" (255).

18 The Stikines were a Tlingit tribe associated with the Stikine River. Their population in 1840 is estimated to have been 1,300 (F.W. Hodge, *Handbook of Indians of Canada* [Ottawa: King's Printer 1913], 440).

19 In *Vancouver's Island: Survey of the Districts of Nanaimo & Cowichan Valley* (London: Groombridge and Sons 1859), Oliver Wells remarked on two Comiaken villages (p. 14). Macdonald also listed two villages: "Que-me-a-kin—chief Loq-ha, 50 [population]" and "He-nip-son— 50 [population]" (Journal, 9 June). In "Cowichan and Its Indians" Jean Arnoup noted: "Comiaken 50 [men] 30 [women]" (*British Colonist*, 5 July 1864).

20 Prior to the arrival of about 100 settlers at Cowichan in Aug. 1863, a "Public Notice" had indicated that settlers should locate land "in such a manner as is not likely to lead to any misunderstanding or difficulty with the Indians" (*British Colonist*, 14 Aug. 1862). Formal arrangements were planned for the autumn, when the Indians had returned to their villages from fishing, with the expectation that "compensation for the lands taken up by the settlers would be made at the same rate as that previously established—amounting in the aggregate to the value of a pair of blankets to each Indian" (*British Colonist*, 22 Aug. 1862). However, it was not until 1867 that Indian reserves in the area were formally established by B.W. Pearse (*B.C. Papers connected with the Indian Land Question, 1850-1875* [Victoria 1875], 165). See also Robin Fisher, *Contact and Con-*

flict: Indian-European Relations in British Columbia 1774-1890 (Vancouver: University of British Columbia Press 1977), 68, 152–3.

21 The arrest of How-a-matcha at Comiaken was reported in the *British Colonist*, where he was described as "a well-known murderer" and "a terror . . . not only to the tribes in that neighbourhood but also to the white settlers" (8 May 1864). In a marginal entry in the journal, dated 22 Oct. 1864, Brown noted: "He has since been pardoned."

22 Blue Camas (*Camassia quamash*), the bulbs of which were steamed and used as a sweetener (Nancy Turner, *Food Plants of British Columbia Indians Part I* [Victoria: British Columbia Provincial Museum 1975], 79–83).

23 Brown had found $2.00 a day to be "the regulation price" when travelling on the mainland the previous year (Journal, 19 Sept. 1863).

24 During the survey of the Cowichan and Nanaimo districts in 1858, an attempt was made to establish a mule train from Victoria to Nanaimo. Despite further attempts to develop a wagon road in 1862, communication by land remained difficult.

25 Macdonald estimated the population of "Qua-m-chin" to be 300 (Journal, 9 June). John Arnoup estimated 247: 87 men, 72 women, and 88 children (*British Colonist*, 5 July 1864). Edward S. Curtis described "Qamutsun" as "the largest village of the Cowichan proper" and noted that it "consisted of thirty-two large houses" (*The North American Indian* [1913; New York: Johnson Reprint 1970], 9, 175). In a journal entry added at this point, Brown noted: "Quamichan or 'Humpbacks' referring to contour of country. The Chief's Name Sem-el-ton."

26 Brown is probably referring to George W. Heaton's census, "Indian population. Cowichan, Nanaimo, Chemainus," presented in a letter of June 16, 1860, to the Colonial Secretary. Heaton estimated a "grand total" population of 2,104: Cowichan, 1,150; Chemainus, 271; and Nanaimo, 399 (Colonial Correspondence, F748/24a, PABC). Other estimates vary considerably. In *Vancouver Island: Survey of the Districts of Nanaimo and Cowichan Valley* (1859), Oliver Wells placed the Cowichan population at 1,100 (p. 14), but J.D. Pemberton maintained in his "Preface" to this publication that Wells had underestimated. Samuel Harris estimated the Cowichan population at "about two thousand" (*British Colonist*, 26 Mar. 1861), whereas Commander R.C. Mayne noted: "Cowitchens . . . numbering between 3000 and 4000 souls" (*Four Years in British Columbia and Vancouver Island* [London: J. Murray 1862], 244). There is more agreement about the population in 1864, following the deaths from smallpox. The Reverend A.C. Garrett remarked: "There are about 1,000 men, women, and children, all told, distributed among five villages" (Herald Street Collection, I, 901, PABC). Macdonald estimated a total population of 800 (Journal, 9 June 1864). John Arnoup estimated 816 (*British Colonist*, 5 July 1864). These later estimates do not, however, cover the total area Brown remarks on here.

27 In 1860, George Heaton estimated the population of "Samena" at 173 (Colonial Correspondence, F748/24a, PABC). Macdonald estimated 150 (Journal, 9 June 1864). Jean Arnoup estimated 190: 75 men, 65 women, and 50 children (*British Colonist*, 5 July 1864). Barnston noted that the village "consists of 7 or 8 large lodges" (Journal, 9 June 1864).

28 Following retirement as Chief Trader at Fort Langley, James Murray Yale (c. 1798–1871) resided at Stromness Farm in Saanich.

29 Whymper remarked on another aspect of Kakalatza's association with colonial society. "[He] has a constable's commission in his pocket," he noted, "which he showed us and is evidently proud of" (Journal, 10 June). However, Brown later associated Kakalatza with the Indian complaints outlined in his journal on 9 June 1864: see also Brown, "On the War-Path," *Cornhill Magazine* 20 (Sept. 1869): 322.

30 For Brown's detailed account of Tsosieten, see his article "The Last of the Chiefs," *All the Year Round*, 12 Mar. 1870:345-7.

31 Brown Collection, III, 1, PABC. George Cruickshank, secretary of the VIEE Committee, advertised himself in the press as "Accountant, Money Broker, Land and Real Estate Agent."

32 In Nov. 1862, members of the Lamalchi tribe had killed Frederick Marks and his daughter when they were travelling to Mayne Island. The following spring a naval bombardment destroyed the Lamalchi village on Kuper Island, and Acheewun and three other Indians were brought to trial. They were found guilty and executed on 4 July 1863. For a detailed account, see Barry Gough, *Gunboat Frontier: British Maritime Authority and Northwest Coast Indians, 1846-90* (Vancouver: University of British Columbia Press 1983), 140-7.

33 "Cultus" is defined as "worthless, good for nothing . . ." and "cultus potlatch" as "a present or free gift" in George Gibbs, *Dictionary of the Chinook Jargon* (Washington: Smithsonian Institute 1863), 3. Brown described his "present" to Kakalatza in his journal entry for 23 June (p. 72 above).

34 In "Memoir on Vancouver Island," Brown explained: " 'King George' men is a term commonly applied to the English by the N. Western Indians as well as in other parts of the world; their acquaintance with that race having commenced in the reign of George III" (Brown Collection, I, 10, 7, PABC).

35 The brothers Joseph Drinkwater (d. 1898) and William Drinkwater (d. 1900) had settled at Cowichan in Aug. 1862. In Oct. 1864, the Land Recorder for the Cowichan area noted that they had made $3,000 improvements on their 300-acre property and that they owned 13 horses, 13 cows, and nine pigs (Herald Street collection, I, 223, PABC). In an obituary, Joseph was described as "an excellent farmer" and "one of the most widely loved men in Cowichan" (British Colonist, 17 May 1898).

36 Samuel Harris made three expeditions up the Cowichan River in 1860. In reporting on the first expedition to Governor Douglas, he remarked: "a short distance before you reach Saclam [Saatlam] in a small creek leading into the main river is a vein of Coal" (Colonial Correspondence, F725/1, PABC). On a second expedition with Langley and Durham, he reported that gold was found on all the bars of the river (PABC, F725/3).

37 For wild crabapple, see Turner, *Food Plants of British Columbia Indians*, I, 202. For salmonberries (*Rubus spectabilis*), see Turner, 217.

38 Near spawning time, the nose of the coho salmon, especially of the male, becomes hooked.

39 For commentary on northwest Indian astronomy similar to Brown's, see Ella E. Clark, "George Gibbs' Account of Indian Mythology in Oregon and Washington Territories," *Oregon Historical Quarterly* 56 (1955): 319-20.

40 Probably the Great Blue Heron (*Ardea herodias*), often miscalled "crane," according to Roger Tory Peterson, *A Field Guide to Western Birds* (Boston: Houghton Mifflin 1961) 19.

41 The place name is a word for penis and refers to a rock in the Cowichan River.

42 Mercury (or quicksilver) may be used to assimilate gold into an amalgam. To separate the gold, the mercury may then be squeezed through a tightly woven fabric.

43 Dr. David Walker (1837-1917), a graduate of the Royal College of Surgeons, Dublin, had arrived in Victoria in 1863, following an expedition in search of Sir John Franklin. He had vied with Brown for the position of Commander of the VIEE. In his application for the position, he had remarked that as a Fellow of the Royal Geographical Society, he had some of their "Travelling instruments," and it seems that he subsequently lent the chronometer to the expedition. Brown was

apparently offended by Walker's confident social manner. He had first met him on 29 Dec. 1963, and noted in his journal: "Walker is giving himself great airs in town." In early Jan. 1865, Brown remarked on Walker's departure: "leaving his creditors in the lurch—after a career of about 18 months distinguished by his pertinacious brag, laziness, gradual loss of reputation & nothing at all."

44 In his letter to Governor Douglas (15 Sept. 1860), Samuel Harris reported that one of his two canoes on the expedition was "broken up" as a result of "misman-agement" (Colonial Correspondence, F725/5, PABC).

45 The place name is the generic term for a waterfall, probably based on a root indicating the making of a noise.

46 In Dispatch No. 2 (23 June), Brown described the Masolomo as "an inland tribe who live for the greater part of the year on this lake [Cowichan Lake]—but whose residence is an inlet on the seacoast." In his *Vancouver Island. Exploration. 1864* (1865), he described them as "a sub-tribe of Nittinahts" (4). Similarly, Macdonald noted: "The Me-sa-la-mos as far as I can learn are from the Nitinatt side" (Journal, 13 June 1864).

47 In his report to Governor Douglas (10 Aug. 1860), Samuel Harris wrote of meeting Tshama, chief of "Mysholomos," at Cowichan Lake at the end of July (Colonial Correspondence F725/3, PABC). The chief, who was at the lake to hunt, reportedly told Harris that many of his people were dying of smallpox and were thinking of "dying gloriously" by attacking the Klallams. According to Harris, the chief said that he would later guide him to gold in the mountains to the north of Cowichan Lake, but when Harris returned in late Aug., the chief was eager to return to the west coast and declined to provide such guidance (PABC, F725/5).

48 In his journal, Brown noted: "Reached some Chinese at Foster's Bar. . . . Wild lonely region abounding in rattle snakes. . . . Only a few Chinese miners" (20 Sept. 1863).

49 "*Shipbuilding* . . . A piece of timber naturally bent, used to secure parts of a ship together" (*Oxford English Dictionary*).

50 A character in Charles Dickens, *Martin Chuzzlewit* (1844), remarkable for in-domitable high spirits. In Dispatch No. 2 (23 June) and in his journal entry for 28 Aug. 1864, Brown described Macdonald as a "Mark Tapley."

51 James Murray Yale arrived at Fort Langley in 1828 and remained there until his retirement in 1859, having become Chief Trader for the Hudson's Bay Company in 1844.

52 Brown copied Leech's report into his journal, following his entry for 3 July. In the report, Leech suggested that the mountains to the north of the lake be known as the Kennedy Range, and those to the south as the Seymour Range—"in compli-ment to their Excellencies the Govs." He also described the rivers entering the Lake and the trees on the shores. Brown also copied into his journal at this point: "Leech's Report on the Journey from Cowichan Lake to Port San Juan" and "Foley's Report of Metallurgy."

53 Macdonald represented the name as "Qui-Quoit." The present-day name is Cot-tonwood Creek.

54 The expedition of Cowichan Lake Prospecting Company—composed of Major Boswell, J. Lawrie, J.W. McDonnell, Tomo, and Kakalatza—was reported in the *Victoria Daily Chronicle*, 16 June 1864. According to this account, the party prospected along Cowichan River (20 Mar.-10 May) and subsequently trekked from Cowichan Lake to the headwaters of the Chemainus River. Their explora-tion would seem therefore to have been more extensive than Brown acknowl-edged. On 28 May, they arrived back at Cowichan River.

55 The "Agreement" drawn up by the VIEE Committee noted: "Sunday is always (as far as possible) to be observed as a day of rest—and it is recommended that

Prayers from the Liturgy be read every sabbath day, and a short prayer every morning before starting" (Brown Collection, I, 6, PABC).

56 William Parsons Sayward (1818–1905) opened a lumber yard in Victoria in 1858, and in 1861 acquired a sawmill at Mill Bay on the Saanich Inlet.

57 The *British Colonist* reported that Lemon had brought into its office a "large lump of rock thickly studded with garnets, some of which are very large and fine" (12 May 1864).

58 In *Water over the Wheel* (Chemainus: Chemainus Valley Historical Society 1963), W.H. Olsen located the copper discovery at Copper Canyon between Mount Sicker and Mount Brenton (36), but it seems unlikely that Brown's group could have travelled this far. Neither was the group heading for the coast, as Olsen supposes. The discovery appears to have been in the region of Mount Landale.

59 In these instructions, Leech is "directed to proceed in charge of a party from the East end of The Great Cowichan Lake to Port San Juan (the Pachena of the Indians) in De Fuca's Strait" (Brown Collection, III, 6, PABC).

60 Brown Collection, III, 1, PABC.

61 In this letter, Brown made no mention of gold discoveries and emphasized his concern with botany, noting that he had instructed Whymper "to make coloured sketches of the trees and shrubs of the country."

62 Whymper's article appeared in the *Daily Victoria Chronicle*, 30 June 1864. In a style reminiscent of *Punch*, he wrote of the *Grappler*'s boilers suffering from "a sick tum-tum"; of an unnamed expedition member (Macdonald) losing six inches in the waist; and of Brown as "energetic and enterprising—a good leader and a good man."

63 Expedition members had agreed to provide "a faithful record of all discoveries . . . and to impart them to our commander for the general benefit of the colony without any reservation whatever or attempt at concealment for exclusive or personal benefit, under pain of peremptory dismissal and forfeiture of pay" (Brown Collection, I, PABC).

64 Thomas Sherlock Gooch, second lieutenant, H.M.S. *Satellite*, accompanied J.D. Pemberton on his expedition from Cowichan Harbour to Nitinat in 1857. In his account, Pemberton noted that Gooch "joined as an amateur, but was afterwards of much service in every emergency" (*Facts and Figures Relating to Vancouver Island*, 149).

65 Brown's basis for this account of the official reservation policy is not clear. Governor Douglas had calculated on a minimum of ten acres per family, but he had also insisted on a flexibility that would permit more than this. (See Robin Fisher, *Contact and Conflict*, 66–8, 156.)

66 In a marginal gloss, Brown notes of "rancheria": "A word very common on this coast derived from California where it is applied to an Indian village, shortly 'Ranch.' Also applied to farms."

67 Admiral Sir George Henry Richards (1820–1900) arrived at Esquimalt in Nov. 1849, and conducted coastal surveys until 1863. Charts based on his surveys were published from 1860.

68 In *Guide to Common Seaweeds of British Columbia* (Victoria: British Columbia Provincial Museum 1967), Robert F. Scagel distinguishes between four species of fucus but does not refer to "Fucus Vessiculous" (158). A vesicle is an air bladder or a float.

69 Of the appearance of Indians in this area, E.Y. Arima writes: "Red ochre, charcoal, and hemlock sap which turns black, were used. . . . Jewellery included ear and nose pendants of abalone shell [haliotis], dentalium shell, copper and trade beads, worn by both men and women" (*The West Coast (Nootka) People* [Victoria:

British Columbia Provincial Museum 1983], 67).

70 "Ik-tah. A thing; goods; merchandise; clothing" (Gibbs, *Dictionary of Chinook Jargon*, 6).

71 "Sit-kum. A half; a part" (Gibbs, *Dictionary of Chinook Jargon*, 22). The reference is therefore to a joint chief.

72 This attack was notorious. W.E. Banfield described it as having occurred in Sept. 1857 and noted that the Nitinats "brought back as trophies twenty heads" (*Victoria Gazette*, 28 Aug. 1858). James Swan also described coming across "the charred remains of an Indian village burned by the Nittinats some two years since, who killed some twenty of the inhabitants of the Clallam or Ehwha tribes" ("A Cruise in a Canoe," *San Francisco Evening Bulletin*, 22 May 1860, in *Almost Out of the World*, ed. William A. Katz [Tacoma: Washington State Historical Society 1971], 88). For Brown's further reference to the conflict, see p. 91 above and note 90.

73 Brown notes marginally: "N.B. Describe at length as a specimen of Indian bargains this 'hyas work.'" "Hy-as" is defined as "large; great; very" by Gibbs, *Dictionary of Chinook Jargon*, 6.

74 That is, the utmost degree of savagery. "Si-wash. . . . French, SAUVAGE. An Indian" (Gibbs, *Dictionary of Chinook Jargon*, 23).

75 "The . . . Clo-oose is a tribe on the Cheewhat River east of Nitinat Lake with territory on the coast from Clo-oose to Carmanah Point" (Arima, *West Coast People*, 5).

76 Frederick Whymper refers to Captain William Spring as Thomas Laughton's partner (Journal, 30 June 1864). Earlier, according to W.E. Banfield, Laughton's partner was Peter Francis (Peter Francis and W.E. Banfield to Governor Douglas, 17 July 1855: Colonial Correspondence F 588a/2, PABC).

77 The Antarctic expedition was presumably that of Captain James Clark Ross, who published an account in *A Voyage of Discovery and Research in the Southern and Antarctic Regions, during the years 1839-43*. While Lieutenant-Governor of Van Diemen's Land, from 1836 to 1843, Sir John Franklin encouraged this Antarctic expedition.

78 In Aug. 1855, Governor Douglas reported to the Colonial Office: "It is estimated that a quantity equal to ten thousand gallons [of whale and dogfish oils] were purchased from the natives of the west coast last year" (cited in R.S. Mackie, "Colonial Land, Indian Labour, and Company Capital: The Economy of Vancouver Island, 1849-1858 [MA thesis, University of Victoria 1984], 53). In Aug. 1858, W.E. Banfield reported of the trade in dogfish oil at Port San Juan: "for the four antecedent years from five to six thousand gallons of oil have been produced from these fish each year, bartered by white traders resident in the bay, sold to H.B. Co., and by them shipped to England" (*Victoria Gazette*, 19 Aug. 1958).

79 Frederick Walker was the leader of an expedition in Australia, 1861-2. An extract from his journal was published in the *Journal of Royal Geographical Society* 33 (1863): 133-50, but Walker does not refer in it to a difficulty with his men over tobacco.

80 The use of red-hot stones set in the chiselled cavity of a cedar tree is described as a felling technique by Hilary Stewart, *Cedar* (Vancouver: Douglas & McIntyre 1984), 36-9, but the use of two holes as described by Brown is not remarked on there.

81 In 1858, W.E. Banfield described the Port San Juan Indians as "a branch of the Nitinett tribe. . . . They were formerly much more numerous, but war with the Songhish Indians has reduced them to this number [about twenty] in connection with the small pox which ravaged them eight years since" (*Victoria Gazette*, 14 Aug. 1858).

82 Brown's account here differs from the subsequent report made by Leech which Brown copied into his journal following his entry for 3 July. Leech notes that on 25 June on the second day of its trek, the group ate slapjacks in order to save the limited supply of flour. Subsequently, on 27 June, he notes that "it was astonishing in these unexplored regions to mark the total absence of game," though later in the day Tomo shot two elk. On 1 July, Meade recorded that the group supped on a pigeon, two young ducks, and a little venison, while the following evening they had only salmonberries.

83 Again, Leech's account is somewhat darker, noting that "the country we travelled over was totally unfit for settlement."

84 Leech's report concluded that "the only advantage" of the terrain passed through was "that it will become a mineral country, from the rich metallurgical indications at the heads of creeks."

85 "Fell & Company" advertised in Victoria newspapers as "Coffee and Spices Merchants;" Samuel Nesbitt, as a "Biscuit Baker."

86 Foley was accompanied by Barnston, Tomo, and three Indians. Brown copied Foley's report, which outlined disappointing findings, into his journal, following his 17 July entry.

87 Perhaps a reference to the fiction published in *Colburn's New Monthly Magazine* or to his editions of "Modern Standard Novelists." Brown seems to refer to an explorer's complaint.

88 Brown outlines this story above (p. 53) and also included it in *Races of Mankind* I, 65–6. The remainder of this paragraph notes topics Brown apparently planned to develop.

89 In a letter of 30 Apr. 1864 to the Colonial Secretary, George Hargreaves and others reported the discovery of coal at Bonilla Point and requested reservation of land there (Colonial Correspondence, F714/1, PABC). Under the heading "Another Coal Company," the *British Colonist*, 22 July 1864, reported plans to develop a mine.

90 In *Races of Mankind*, Brown elaborated on this reference to the conflict between the Nitinats and the Elwhats (I, 72–5). The sick "tum-tum" is there glossed as a saddened heart caused by the death of a brother. To allay his sorrow, Moquilla is described as killing a member of his own tribe with whom his brother had quarrelled, and then, apparently as a diversion, attacking the Elwhats across the Strait of Juan de Fuca, having dredged up an "unavenged insult" as a motive. The account concludes with a fictionalized narrative of L[aughton] and a visitor defending their settlement at Port San Juan from the Elwhat's attempt at revenge—a narrative that Brown had first presented in "Saving a City," *All the Year Round* 23 (9 Mar. 1870), 377–8.

91 Foley's "Report upon the coal seams . . . on S.W. Coast of V.I." refers to "the recent discovery of coal in Clallam Bay, W[ashington] T[erritory] . . . from here 15 m.S." The discovery is reported in detail supplied by Allen Francis, U.S. Consul, in *British Colonist*, 24 May 1864. Brown included in his journal a rough sketch of the geological formation near Sheringham Point.

92 This settler's name is variously rendered in the explorers' journals: Brulais (Barnston), Brulé (Whymper), Breuilly (Meade), and Brule (Macdonald). The name does not appear in the early lists of settlers pre-empting land in the area.

93 Brown Collection, III, 6, PABC.

94 Brown provided various explanations for his temporarily leaving the expedition and journeying to Victoria. In his official report, *Vancouver Island. Exploration. 1864*, he remarked that (1) better supply arrangements needed to be made; (2) his "English mission" needed attention; and (3) there was a threat of "mutiny" among the explorers if commercial development of their discoveries were per-

mitted before completion of the expedition (11). However, at least one member
of the VIEE committee was critical of Brown's conduct. At a meeting on 18 July,
Charles B. Young remarked that Brown had returned to Victoria "without any
ostensible reason," and he proposed "that a strong resolution should be passed
conveying the feelings of the Committee on the subject." The proposal was
overturned by a motion that expressed "satisfaction" with the expedition's
progress (Brown Collection, III, 8, 41, PABC).

95 The Honourable David Cameron (1804-72) was formally appointed Chief Justice of the Colony of Vancouver Island in 1856 and retired in 1865. His home,
Belmont, was situated on the western side of Esquimalt Harbour. Brown's trek
from Sooke to Victoria is described in *Countries of the World*, 271-83.

96 Henry Fry is reported in the *British Colonist*, 22 Sept. 1863 as having leased
"the fine new hotel at North Saanich" from Charles Street. Subsequent press
advertisements describe the hotel as eighteen miles from Victoria and as ser-
viced by a stage coach three times a week and by a ferry to Cowichan. The farm
extended to 400 acres.

97 For James Murray Yale, see note 28 above. Like Henry Fry, Peter Lind was also a
hotelier, having recently opened the South Saanich Hotel. Thomas Harris, Victoria's first mayor, had purchased 513 acres in North Saanich in 1861.

98 Brown's subsequent remarks on the manufacture of turpentine appear to be
derived from two newspaper articles: *British Colonist*, 20 June and 1 July 1864.

99 The Land Recorder for Cowichan noted that H. Marriner settled on 108 acres at
Cowichan on 4 May 1863, and that he made $60 worth of improvements by
"some clearing of bush" (Herald Street Collection, I, 223, PABC).

100 Similarly, the Reverend A.C. Garrett remarked in 1864: "There are altogether
3,500 Acres of Indian Reserves in Cowichan Valley. Of this about 50 Acres are
in cultivation" (Herald Street Collection, I, 901, PABC).

101 Following the treaties of 1850 arranged by Governor Douglas, the Songhees
leased parts of their reserve. According to Wilson Duff, "the leasing arrangement seems to have worked successfully until Douglas retired in 1864, after
which disputes over the legality of the leases resulted in their cancellation.
There followed a long series of negotiations whose purpose was to move the
Songhees away" ("The Fort Victoria Treaties," *BC Studies* 3 (1969):43).

102 Patrick Brennan, the Irishman, remained a troublesome presence at Cowichan.
In "Report of visit to Cowichan relative to Patrick Brennan" (14 Sept. 1864),
Magistrate A.F. Pemberton dealt with Brennan's contention that Indians had
"maimed and injured" his cattle. "The complainant Brannen [sic] is a squatter
upon the Indian reserve," Pemberton remarked. "From his own statement and
from the general character he bears in the country, he seems to be very violent
and harsh in his treatment of the Indians. I think it desirable that he should be
removed." Pemberton also recommended that Brennan should be compensated
if he was accurate in maintaining that the Surveyor General and Douglas had
earlier granted the land to him. Brennan's statement in the report noted that he
had been resident at Cowichan for four years, and it included a copy of the
Surveyor General's statement, dated 27 July 1861, granting him "a legal claim . . .
to not less than 200 acres of land improved by him at the entrance of the
Cowichan river, on Indian reserve." Also included in the report is a statement by
Bishop Demers, remarking that "the Indians have continually complained of the
harsh and unjust way in which he [Brennan] treated them," and noting in
particular Brennan's having recently shot an Indian's dog. According to the
Cowichan Land Recorder, Brennan had by Oct. 1864, made $700 worth of
improvements and had two oxen, thirty cows, eight pigs, and two horses (Herald Street Collection, I, 223, PABC). Several years later, Brennan was charged

with threatening to shoot a settler and stealing cattle (*British Colonist*, 20 June 1868). Finally, in 1871, he was sentenced to two years' hard labour for shooting at Henry Shaw, another settler (*British Colonist*, 28 Oct. 1871).

103 In this dispatch, Brown reports the gold discovery "on the banks of one of the Forks of the Sooke River—about 12 miles from the sea in a straight line in a locality never hitherto reached by white men." This discovery, he asserts, "cannot fail to prove of the highest importance to the prosperity of the colony & the further upbuilding of the City of Victoria."

104 Brown later added in his journal: "I asked him to deliver a letter to the Exploration Committee which he never did."

105 In his private dispatch, Brown remarked: "Foley . . . looked upon the whole Expn. as wholy a mining party & that nobody knew anything but self & anything out of mining a mere waste of time & the master an ignoramus. . . . Take care of him—he is treacherous & has cursed every member on the Committee for one thing & another." Brown's suspicion that Foley had joined the expedition for private ends gains some credibility from Foley's promptly setting up a guide service to the diggings at Sooke—"the new El Dorado," as he advertised the service in the press.

106 In *History of the Catholic Church in Western Canada from Lake Superior to the Pacific, 1659-1895* (Toronto: Musson 1910), the Reverend A.G. Morice wrote of four Sisters of St. Ann as connected with the mission at Cowichan: Sisters Mary of the Sacred Heart, Mary Angéle, Mary Luména, and Mary of the Conception (II, 304). Father Rondeault had pre-empted land for the school on 12 Sept. 1862 (Herald Street Collection, II, 137, PABC).

107 J. Humphreys had settled at Cowichan on 18 June 1863. In Nov. 1863, the Land Recorder reported that he owned four pigs and that he had done "nothing" to improve his "2nd Quality" property. In his report of 22 Oct. 1864, he credited Humphreys with a 142-acre property, five cows, six pigs, and $125 worth of improvements (Herald Street Collection, I, 223, PABC).

108 In this dispatch, Brown expressed fear that the explorers would desert unless they were rewarded for their discovery of gold on Leech River. "There is great growling in Camp," he wrote, "and I tell you plainly I have a difficult job to keep them together" (Brown Collection, III, 4, 1, PABC).

109 Brown has added at a later time: "Tom or Stashul. He was hung in Victoria in December 1864 for murdering some Hydahs." *British Colonist* (5 Dec. 1864) reported the execution on 3 Dec. of two unnamed Chemainus Indians "for the cold-blooded murder of five "Tsimpsean Indians."

110 Bannerman is listed among those who pre-empted land on the "Cowichan Expedition of Augt. 18th 1862" (Herald Street Collection, II, 137, PABC).

111 William Smithe contributed several letters to the *Victoria Daily Chronicle*, in which he reported on the settlement at Cowichan. In a letter published 3 June 1864, he remarked on the increase in the amount of cultivated land in the district and of the intention to form a cricket club. In a letter published 16 July 1864 (under the address: "The Hermitage, Somenos, Cowichan"), he wrote of "Cowichan Grievances"—specifically, of the difficult relations of the settlers with the Indians. In 1871 he was elected to the Colonial Legislature and was premier from 1883 until his death in 1887.

112 Major Biggs was Justice of Peace of the region (*British Colonist*, 13 May 1863). There seems to be no record of his return to the region.

113 James Habart (1833-91) pre-empted 100 acres at Chemainus on 13 Oct. 1862 (Herald Street Collection, II, 137, PABC). Just prior to Brown's visit, the *British Colonist* (2 July) reported: "Messrs. Stafford & Hobart have about 75 head of

fine cattle on their ranch at Chemainus, among which number there are 20 milch cows."

114 Brown's subsequent reflections in his journal on the relationship between Indian potato cultivation and settlers' land relate closely to D.W. Minguay's plight, which culminated in his formal complaint in 1867. William Pearse, Acting Surveyor-General, then interceded on Minguay's behalf, noting in a letter to William Young, Colonial Secretary (17 May), that "great inconvenience is felt by the white settlers from the constant, and in one instance forcible trespass of the Penal-a-Khuts [from Kuper Island]," even while he also acknowledged that Indians had visited the Chemainus valley from time immemorial to fish and raise potatoes. Minguay, he remarked further, had acted in difficult circumstances "with a good deal of patience and discretion" (Colonial Correspondence, F949/4). Young did not immediately concur with the recommendation that Indian potato cultivation should be restricted to Kuper Island, and subsequently (5, 24 June 1867), he proposed a land exchange (Colonial Correspondence, F949/6 and 8). Minguay was prepared to give up his home and 40 acres (valued at $200 minimum), in exchange for two islands at the mouth of the river and about 126 acres. This exchange is reflected by the present day name: Mainguy Island.

115 Following protracted negotiations with the Colonial Government concerning mineral rights in the area, George Charles Deverill reported: "I have commenced to put down expensive bores" (23 July 1864). Subsequently, on 29 Aug. 1864, he noted that he has had "six to eight men constantly at work" (Colonial Correspondence, F460, PABC).

116 Macdonald further defined this location: "to the North of the Most Northern of the Chemainus Villages, nearly opposite to Sie-ex-in on Valdes Island" (Journal, 5 Aug. 1864).

117 On 4 Aug. 1864, the *British Colonist* reported the discovery of this nugget: "It is of oval shape, with a smooth surface, and about the size of a small hen egg. On being weighed it was declared to contain 4 ounces, 6 dwts. or $73.20!!"

118 John J. Landale was described by Brown as "a most competent Scottish mining engineer" ("On the Geographical Distribution and Physical Characteristics of the Coal Fields of the North Pacific Coast," *Transactions of the Edinburgh Geological Society* (1868-9): 5). Brown noted that Landale was active in Clallam Bay on the Olympic Peninsula and at Koskeemo on Vancouver Island (13).

119 Following the resignation of Foley, the VIEE Committee resolved on 30 July that "two efficient miners" be appointed as replacements, and $230 was collected for this purpose. On 1 August Richard Drew and William Hooper were engaged "at a Salary of Eighty Dollars per month with Rations" (Brown Collection, I, 9, PABC).

120 Captain William Franklyn (1816-74) had served in the merchant navy prior to arriving in Victoria in 1859. He was magistrate at Nanaimo from 1860 to 1867.

121 In a dispatch of 30 Aug. sent with a further volume of his journal, Brown described the journal as "a private Document to prepare a condensed report from."

122 Nanaimo was originally named after Andrew Colville, Governor of Hudson's Bay Company, 1852-6. Captain John T. Walbran remarked: "After [1859] . . . the name [Colville] was gradually discontinued and has not been used since 1860" (*B.C. Coast Names*, 349). Other visitors to Nanaimo in 1864 attest to its growth. A writer in the *Victoria Daily Chronicle* (19 July) remarked: "Among the solid evidence of prosperity at this town, we learn that there are thirteen handsome and substantial buildings in the course of erection." Those on an

"Excursion to Nanaimo" are also described as "surprised" by the town's size, since they "expected to find a place of much smaller dimensions" (*Victoria Daily Chronicle*, 28 July). There seems to be no record of Brown's earlier visit to Nanaimo, but he presumably visited during an expedition to Sangster Island with some mining prospectors on which he set out from Victoria on 29 Jan. 1864.

123 W.H. Franklyn formed a branch committee of the VIEE at Nanaimo on 6 June 1864. The committee was especially eager that a second exploration party should set out from Nanaimo, and it was therefore pleased with the plan Brown outlined at a meeting on 8 Aug., whereby a group would explore the Nanaimo River (Brown Collection, III, 12, PABC).

124 With the arrival of about twenty-four families from Staffordshire, England, on 27 Nov. 1854, Nanaimo became established as a coal-mining centre. In 1862, the Vancouver Island Coal Mining and Land Company replaced the Hudson's Bay Company as owners of the mines.

125 Mr. Fowler, Secretary of the Nanaimo VIEE Committee, wrote to the Committee in Victoria on 12 Aug. 1864, indicating that the expedition's delay at Nanaimo was partly "owing to the Indians refusing to work with a half breed [Tomo] who . . . has been constantly drunk during his stay here, and who the Indians are afraid of" (Brown Collection, I, 12, PABC).

126 Charles S. Nicol, J.P., was the Treasurer of the Nanaimo VIEE Committee, manager of the Vancouver Island Coal Company, and Nanaimo Agent of the Bank of British Columbia.

127 Thomas Crosby became a lay missionary among the Indians at Nanaimo in 1863. In *Among the An-ko-me-nums or Flathead Tribes of Indians of the Pacific Coast* (Toronto: W. Briggs 1907), he outlined his disagreement with Brown: "An exploring party, sent by the Government, was preparing to start from Nanaimo across the Island. They hired a number of Indians as packers and guides. After having engaged these natives they hung around the town for some days doing nothing. When the week came to a close they immediately became active, and wanted to make a start on Sunday morning, but the Indians refused to go. The first intimation we had of the difficulty was through a letter, written by the head of the party and published in the *Daily Chronicle* [19 Aug. 1864], in which he stated: 'Thanks to Brother Crosby, the Indians would not travel on Sunday, so we were set out another day'" (167).

128 The Harewood Coal Company was named after the family name of Lieutenant Commander the Honourable Horace Douglas Lascelles (1835–9) of the gunboat H.M.S. *Forward*, 1862–5, who formed the coal company in 1864. Brown wrote elsewhere: "Behind, and out of the limits of the present Coal Company's grant [i.e., the Vancouver Coal Company], the beds of coal crop out again, showing in one place a clear face of 11 feet of pure coal. This has been taken up by the 'Harewood Company'—an English concern, but as yet nothing has been done to develop the mine" ("On the Coal Fields of the North Pacific Coast," *Transactions of the Edinburgh Geological Society* [1868–9], 12).

129 Brown's instructions to Leech indicate his new concern with gold prospecting: "You will ascend the Nanaimo River to its source—prospecting—& exploring the geography of the neighbouring country, but will pay particular attention to the discovery of profitable gold fields & you will make all other mineralogical researches subservient to this" (Brown Collection, III, 6, PABC).

130 Captain Hugh McKay had arrived in Victoria about 1852 and engaged in such various activities as cooperage, fishing, and mail delivery between Victoria and Olympia. In 1859, he purchased the *Surprise* for trade along the west coast of Vancouver Island. (See Walbran, *B.C. Coast Names*, 330.)

131 The Reverend John Booth Good (1833-?) had arrived at Nanaimo in Sept. 1862 as a missionary for the Society for the Propagation of the Gospel. In his unpublished work, "Utmost Bounds of the West / Pioneer jottings of Forty Years / Missionary Reminiscences of the Out West Pacific Coast / A.D. 1861 to A.D. 1900," Good wrote of his journey to Comox: "My first visit to this young community of our countrymen was in connection with Dr John [sic] Brown's Exploration Expedition through the northern part of Vancouver Island. . . . We formed quite a large party with abundant supplies needed for such an enterprise" (24, holograph, PABC). See also F.A. Peake, "John Booth Good in B.C.," *Pacific Northwest Quarterly* 75:2 (1984):70-8.

132 *North American West Coast Vancouver & British Columbia Strait of Georgia— Sheet 2 (E.N.E. of Texada I[sland] to Johnstone Strait Surveyed by Capt G.H. Richards, RN 1860*. In 1864, this chart was reissued "with additions" and the notation: "The Lakes between Stamp Hr. & R. Courtenay from the Explorations of Mr. Brown, Botanist, 1864."

133 Malcolm Munro, the contractor, and six "choppers" are reported as setting out for Comox to work on this trail (*British Colonist*, 13 Mar. 1863). The return of Munro and eighteen men to Victoria is subsequently reported in an article which describes the trail as "first class" (*British Colonist*, 9 May 1863). Accounts of Department of Lands and Works record: "1864. Comox Road. Expenditure. Vote $5,000.00" (Herald Street Collection, I, 25, PABC).

134 Francisco de Eliza (and Jose Maria Narvaez) explored the Strait of Juan de Fuca and the Gulf of Georgia, 1790-1. The reference is probably to Englishman River, as noted by Henry Wagner, *Cartography of the Northwestern Coast of America to the Year 1800* (Berkeley: University of California Press 1937), 2:364.

135 "San Leonardo, Punta, a name no doubt given by Narvaez to a point on Vancouver Island nearly opposite the southern end of Denman Island, perhaps Maple Point" (Wagner, *Cartography*, 2, 503). The map based on Spanish charts is probably J. Arrowsmith, *Map of Vancouver Island and the Adjacent Coasts, Compiled from the Surveys of Vancouver, Kellett, Simpson, Galliano, Valdes &c &c &c* (1858). The large survey presumably refers to the chart indicated in note 132 above.

136 Adam Horne, a Hudson's Bay Company trader, has been described as the "First white man" to cross Vancouver Island, having journeyed from Qualicum River to the head of Alberni Inlet in 1856 (Walkem, *Stories of Early British Columbia*, 38). At the conclusion of the 1864 expedition, Brown crossed from Alberni to Qualicum on this trail and described the experience in *Races of Mankind*, 41-7.

137 The Reverend Jordayne C. Browne-Cave was appointed probationary catechist to the Nanaimo Indians in Nov. 1862. From 1864 to 1866 he served at Comox, where he arranged the building of a church and a parsonage. He then became deacon at New Westminster, and following his ordination as priest in 1868 became vicar of Saanich. In Aug. 1870 he returned to England.

138 Edward Parke Bedwell was second master on H.M.S. *Plumper* during its surveys of 1856-60. He became a Master in 1860 and was appointed to H.M.S. *Hecate* when it took over surveying duties that year. The drawing remarked on here is not listed among Bedwell's known works in Helen Bergen Peters, *Painting during the Colonial Period*, 66-7.

139 *Macbeth*, I.v.38 and Edgar Allen Poe, "The Raven."

140 Macdonald noted that the village belonged "to the Puntledge Tribe who are now reduced to about ten or twelve men by the Euclatas and have since joined the Comox Tribe" (Journal, 19 Aug. 1864). Wilson Duff also connects the village with the extinct Pentlatch, noting that they joined the Comox after 1850 (*Indian History of British Columbia*, 25).

141 The Colonial Government organized settlement at Comox in the fall of 1862. A report in the *British Colonist* commented: "Some 35 settlers have taken up claims in the vicinity of Courtenay river and express themselves delighted with the prospect. The land is of the richest character with scattered prairies from five hundred to a thousand acres, well watered, and abounding with game" (10 Oct.). By 1864, the news of agricultural development is described as "very favourable" (*British Colonist*, 23 Apr. 1864), and a couple of months later some specific details are provided. A hundred pounds of butter had just arrived from the settlement—"the first but let us hope the precursor of many hundred kegs more of that commodity" (14 June). Eighteen tons of hay of "splendid quality" had also been sent to Chemainus, with "plenty more of it on hand" (25 June). For Brown's detailed assessment, see "Comoucs Country Settlers & Indians" (pp. 120-2 above).

142 According to a government survey in 1864, J. Robb had pre-empted 180 acres on 9 Oct. 1862, cultivated 3 acres, and made improvements of $475 (Colonial Correspondence, F910/1, PABC). In the *British Colonist*, 23 Apr. 1864, Robb is reported as having "10 to 15 acres in crop." Later in 1864, the *Colonist* reported that "great complaints" were being made about Robb's conduct as Land Recorder. "Those in Cariboo have had claims jumped—he himself having appropriated one or two of the best" (11 Oct. 1864). He is described as a fifty-year-old settler from Aberdeenshire and of a "masterful character" (Eric Duncan, *Fifty-Seven Years in Comox Valley* [Courtenay, B.C.: Argus, c.1934], 4, 26).

143 G. Mitchell is described in the *British Colonist*, 23 Apr. 1864, as "one of the principal settlers" at Comox, with about 40 acres under cultivation and 18 head of cattle. According to a government survey in 1864, he had pre-empted 150 acres on 11 June 1862, fenced 25 acres, cultivated 18 acres, and made $700 in improvements (Colonial Correspondence, F910/1, PABC).

144 William Walker had seized power in Nicaragua in 1856 after intervening in an internal dispute. He was subsequently expelled and killed when attempting to return to the country in 1860.

145 On 10 June 1864, William Burrage had formally complained about James Hart's infringement of liquor regulations (Colonial Correspondence, F594/10, PABC). Hart was sentenced on 27 Dec. 1864, to one year's imprisonment (Colonial Correspondence, F597/4).

146 Ford is described as having eight to ten acres under cultivation (*British Colonist*, 23 Apr. 1864).

147 According to a government survey in 1864, S. Gunderson had pre-empted 100 acres on 4 Mar. 1864. He had fenced ten acres, cultivated two acres, and made $300 in improvements (Colonial Correspondence, F910/1, PABC).

148 Brown includes in his journal "List of Lands Preempted in Comox" (note 167 below). Blakely is there noted as having pre-empted 100 acres in 1862. "Funly" may be represented in the list as "Fairly"; he is noted as having taken up "all spare ground" between two other settlers.

149 According to a government survey in 1864, W. Harmston had pre-empted 220 acres on 27 Apr. 1863. He had fenced eight acres, cultivated one acre, and made $430 in improvements (Colonial Correspondence, F910/1, PABC). In Eric Duncan's *Fifty-Seven Years in Comox Valley*, Harmston is described as thirty-eight years old when he arrived at Comox with his wife and two children, and is said to have settled there for four years (22).

150 "Til-i-kum. . . . *People*. Applied generally, it means those who are not chiefs. Cultus tilikum, *common* or *insignificant* persons . . . nika tilikum, my relations" (Gibbs, *Dictionary of Chinook Jargon*, 26). In this context, the reference is probably to a companion.

151 According to a government survey in 1864, J. Baily had pre-empted 250 acres on 2 Sept. 1862, fenced and cultivated nine acres, and made improvements valued at $450 (Colonial Correspondence, F910/1, PABC).

152 On a facing page in his journal, Brown noted: "These Coguells are notorious scoundrels and pirates. Davis' adventures at Rio de Grullas. Scouting canoe full of Warriors." He elaborated on Davis's experience in "Up a Tree," *All the Year Round*, 9 July 1870: 127–32. In this narrative, Jim, who is described as "kind of an odd man on an exploratory expedition . . . on the coast," records his encountering a band of drunken Euclataws near the Rio de Grullas and his concealing himself up a tree.

153 In Dispatch No. 11 (26–7 Aug. 1864), Brown wrote: "I am fortunate enough to be able to report the existence of the finest seams of coal hitherto discovered . . . on the Pacific Coast. . . . The party insisted in naming the River after me & though I am as a matter of principle opposed to have anything named after the Commander . . . and though I am perfectly well aware that this is quite common . . . and that the strict laws of scientific nomenclature allows of no name to be cancelled when it has the priority, I have more than once changed the names of parts of the country discovered by us when the detached party had named them after myself, I hope you will not accuse me of egotism if at the earnest solicitation of the Expedition I allow the seat of this rich coal field to bear the name of Brown River" (Brown Collection, III, 1, PABC). The river continues to bear Brown's name.

154 Davis's experience in the Indian Wars may be rendered in "The Free Trapper," *All the Year Round*, 15 Jan. 1870: 160–1, where Brown wrote of Seth Baillie "piloting . . . a troop of United States cavalry for service in the Indian war of 1855."

155 In a report by W. Pearse, Acting Surveyor General (6 Jan. 1865), thirty eight settlers are listed (Colonial Correspondence (F910/1, PABC). As for total population, a letter in the *British Colonist*, 8 Dec. 1864, fixed the number at 62, noting 19 new settlers in the past year.

156 In a census of the area taken on 31 May 1865, and forwarded to the Colonial Secretary, 3 Oct. 1865, J.C.B. Cave noted a population of "34 English, 8 Canadian, 13 Scotch, 1 Israelite, 2 Norwegian, 2 American, 1 Portuguese, 6 Irish, 1 Swede, and 2 Half-Breeds" (Colonial Correspondence, F280, PABC).

157 In Charles Dickens's *David Copperfield*, Wilkins Micawber alternates between elation and depression over his financial affairs. When attempting to sell corn upon commission, he declares to David: I have now an immediate prospect of something turning up" (Chapter 27).

158 Brown's subsequent account of the Puntledge and Comox Indians concurs essentially with that of more recent commentators. Wilson Duff writes of the extinct Pentlatch: "Before 1850 three groups lived on Comox Harbour, Denman Island, and Englishman River" (*Indian History of British Columbia*, 25). Similarly, of the Comox, he writes: "Several tribes . . . before 1850 lived in Quadra Island area; remnants driven south to Comox by Euclataw" (25). Brown's contemporary, R.H. Pidcock, in "Adventures in Vancouver Island" (1862) (unpublished, holograph, PABC) also remarked that the Puntledge were now "amalgamated with the Comox though they have a different language and were formerly a very strong tribe" (80).

159 Of "Comox," Walbran writes: "the name has been spelt variously and also gradually shortened. Komoux, Comuck, Comax and finally Comox. The tribes residing here are the Puntledge and Sloslute, both of them nearly extinct" (*British Columbia Coast Names*, 104). Macdonald remarks in his journal: "E-yees . . . informed us that the right pronuncation is Koo-moox which is a

name given them by their enemies the Euclatas. That their right name is Sa-shool-tuch" (20 Aug. 1864).

160 A correspondent in the *British Colonist* [Victoria] wrote of the Euclataws: "This tribe whose proper locality is Cape Mudge, has almost continually a large force camped on the Indian Reserve at Comox, amounting sometimes to over 300 and seldom falling short of 100" (18 Feb. 1864). Similarly, on 2 Mar. 1864, the *British Colonist* reported further: "The Euclataws, who have for some time been threatening to drive out the Comox Indians, now say they will do it in earnest, and warn the white people to keep out of the way." H.M.S. *Forward* then "visited" the area, and on 23 Apr. the region was described by the *British Colonist* as "quiet and peaceable."

161 Probably the William Jones who was remanded on a charge of robbing a drink-ing companion of $153 in 1860 (*British Colonist*, 28, 30 June and 7 July). (The case was dismissed when a witness failed to appear.) William Jones died a pauper in 1861 (aged about 35 years), and an inquest concluded that the death was "hastened by the too frequent use of ardent spirits" (*British Colonist*, 8 Jan. 1861).

162 Augustus Frederick Pemberton (c. 1808–91) was "Stipendiary Magistrate at Vic-toria and Chief Commissioner of Police" (*British Columbia and Victoria Direc-tory 1863*, 86).

163 A reference to the Reverend Thomas Crosby (see p. 104 above). Chadband is a religious (and loquacious) hypocrite in Charles Dickens's *Bleak House*.

164 Brown has added on the facing page: "A commission from which every Hud-son's Bay Co servant ought to be excluded—and only examined as a witness on oath."

165 Brown presented his considered notions on American Indian policy in "On the War-Path," *Cornhill Magazine* 20 (Sept. 1869): 313–26.

166 Of Courtenay, Walbran writes: "After Captain George William Conway Courte-nay, H.M.S. *Constance*, 50 guns. On this station, 1846-49. . . . Name adopted, circa 1860" (*British Columbia Coast Names*, 115–16).

167 Brown here includes in his journal: "List of Lands Preempted in Comox / Burrage 50 acres Act of 1862. Entitled to ten claims wide / Mitchell 150 acres–1861-24.50 x 61.24 / Hairup 100 acres–1862-20 x 50 / Fairly—all spare ground between Hairup and McNish / McNish 100 acres–1862-20 x 50 / Murphy 100 acres–1862-20 x 50 / Fletcher 100 acres–1862-20 x 50 / Green 100 acres–1862-20 x 50 / Duncan 150 acres–1861-24.50 x 61.24 / Pidcock (Mission) 100 acres–1862-20 x 50 / Britain—understood but not pre-empted—none to spare, gone to Cariboo / Wilson 150 acres–1861-24.50 x 61.24 / Lau-rence 150 acres–1861-24.50 x 61.24 / Harmston 150 acres–1862–not decided / Blakely 100 acres–1862-20 x 50 / Carmthen 150 acres–1861-24.50 x 61.24 / Baily 150 acres–1861-24.50 x 61.24 [Also] purchased 100 acres–1862-20 x 50 / Farland 100 acres–1862-20 x 50."

168 Brown noted his first meeting with "old Quassoon—the famous hunter" in his journal on 23 June 1863. At that time he engaged him as a guide for the exploration of Sproat Lake and Central Lake. In his introduction to *Adventures of Jewitt* (1896), Brown described Quassoon as "a shaggy, thick-set, and tremen-dously strong individual" (23). Gilbert Sproat gave his age as forty-five and included him among the "Important men" in his list of the Opetchesahts (*Scenes and Studies of Savage Life* [London: Smith, Elder 1868], 308).

169 Meade described the seam as in "some places 3 feet thick & forty feet long, other places 70 feet long & 1 foot thick" (Journal, 24 Aug. 1864).

170 William Fawcett had reported in the *British Colonist* 30 Apr. 1864, the discov-ery of coal of "very superior quality" at Valdez Inlet (i.e., Comox Harbour).

Fawcett claimed "large practical experience" in coal mining in the United States and maintained that Vancouver Island would as a result of the finding become "one of the richest coal-bearing districts of the world."

171 On the facing page of his journal, Brown has noted of this passage: "Concerning the dignity of putting a Commander's shoulder to the wheel."

172 In *Testimonials*, Brown noted his joint authorship of "On the Natural History of the *Castor Canadensis* Kuhl.," *Journal of the Royal Physical Society* (1868), xii.

173 Several sentences that follow are incoherent and have been omitted here. Robert Brown has noted marginally: "What does Martin who copied this mean? I can't make it out."

3
A GUEST at a POTLATCH

Robert Brown attended a potlatch given by a member of the Opetche-
saht tribe for a group of Sheshahts towards the close of the Vancouver
Island Exploration Expedition in the fall of 1864. The expedition party
was at this point based in Alberni, awaiting further directions from the
organizing committee in Victoria. Brown's journal for the period has
not survived, but the journal of another expedition member notes that
Brown was about to set out for the potlatch on 11 October. He appar-
ently returned on 13 October since on the following day the expedition
party began its return journey to Victoria.

Brown's account in The Races of Mankind *is remarkable, first of*
all, for its sympathetic approach to the ceremony and for its attempt
at understanding. A guest rather than a detached observer, Brown
displays none of the inclination to denounce the potlatch as a heathen
custom that was common among missionaries. Admittedly, he could
not entirely escape the tone of moral superiority that permeates
Victorian prose, but he also checked this drift to moralizing. His
careful consideration contrasts with the dismissive gesture of a con-
temporary clergyman who remarked: "To enumerate the grotesque
antics prevalent on these gala occasions would be a tax on the pa-
tience of the reader."[1]

The detail of Brown's account is another of its distinguishing char-
acteristics. Earlier accounts, such as that in The Adventures and
Sufferings of John R. Jewitt, Captive among the Nootkas 1803–1805
(1815), are usually brief; indeed, it is not always clear from them that

a potlatch is being described.[2] *In contrast, Brown draws on his own
recollections and on the notebook of a companion who was familiar
with the Indian language of the region. The result is a description
that was to remain without parallel until the accounts of Franz Boas
over thirty years later.*

IF I WERE ASKED what constitutes the most peculiar feature in the
economy of these North-western Indian tribes, I should certainly
reply, these great gift-feasts; or, as they are known to the white
traders, their *potlatches* (or "givings away"), a term derived from the
Chinook jargon word *potlatch*, "to give." Gambling is an every-day
amusement, while horse-racing can only be indulged in by some of
the interior tribes; but a *potlatch*, combining glory, amusement, and
the gratification of vanity, can be given whenever the donor has
property enough.

These coast Indians are very avaricious in the acquisition of property, blankets being the standard of riches amongst them, as horses
are among the interior tribes. Though muskets, canoes, &c., are all
carefully collected, yet most of these articles owe their acquisition to
blankets, and an Indian, in describing the wealth of another, will
indicate this by telling how many *pessisse* (or blankets) he has. This
hoarding up of blankets is the engrossing passion of these people in
time of peace, and the exciting cause of their wars is often the desire
of obtaining prisoners as slaves, by the sale of whom, or by whose
labour, they may add to their hoard. I have often commiserated a
poor-looking man lounging about, his only covering a threadbare,
tattered blanket, and on inquiry would be surprised to learn that he
was one of the wealthiest men in the tribe, and had several hundred
new blankets stored up in air-tight boxes, of native manufacture, in
his lodge. I was once sneered at as "no great chief" because, forsooth,
I had only one pair of "Mackinaw" blankets in my canoe, when halt-
ing at a village of Indians who had little intercourse with the whites,
and were accordingly in a primitive condition. To obtain these
blankets, there is no act of self-denial at which the coast fisherman
will hesitate; I might almost say no crime which will deter him, if he
sees blankets likely to be the result of it. The end of all this scraping
and hoarding is to give away the property again at some *potlatch*, at
which in a few hours the labour of years will be dissipated. These
feasts are often given by the chief men of small tribes as a sort of

peace-offering to more powerful ones; but most frequently they are looked upon in the light of gratifying the vanity of the giver and of adding to his personal consequence. His praise sounds far and near. He accordingly assumes a sort of parvenu rank in the tribe, very different, however, from the hereditary aristocracy already referred to. The chiefs are under the necessity of frequently giving these *potlatches* in order to preserve their popularity, just as the old knights used to scatter largess to their followers; and accordingly we generally find these dignitaries about the poorest men in the tribe.

It is, as I have said, at these gatherings that Indian character is seen in its most attractive, if not most characteristic aspect. I, therefore, think it might be amusing and instructive to describe at some length one of the principal at which I was fortunate enough to be present, more especially as it will give me an opportunity of alluding to some Indian customs as yet untouched on. The occasion of the entertainment was the hospitality of a rich Opichesaht named Kayquash,[3] who having a large store of blankets and other things, invited some eight or ten of the leading Seshahts[4] to come and receive presents from him. The Indians always make the most of these occasions, each one invited bringing his canoe full of friends. Thus nearly the whole tribe is present, including the women, who are escorted by one or two men, in one large canoe by themselves. The Opichesahts live in a little village romantically situated on the beautiful Somass or Klistachnit River, arising in Sproat's Lake and flowing into the sea at the head of the Alberni Canal. Accordingly, a companion[5] and I gladly accepted the invitation of one of the Seshahts to accompany him to this great feast in his canoe.

It was on a bright October morning that we left the Seshaht village on the seashore and entered the mouth of the river. The banks were densely wooded down to the water's edge by a tangled maze of forests of the beautiful dog-wood (*Cornus Nuttallii*), and the broad-leaved maple (*Acer macrophyllum*), now in its autumnal yellow leaf, reflected in the waters of the little river, added variety to the otherwise sombre scenery of the forest-clad hills, over which the grey morning mist was just hovering. Every now and then, as we turned the bend of the river, we would come in sight of some little prairie, with a solitary Indian lodge, the site having been selected as a good hunting or fishing station. There was, however, little hunting on that morning, for all were astir for the Opichesaht feast, and the inmates now joined our little fleet of canoes on the river. We reached the Seshaht fishing-

28 Frederick Whymper, *Alberni* (Yale Collection of Western
Americana, Beinecke Rare Book and Manuscript Library)

29 *"Quatjenam & wife Opischesaht
tribe, Alberni,"* photograph by
Gentile, c.1864 (Yale Collection of
Western Americana 525, Beinecke
Rare Book and Manuscript Library).
In *Races of Mankind*, Brown described Quatjenam as the "second
chief." Sproat described him as the
"most influential chief" in *Scenes
and Studies of Savage Life*. As in
Whymper's drawing of the Pachee-
naht Indians (18), this photograph
shows a medley of dress: the bare
feet, the Hudson's Bay Company
blanket, and the well-worn coat and
trousers suggest again the transition
in Indian society. The deliberately
savage appearance which Whymper
worked up for publication (17) is in
striking contrast.

village at the rapids of the river about nine in the morning, and the
chief ran down to meet us, and carried me to the shore on his back.

The same kind office was done for my companion by Tueckbacht, another Seshaht, who had accompanied us in the canoe, and by whom we were to be introduced to the day's entertainment. The office of carrying us ashore was merely a point of politeness, as we could easily have stepped from the canoe to the bank, but it is, no doubt, a remnant of some stately bit of Asiatic courtesy. We found the Seshahts busy in making preparations. Some were polishing up their wooden masks, some painting their faces, others arranging the fashion of dress, or that near approach to nudity which they seemed to think individually most becoming. We left them thus engaged in order to precede them to the Opichesaht village, where we might observe the whole ceremony of their first approach.

When we got to Opichesaht we saluted the chief and others, and were very kindly received. Circumstances threw us rather more into the company of the second chief[6] than the first, as the Seshaht Tueckbacht had married into the second's family; and I fancied we could see a *little* coldness on the part of one or two on account of this, but it speedily wore off as the day advanced. We occupied ourselves for some time conversing with one and another and viewing the house where the entertainment was to be held. It belonged to Kayquash, and was swept out and supplied with two tiers of seats or boxes. One end of the house was intended for the Opichesahts and their performance, the other for the Seshahts.

There now began to be some movement in the camp, and whispers were heard that the Seshaht canoes were coming up the river. The ceremony of arrival consisted of a sham attack upon the Opichesaht village by the Seshaht visitors.[7] A free discharge of muskets was heard in the distance, and they were soon replied to by our party, to show that they were ready for the friendly fray. The plan of assault which gradually unfolded itself was that, while the canoes came up the river, others lying in ambush on the opposite bank should, at a given signal, ford the river and join the attacking party. As the canoes came rapidly up, the Opichesaht scouts, consisting chiefly of young boys, withdrew to the village, the chief's son in a small canoe being the last to go. All the attacking canoes were now in sight, and the last to round the point at some distance from the rest was the canoe of women. This canoe was to be considered as showing by its womanly freight that the whole proceeding was to be taken as a friendly jest and not in earnest. The women were standing and dancing in the canoe, keeping time to a song of a sweet high-pitched tone, which they did not cease for a moment. Their heads were plentifully covered with white, downy feathers. I could find out nothing more about this custom, so universal among all Indians, than that it indicates lightness of heart, joy, and feasting.[8] The canoes now ranged themselves in a line right in front of the village, and were soon joined by the men in ambush, among whom was the Seshaht chief himself. Now there began to be an appearance of increasing hostile feeling; the men in the canoes flourished their sticks and brandished knives, and exhibited great horse-pistols, while a fire-eater, with face entirely blackened, exhorted them to the attack. They answered his shriek with a deep single note, like the roar of a hundred wild beasts in unison, and which, once heard, one could never forget. I remember the same note from a much larger body of men at the Tsongeisth entertainment at Victoria to the S'calams and other tribes. This peculiar note, which was repeated more than once afterwards, always meant a readiness and impatience to do what was proposed. On one occasion in the house when food was proposed the people gave their eager assent in the same manner. All this time the women's canoe kept at a little distance, and like the chorus in a Greek play, with its sweet song and holiday appearance, gave a peaceful interpretation to the savage scene. The name of this song and dance, whether carried on in the canoe or on shore, is *chees cheesa*.

While this went on among the Seshahts, the Opichesaht women and the host were dancing and singing a welcome on the roof of the house nearest the water,[9] and those who remained below were supposed to exhibit the appearance of persons alarmed by the attack and afraid to resist it. In a moment, on a given sign, the Seshaht canoes were thrust upon the land, and a number of men with a leader leapt out and marched upon the village. At least half, however, remained behind, as if afraid, and the men who had run to the attack returned and seemed to upbraid them with their cowardice. Upon this nearly all climbed the bank, and after some apparent difficulty, entered the house, and at this point the pretended hostility was exchanged for a better understanding. A little acting now went on among the people on the roof of the house. A man in an immense wooden mask made his appearance, bending so low that hardly anything but his head was seen. The mask had a long open nose like a trunk, and the performer, who feigned drunkenness, often bent his head down, which caused a bottle to run down his nose, and then turning his head back like a fowl drinking, he would draw the bottle back again. After this an Indian came upon the roof, made a speech, and threw a blanket down to the ground, which was quickly taken up by one of the Seshahts, who came up from one of the canoes near which they were all assembled. The canoes, although aground, were not completely drawn up, and until that occurred the reconciliation of the supposed combatants was not considered to be consummated. Two Seshahts now came forward, dancing lightly with blankets in their hands. They said a few words with great force, the burden of their speech being to name the persons for whom the blankets were intended, and to say, in reference to the blankets which they threw down, "We don't know where they came from—take them." Two Opichesahts (not necessarily those to whom they were given) came forward to receive them, and immediately delivered them to the persons for whom they were intended. The same thing was done by the same dancers some eight or ten times, always accompanying the gifts with some short remark, such as, "Don't have a bad heart," "We give you many blankets," "We mean to give plenty," "We have a good heart," "We give plenty," "King George men (Englishmen) do not give." The real giver of all these was the Seshaht chief. After this the Seshaht women stood up upon the shore, and in order came forward and invited the Opichesahts to come down to see the *chees cheesa*. The dance was then carried on in exactly the same manner as it was before, the women being ranged in a half-circle. I should say in performing it the women do not leap up, but rise on their toes and fall again, hardly moving, and on some occasions not at all, but remaining on one spot all the time. Their elbows are kept down to the sides, the fore-arm extended upwards, and the hand and fingers held flat with the palm up.[10] After this had lasted some time, and the Indians of the two tribes had mingled freely in various groups, the last act and complete consummation of good fellowship was completed by an old Opichesaht coming forward on the house-roof, and shouting welcome to the Seshahts who were below. At this moment the Opichesahts ran down and performed the friendly act (always done to welcome guests) of assisting to haul up the canoes upon the beach.

At this moment of greatest friendship, we had an opportunity of contrasting the pretended animosity of the earlier part of the day with an exhibition of real anger, which at one time assumed a very serious aspect. One of the Opichesahts, in the friendly exercise of his strength while hauling at a canoe, unwittingly pulled off the projecting nose or bow, which in the canoes of this part of the coast forms a piece by itself. In a moment a shout was raised, and he was grappled by the owner. At first there were a good many who tried to separate the combatants; but as the excitement increased men ranged themselves on the sides of their friends, and every moment the storm of lowering brows and crowd of fighting-men increased. I saw the massive face of old Keekean, one of the Seshaht chiefs, as he began to press into the crowd. We touched him and told him it was foolish work, and asked him not to join in. In a moment his features relaxed into a good-natured laugh. With another, an Opichesaht, of a generally good character, but known for his fierceness, we were not so successful. He was very stern and angry, and we could not get him to smile, and we noticed that he carried a small knife concealed in his hand. To the general absence of knives was probably owing the fact that the quarrel had no serious termination.

After a considerable time had been spent on it, and some of the more respectable and peaceable Seshahts had been driven away by the prospects of a general fight, a partial pacification was made between the angry men, and though the quarrel was now and again stirred up with the strife of tongues, chiefly carried on by women, a hearing was at last gained for a Seshaht orator, who spoke with great force and at considerable length. Peace was restored by an exchange of presents— on the Seshaht side, five blankets given by the chief, on that of the Opichesahts, a new canoe by the man who had been the cause of the injury. The vulgar expedient of deciding the amount of the actual damage would never enter into the heads of these people; it was not the injury done to the canoe, but the pride of the man who owned it which had to be paid for.

I may mention here that those who would properly appreciate the Indian character must make proper allowance for their degradation, but be sufficiently on guard against their hostility; it is a great lesson to see them not only in their moments of friendship, or quiet guile, but also when transported by rage. Reason appears for the time to be quite obliterated, and there seems to be no restriction nor check but superior force to prevent their uncontrolled passions proceeding to the greatest extremity.

With this exception, the whole proceedings, both before and afterwards, were carried on with the greatest good humour. Quarrelling among Indians is serious, and perhaps for that very reason rare. To this I may add, that neither by night nor by day was there the slightest approach to indecency. Of course, the nudity not unfrequently exhibited is not in accordance with our notions of delicacy, and, in fact, leads to a coarseness of mind and degraded condition; at the same time it is accompanied by the most entire absence of self-consciousness.

Up to this time about eighteen good and perfectly new blankets had been given away by the chief of the Seshahts, but only two or three by the chief of the Opichesahts. These, however, were only the preliminaries. The people of both tribes now repaired to the house of the host. The Seshahts ranging themselves round one end and the Opichesahts the other. All were seated on the boxes placed around the room, the rest of the space being left for the dancers.

THE "PACHEETL"[11]

This, which constituted the longest part of the entertainment, consisted of a mutual giving away, accompanied by dancing and short speeches. In some parts, as will afterwards be noticed, it differed markedly from the other sort of giving, which goes by the name of *noosheetl*.[12] The Seshahts commenced the *pacheetl*. One tall Indian, with a good voice and ear and ready hand, was the conductor of his tribe. He gave the time and exerted himself to keep things going in a proper manner. A good many of the Seshahts gave presents of blankets and smaller things to their friends of the other tribe. First came the giver's dance, in which he did not usually figure alone, but generally in company with one or two more. The whole tribe were seated round, beating time with sticks with all their force, and with a song by one and afterwards taken up by all. When the dance was over, one or more men (but never the giver himself) came forward with the presents; one always made a short speech, named the person for whom each gift was intended, and generally said something in praise of the giver. There were always persons ready to run forward with great appearance of alacrity to receive the gift, and the answer, "Klak-koh howilth!" was shouted back. *Howilth* is the word for "chief," and *klak-koh*, though I do not know how it should be translated, is evidently intended as a gracious acknowledgment.[13]

Many persons made gifts, and consequently there were many songs and many dances, which lasted a long time. Some of the dancers were light and graceful in their movements. In some instances performers wore wooden masks, made effective in appearance by black paint. The most striking of these representations were of deer or other pointed-nosed animals, which were not worn over the whole face, but set upon the forehead like a horn. The unicorn sort of appearance which this gave the face was very striking, and was much added to by the style of dance in which they were used. In these dances the performers by turns seemed to be pursuer and pursued, and while they sped quickly round in one direction, turned the head sharply, and with a searching gaze in each other's faces fled in another direction. In these dances, in which speed, watchfulness, and pursuit seemed to be objects aimed at, the performers generally had a bunch of eagles' feathers in their hands, which they shook out, and threw out before themselves with a quick vibratory motion. The feathers probably either represented wings supposed to belong to the dancers, or were merely intended as emblems of rapid flight. Two young boys were among those who made presents, and therefore had to dance. One was a bold, stout youth who, if he felt any natural diffidence, hid all his blushes under a mass of red paint, which made his countenance glow like a furnace. He wore one of the horn-like masks on his forehead, and did his part very well, having the conductor himself for his company in the dance. The other boy was younger and more timid, and seemed to feel his conspicuous position, as he stood up alone to dance with all eyes on him, and all hands and voices ready to give the tune to his steps. He danced without any freedom of action, but with great care, and seemed very glad when it was over.

The largest number of presents made at this time was by a young girl who had reached the stage of womanhood.[14] She danced the *chees cheesa* in company with the other Seshaht women, her great modesty keeping her behind all the rest, so that one could hardly get a sight of her features. Her gifts consisted of eight blankets, nine bunches of brass wire bracelets, with from three to six bracelets in a bunch, five long strings of beads, one bunch of brazen ear-ornaments, and one coat. In the next dance a small child (the grandson of Wickaninish,[15] a chief only a few months dead, and who had been second to the present chief of the tribe) was carried about in the arms of one of the performers. The child's gift seemed at first a curious one. One of the Seshahts came forward, making a speech, and finally presented a piece of bark, which was taken by an Opichesaht with as much alacrity as any of the other things. This piece of bark represented a canoe, which could not have been brought conveniently into the building. It was, in fact, a sort of promissory note payable "on demand." Scarcely anything was given away but what was really good and worth receiving. The two or three exceptions to this rule consisted of an old blanket and one or two very small strings of ornaments, which fell to the lot of a little boy, a slave of one of the Opichesahts. This child, though despised, and I dare say a good deal kicked about by the other children, was not really badly off, nor was he in danger of being overworked, for to set him full tasks would be a mental exertion far too great for his masters. While these small gifts were being given and received, a sort of murmur of appreciation was heard among the Seshahts, especially from the women; but the Opichesahts seemed rather to dislike it, as lowering to the dignity of the free-born recipients of presents. To me it was the most humanising feature of the day. Two of the Seshahts' gifts towards the end of their part of the entertainment were made with great mystery. Once and again men came forward with their present concealed in a blanket, those who received it having also a blanket in their hands, so that the presents passed from one to another without any one seeing them. These gifts were really two masks, which were not exposed to public view, that they might appear with more effect when the Opichesahts began their part of the *pacheetl*. From the time that they entered the house up to this point, the Seshahts had given away about fifty blankets, besides a canoe, and a good many other presents of various sorts, such as camp-kettles, bracelets, muskets, &c.

At a lull in the entertainment a noted hunter came round and presented each of the women with a cake of elks' tallow to dress her hair with, and afterwards distributed pieces of dried venison; after which, teased-out bark of the cedar (*Thuja gigantea*) was handed round in lieu of napkins, for the guests to wipe their hands and mouths on. The heat and noise combined, superadded to the labour I had undergone during the few previous days, had rather inclined me to drowsiness, and I nodded frequently, to the great amusement of the wide-awake women and youngsters, who seemed to watch for this kind of weariness with keen attention; and immediately on noticing it, those nearest would nod in a comical manner, and shout good-naturedly that "Yakapis" (or the bearded one) was falling asleep. A good many of the guests were in much the same condition, and by general consent the assembly was adjourned, and though desultory eating had been going on at intervals, the company now separated to sup with their different friends. We had been somewhat afraid of the items of Indian hospitality, and had rather hastily declined a meal, which we were sorry for when we saw the great pot of well-cooked venison from which each supplied himself.

Later in the evening, Quatjenam, the second chief, who had, in company with his wife, been my companion in many explorations on Sproat's Lake, invited us to pass the evening in his lodge. A clean mat of cedar-bark and rushes, rolled up at one end into a pillow, was spread on one of the raised benches on either side of the fire; new blankets were produced from a box, where they had lain since they were bought from the Alberni trader, to wait a *potlatch*, and a most comfortable bed to weary men was made up. Quatjenam and his wife reposed on the corresponding bench on the other side of the fire, his family lay somewhere at our feet, and throughout the capacious lodge there must have been twenty or thirty people sleeping. The smell of bark-smoke and of dripping salmon stored for winter feasts overhead was something overpowering; but we were weary, and slept soundly until we were awoke at daylight by the squaws lighting the fires, and the little children peering round at us and shouting, "Mammathle! Mammathle!" ("white men! white men!"—literally, "men who have come over the sea in houses.")[16]

As we went out in the chill morning down to the river to make our ablutions, we found the patriarchs of the village already up, sitting, Indian fashion, in a row against the lodges, with their noses in their blankets as a protection from the chill morning air, and talking in their low, quiet way about last night's adventures and the remaining part of the programme. They saluted us cheerfully, but seemed to be rather astonished at our washing in the river, the fog from which concealed the sun from view, or rather at washing at all. The "dew and mist of morning" in these regions is indescribably strange, and with the solemn scenery and such curious surroundings the whole of the incidents are impressed on the memory in a manner not easily to be effaced. As we sat talking with the elders of the people, a sturdy hunter, my companion in many a forest journey, and who afterwards crossed the colony with me, invited us to his lodge to have breakfast. If hunger had left any squeamishness in us, assuredly the sight of Quassoon's breakfast equipage quite dissipated it. It was not extensive, and certainly was not grand, and in its excessive newness bore marks of having been only recently procured, possibly in honour of his expected guests; but it had that crowning virtue—not always found in things aboriginal—cleanliness. On a clean cedar-plaited mat, placed over a box, were three cups and a pot of tea, with a native carved vessel full of splendid potatoes and a fine, whole, fresh-boiled salmon. We were invited to fall to while the host and hostess held bashfully aside, waiting on their guests, somewhat after the graceful but embarrassing custom, now and then, but at one time very commonly seen in Scandinavia. We begged them to share with us; but as it was evident that they were not at home in this method of breakfasting, we allowed them to wait until we had finished, when they attacked the remainder with a hearty good will.

Our morning repast over, we adjourned to the house of entertainment. What followed need not be particularly described here, as there was much the same style of dances, songs, and presents on the part of the Opichesahts as we had witnessed the night before on that of the Seshahts. Some of the dances were, however, rather peculiar; many of them being carried on with such energy that the perspiration poured from the dancers. The weird-like appearance of some of them, heightened by the glare of the torches of resinous pine which flared around the lodge, was remarkable. In some, an accompaniment was kept up with a sort of drum, and the beating with paddles or sticks was continuous. When a more than ordinarily popular dancer or chief got up, he was applauded by the beating of paddles against the lodge-boards. One of their *nooks* (or dances) seemed to be the sorcerers' or *oostilukyn* dance;[17] and certain sleight-of-hand feats were practised on a slave-boy. This boy suddenly ceased dancing and fell down as if dead. The face was pale and bloodless, and the pulse scarcely beat; altogether he presented a most ghastly appearance. Blood flowed from his nostrils and soon covered his face. The dances of the "medicine-men" continued furiously around him; his feet were laid to the fire, the blood washed off, the people beat drums, danced and sang, and suddenly the patient sprang up and joined in the dance. Certainly it was a most consummate piece of acting, and was, no doubt, due to the training and skill of the sorcerer. In the earlier part of the day I had seen him in close conversation with this youth, whose servile condition would render him unlikely to be on intimate terms with men of that rank, except to serve some purpose. All of the Indians seemed implicitly to believe in this display of the medicine-man's power and it was triumphantly pointed out to us as a refutation of all our sneers.

Another dance was the "roof-dance."[18] The greater number of the performers having ascended the flat roof of the lodge, while the dances and songs were going on below, leaped up and down between the roof-boards—pushed aside for that purpose—making a noise like thunder. After the dance was finished, an old Seshaht came forward and remarked that it was a dance peculiar to his tribe, it could not be omitted, but that it was very injurious to the roof, and feared their friend's house, which was of great antiquity, had suffered considerably from their performance. In order to make recompense, he would present a board to him, at the same time throwing down a piece of stick as a promissory note. Several others followed his example, and the old man gravely bowed his acknowledgments.

The last dance which I shall notice was characterised by having a greater number of dancers, and a movement of the song which, though cheerful, was not so quick or loud as those which had preceded it. The dancers moved softly but actively about, and seemed to address each other in praises of the building; they looked cheerful, and then turned their heads quickly, as if speaking first to one and then to another, and sang, "It is a very great house, a very great house—a *very* great house!" Upon a movement of the conductor, who with voice and arm never failed to direct all the performances of the company, they changed their words (while they kept the same tune, certainly the most pleasant one of the entertainment) to, "It is a very warm fire, a very warm fire, a *very* warm fire!" and finally ended by praising the household furniture—such as it was—"These are very nice things, very nice things, *very* nice things!" On the whole this dance-song was the most pleasing of those we witnessed; there was something dramatic in the way in which those rudely-painted and half-naked savages attempted to represent in dance and song the idea of an animated conversation.

THE "NOOSHEETL"

Hitherto the two tribes had taken an equal part in the proceedings, and given and received about an equal number of presents. The same morning the *noosheetl* commenced. This differs from the *pacheetl* in not being made with any expectation of a return, but really of the nature of a gift. In this instance the presents were all made by one man, Kayquestl. The blankets and other things were given according to the rank of the receivers; some getting four blankets, others three, and so on. Besides gifts, payments were made to such of the common people as had come to swell the train of their chief. The liveliness which characterised the *pacheetl* was entirely wanting in the *noosheetl*. The people did not come forward to receive their presents, but sat sullenly until they were brought. There were no more songs and dances; the cheery *klak-koh* was seldom or ever heard, and the whole affair seemed to imply feelings rather mournful than otherwise.[19]

Just as the entertainment was drawing to a close, a loud buzz went through the house, and all eyes were directed to Mr. Knipe and myself. At the same time a young chief danced into the middle of the room, and after loud praises chanted by the women and the children, and echoed by the men, a bear-skin was presented to each of us. Then, amid the applause of the assembled guests, we dismounted from the dais and made a few remarks, short enough it is true, but as appropriate as our very limited knowledge of the language would admit. An Indian only makes a present with a view to another in return, and if ever, as in this case, they trust a white man so far as to part with one, without the immediate prospect of a substantial return, it must be looked upon as a peculiar mark of confidence. Our Mentor, however, warned us that if on this occasion we showed any desire to make any return it would be looked upon in the light of an affront, but he naively added, if ever we gave a *potlatch*, Kayquestl would expect to be invited. As we never did give a *potlatch*, I may remark that we took an opportunity of rewarding the donor before many days passed without in any way offending his dignity. On afterwards showing the skins to the Alberni trader, he assured us that they were two of the finest he had ever seen. Admire the good sense displayed in this arrangement. They did not give us blankets, or muskets, or canoe, knowing that these would not be appreciated; but though such things as furs were not a part of the articles distributed, yet as they knew we should value them most, this delicate compliment was hit on.

Owing to the absence of any festive accompaniments, the *noo-sheetl* did not last so long as the previous part of the entertainment, and presented no marked features. The host himself gave away about fifty blankets (of about £25 value), one shaft of a salmon-spear, a large quantity of clothing, four looking-glasses, a great many iron basins, bracelets, plates, and strings of beads.

This feast presented many interesting features of such entertainments, and being between two tribes as yet little (if at all) altered by the customs of civilisation, may be taken as the type of all. Still, however, the property distributed, owing to the small number and poverty of the people, was not so great as in some others I have been a witness of. There is a chief near Clayoquot Sound, well known to the traders as "Trader George of Clayoquot," but who is called by the

Indians by a name signifying "the man who takes everything and gives nothing." When I last heard of him he was said to have between 700 and 800 blankets, beside a vast accumulation of other property. Yet this abominably cruel wretch has been known to cut off young slave children's heads just to show how careless *he* was of valuable property![20] On these festive occasions I have known them to smash canoes, break muskets to pieces, and burn large numbers of blankets, their object being to show how little they cared for wealth. At a great feast of this nature given by the Thongeisth tribe at Victoria, in 1863, a slave was presented. On this occasion the blankets were pitched by a pole from an elevated platform. But the customs of the east coast tribes differ considerably from those of the western shores of Vancouver Island, and likewise on this occasion a desire to make as great a show as possible before the crowd of whites was evident. At these feasts, as all the world over, the greatest man gets the most, while the poor people come off with a very small share, and sometimes this is only a strip of blanket. Hence Indians may be seen with a blanket composed of these shreds sewn together like the capelets of a cabman's coat.

Soon after the festival the party broke up, and left without any general formal leave-taking, and as if they were glad to be off, showing a great contrast to the exciting scenes which had attended their arrival. We soon followed suit, and swiftly glided down the rapid river, arriving at our camp with really pleasant memories of the Opichesaht *potlatch*.

Among some of the comparatively rich northern tribes these *potlatches* are on a much greater scale, as many as 800 blankets, hundreds of yards of cotton, and at one, which I know of, several furs, including two sea-otter skins, worth from £15 to £20 each, were given away. Individuals will often travel great distances to be present at one of these feasts; but people of the same *totem* (or crest) are not invited to each other's feasts. They are, however, much more particular than the southern tribes as to whom they invite to their feasts; and at some great ceremonials men and women are served separately, the women (curiously enough) taking precedence. All, however, are just the same—only an interchange of presents; for an Indian, if he is overlooked at one of these, or is presented with something inferior to what he gave, will not be backward in informing his host of the fact, and demanding something better. Among the northern tribes *rum* feasts are now beginning to be given, and most demoniacal orgies they are.

There are other feasts—at the end of the salmon season, &c., or when a new house is built—in fact, a sort of "house-warming." Any Indian who values his reputation always invites his friends to partake of a seal or a deer which he has killed, or to share any other food at all above the common which he may have come into possession of. The guests go early, and sit chatting while the food is being prepared—of course, before their eyes, since there is only one compartment in the house, or the young people amuse themselves in various ways. They eat in silence; going away one by one, each taking what has not been eaten of his allowance in a corner of his blanket—a habit which we shall see, by-and-by, is common to the Japanese, and some other more or less civilised nations. After a whale is killed, about a hundred-weight of the best parts is cut off and presented to the chief, and the harpooner, fish-priest, and other dignitaries each receives his share, the rest being distributed among the people according to their rank. Those who have received the larger portions are, however, expected to give feasts all around. Messengers, with red and blue blankets tastefully put on, go to each house, and in a loud and official tone of voice invite the different guests; but the women are not invited to feasts of this nature, only to the *wawkoahs*, or *potlatches*, already described.

From *The Races of Mankind* (London: Cassell, Petter, and Galpin [1873]), 1, 75-90

NOTES

1 Matthew Macfie, *Vancouver Island and British Columbia: Their History, Resources, and Prospects* (London: Longman 1865), 431.

2 *The Adventures and Sufferings of John R. Jewitt, Captive Among the Nootka 1803-1805* (Toronto: McClelland & Stewart 1974), 36-9. Derek G. Smith, the editor, remarks that Jewitt may describe here "a potlatch or something closely related to it" (39n).

3 The Opetchesahts may originally have been a Salishan group who settled at Sproat Lake and Great Central Lake, and moved down the lower Somass River in the 1860s (Alan D. McMillan and E. St. Claire, *Alberni Prehistory* [Alberni: Theytus Books, Alberni Valley Museum 1982], 12-13). Elsewhere, Brown described the Opetchesahts as "an offshoot of the Sehsahts" and noted that they had been reduced to seventeen men following an attack by the Qualicums (Introduction, *The Adventures of John Jewitt* [London: Clement Wilson, 1896], 23). He

further remarked that three Opetchesahts were entitled by descent to the rank of chief: "Quatgenam, Kalooish or Kanash [subsequently referred to here as Kay-questl and Kayquash], and Quassoon." Gilbert Malcolm Sproat estimated the total Opetchesaht population to be forty four (*Scenes and Studies of Savage Life* [London: Smith, Elder & Co. 1868], 308–9). His list included: "Kal-lowe-ish . . . 45 [years] Hereditary chief" and "Klay-klay-has . . . 25 [years. Listed among] Inferior men" (309).

4 The Sheshahts had apparently established settlements on the lower Somass River in fairly recent times—according to Brown "not . . . until the whites came to Alberni in August 1860" (Introduction, *Adventures of Jewitt*, 23n). They had formerly lived solely in Barkley Sound (*Alberni Prehistory*, 14). Brown estimated the "fighting men" at "not over fifty men" (*Adventures of Jewitt*, 23), whereas Sproat fixed the male population at seventy (*Scenes and Studies*, 308). Richard Charles Mayne set the total population at one hundred and fifty (*Four Years in British Columbia and Vancouver Island* [London: J. Murray 1862], 25).

5 The Reverend C. Knipe, a missionary for the Society for the Propagation of Christian Knowledge, had volunteered his services to the Columbia Mission in 1860 (*Report of Columbia Mission*, [1860], 103). In the 1861 Report, he is listed as a missionary in the "Gold Fields, Cariboo," and in the reports for 1862 and 1863 as at Alberni. He is not listed in subsequent reports. In 1868, he anonymously published *Some Account of the Tahkaht Language, as Spoken by Several Tribes on the Western Coast of Vancouver Island* (London: Hatchard 1868), a work that is valuable both for its ethnographic introduction and its vocabulary.

6 Subsequently identified as Quatjenam. Brown had travelled with him in 1863 when exploring Sproat Lake (*Adventures of Jewitt*, 23). Sproat noted; "Quichee-nam . . . 55 [years] Most influential chief" (*Scenes and Studies*, 308).

7 In *Adventures of Jewitt*, the firing of recently acquired arms by the host group is described as a welcoming salute "in the European manner" ([1974], 37). Closer to Brown's account is that of Boas, who described the visitors to a Kwakiutl potlatch as singing war songs as they approached ("Contributions to the Ethnology of the Kwakiutl," *Columbia University Contributions to Anthropology* 3 [1925]: 159). Drucker also noted that "the approach of the guests was heralded by singing and in historic times by gunshots" (*The Northern and Central Nootkan Tribes* [Washington: U.S. Bureau of American Ethnology 1951], 378).

8 Recent commentators have also found the import of down difficult to describe. Derek G. Smith has suggested that it connotes "peace, harmony, gentleness, and 'sacredness'" (*Adventures of Jewitt* [1974], 38n).

9 Jewitt similarly described Maquinna as ascending the roof of his house and "drumming or beating upon the boards with a stick most violently" (*Adventures of Jewitt* [1974], 37).

10 The description is strikingly close to that of George Clutesi: "Their arms outstretched at an easy angle and their hands held with palms turned upward to denote friendship, good will and acceptance to all guests" (*Potlatch* [Sidney, B.C.: Gray's 1969], 26).

11 "*Pacheetl*. To give" (Knipe, *Account*, 49).

12 "*Noosh-itl*. A great giving away, an entertainment for making presents" (Knipe, *Account*, 47).

13 "*Howilth* is the word for 'chief,' and *Klak-koh* is evidently intended as a gracious acknowledgment" (Knipe, *Account*, 82). Drucker represents the phrase as "La-'kao, La'kao, ha'wil" and glosses it "Thank you, thank you, chief" (*Northern and Central Nootkan Tribes*, 379).

14 Brown seems to recognize here and in the preceding reference to two young boys a link between the west coast potlatch and puberty rites that later commentators

have stressed. See, for example, Edward Sapir, "A Girl's Puberty Ceremony among the Nootka Indians," *Proceedings and Transactions of the Royal Society of Canada* 7 (1913):80. Diamond Jenness also remarked that "the Nootka reserved their most elaborate potlatches, not for marriages or accessions to chieftainship, but for the coming of age of their daughters" (*Indians of Canada* [1932; Toronto: University of Toronto Press 1977], 346).

15 The most celebrated bearer of the name Wickaninish was chief at Clayoquot Sound when the *Tonquin* was destroyed in 1811. Brown's reference here is to "a Sheshaht chief who died at middle age in 1864" (Knipe, *Account*, 4).

16 "*Mahmathleh*. A term applied to any persons not Indians, and meaning 'house-like,' from the ships in which foreigners first visited the natives. Some years ago the word *Mamatle* (no doubt the same) was used in the Chinook jargon to signify a ship" (Knipe, *Account*, 18, 44).

17 In his subsequent description of this dance, Brown appears to be indebted to Sproat's account of "the doctors' (Ooshtukyu) nook" (*Scenes and Studies*, 68). Knipe glosses *nook* as "a song" (*Account*, 47).

18 In this and the following paragraph, Brown follows Sproat closely (*Scenes and Studies*, 70-1). Sproat, however, did not claim to be describing a potlatch.

19 In *Adventures of Jewitt*, there is also mention of the "very stern and surly look" with which gifts were received ([1974], 39).

20 On the testimony of a "trustworthy eye-witness," Sproat wrote of the "bloody act of George . . . the rich merchant of Klah-oh-quaht" who beheaded a young captive girl brought back by a warring party (*Scenes and Studies*, 154).

4

A COLLECTION of INDIAN MYTHS and LEGENDS

In his own time, Robert Brown's knowledge of Indian myth and legend was well recognized. Eleanor C. Smyth acknowledged her indebtedness in An Octogenarian's Reminiscences *(1916) when she presented "A Group of Indian Legends" (Chapter XII).[1] More significantly, Gilbert Sproat described him in* Scenes and Studies of Savage Life *(1868) as an "active and observant traveller . . . with extensive information on this subject."[2] Unfortunately, Brown's only publication concerned with Indian mythology was incorporated in a popular educational enterprise entitled* The Races of Mankind *(1873-6), which seems now to have been entirely forgotten. This is the more unfortunate since Brown was among the earliest collectors on the northwest coast.*

Brown's most rewarding period as a collector of myth and legend was probably during the four months of the Vancouver Island Exploration Expedition in 1864, and he was later to acknowledge his indebtedness to two Indians associated with the expedition. First, there was Kakalatza, a joint chief of the Somenos who accompanied the exploratory party from Cowichan Harbour to Cowichan Lake. "Every dark pool suggested a story to him," Brown remarked, "every living thing had a superstition, and hour after hour we lay awake listening to the strange story of Kakalatza, Lord of Tsamena."[3] Second, there was Tomo, who joined the expedition at Cowichan Harbour and re-

mained with it until the conclusion. Tomo had lived for some years in the Cowichan area, and this is reflected in the myths Brown records, but Ranald Macdonald had earlier known Tomo at Fort Langley on the Fraser River, and two of the myths recorded by Brown are explicitly related to this region. In his journal, Brown several times refers to his interest in Tomo's narratives. "Miserable wet stormy day," he notes on 8 September. "Spent it as I spend most stormy days, in drawing from Tomo's extensive store of Indian lore and tradition and committing them to paper." And a few days later (13 September): "Sat round the fire till late, [Tomo] telling me stories of Indian life & warfare."

Brown's renderings of Indian myth and legend are scarcely "the unedited and unwritten tales" from his notebook that he claims them to be. The heavy hand of Victorian moralizing is laid on them at numerous points, and he also appears to be indebted to Sproat's Scenes and Studies of Savage Life (*1868*). *All the same, Brown clearly responded to the power of the legends, as evidenced, for example, by his fascination with accounts of youths "seeking their medicine." Within a few days of setting out on the 1864 exploration, Brown remarked on "the curious store of lore and traditions . . . [the Indians] possess" (10 June). "Few ever take the trouble to learn about them," he continued. As his collection of myths and legends indicate, this could not be said of Brown himself.*

"Tell me the songs of a nation, and I will tell you their history," is an old truism. It is equally true regarding a savage race, that their traditions are their songs, their history, their metaphysics. Without a written history, historical events soon get into the region of myths, and therefore we find few events which can be distinctly classed as history. Many of their traditions are myths of observation—such as the natural features which may have struck a people as peculiar, and accordingly they have set their imagination to work to devise an explanation. Another set of traditions have a deeper origin, and may be classed as world-wide, and as pointing to the Asiatic origin of the Indians. All of them are very imaginative, and may serve to "point a moral" while "adorning a tale" in an Indian wigwam. A few of them are local, but the greater number are found widely scattered, under different versions, among the Indian tribes, but in few cases is the disguise so deep as to conceal the original outline of the tale. These traditions and myths are so numerous that even was my knowledge sufficient, the space at my disposal would only admit of a few of the more characteristic being given in this place. Nowadays, as the young people affect to despise these idle tales, and only a few of the old people know them, they are dropping fast into oblivion, as the more ignorant class of the whites, who have opportunities of collecting them, look upon them as so many foolish Indian stories, without being aware that they form some of the treasures of that unwrought mine of Indian mythology which, followed out in the same spirit of investigation as that adopted by the Brothers Grimm in studying the European folk-lore, is capable of yielding so much to the stores of science. It is not always possible to obtain these tales, for an Indian, even if he is not too lazy or too ignorant to be capable of imparting this information, is so afraid of being laughed at that it is with the utmost difficulty he can be induced to tell the traditions of his people. I have often heard part of a story, and have had to wait weeks before hearing the end of it, if even then so fortunate. To add to our difficulties, few of the Indians have the same version of the same tradition. Our Indian hunter, Tomo, was noted for his skill in this style of narrative, and among the many scattered through my notes, I give the following as specimens of these unedited and unwritten tales:—

THE INDIAN STORY OF "JACK AND THE BEAN STALK[4]

Once on a time long ago (this was in the days no more remembered, when the heavens were nearer earth, and the gods were more familiar—it never happens nowadays), two Tsongeisth girls were gathering gamass,[5] at Stummas (near Elk Lake, Vancouver Island), and after the manner of the gamass-gatherers they camped on the ground during the season. One night they lay awake, looking up at the bright stars overhead, thinking of their lovers, and such things as girls, Indians or English, will talk about. The Indians suppose the stars to be little people, and the region they live in to be much the same as this world down below. As one of the girls looked up at the little people twinkling overhead, one said to the other, looking at Aldebaran, the red eye of the Bull, "That's the little man to my liking; how I would like him for my lover!" "No," said the other, "I don't think I should; he's too glaring and angry-looking for me. I am afraid he would whip me. I would better like that pale, gentle-looking star, not far

*from him." And so the gamass-gatherers of Stummas talked
until they fell asleep. But as they slumbered under the tall
pines, Aldebaran and Sirius took pity on their lovers and
came down to earth, and when the girls awoke in the morning it was in Starland, with their lovers by their sides, in the
country up in the sky. For a while all went well and happily,
until, after the manner of their race, they wearied to see their
friends at Quonsung ("The Gorge," in the Victoria Arm) and
Cheeuth (Esquimault) [Esquimalt], and their gentle husbands
grew sad at their melancholy wives. One day one of the sisters
came upon the other busily engaged in Starland, and she said,
"What are you doing, sister?" "I am twisting a rope," she
said; "a rope of cedar bark, by which to get back again to
Quonsung. Come, sister, our husbands are asleep, help me."
So the sisters fell to work, and while their husbands slept they
wrought, until they had twisted a rope long enough, in their
opinion, to drop themselves down to earth again. This they
concealed in the woods, and then commenced to dig a hole in
the vault of heaven with a pointed stake. For many days they
dug, until they heard a hollow sound, and then they knew that
they were nearly through; and next day they finished their
work (at a fitting time), and saw the clouds beneath, but the
earth was a long way down. All this time their husbands were
out hunting, or asleep in the lodge. They then fastened a stick
transversely over the hole, and to this they attached the rope,
and commenced to slide down. For long they slid, but yet did
not come to the earth, and they began to fear for the results,
for the rope was nearly ended, but Satitz (the east wind) took
pity on them, and blew them to the earth, and they knew not
what had happened, but on recovering their senses they
found themselves near the valley of the Colquitz—not far
from their own home—with the rope lying beside them. So
they coiled it up, and Haelse*[6] *made it into a hill as a monu-
ment, to remind mortals not to weary for what is not their
lot. And after this the girls went back to Quonsong, and
became great medicine-women,[7] but remained single, all for
love of the "little people" above.*

The stars, however, are gentle little folks, and were not at all angry with their wandering brides, and used often to visit them on earth again, when Seam Seakum (my lord the sun) has ended his travels over the great plain of the earth, for See Seam, my informant, told me, "don't you often see at night the stars coming to earth?" and as he referred to the "falling stars," I bethought me that the philosophers of "King George's Land," while giving no more sensible explanation of that phenomenon, had given one which appealed not half so well to the imagination. If I were to draw a moral from this little Indian story, I should say that it teaches us not to wish for things that are out of our reach. There is, however, a far deeper interest attached to it, and for this reason I have styled it the Indian story of "Jack and the Bean Stalk," for I believe it to be the American analogue of that tale (widely altered, no doubt), which I need not tell mythologists is not, as is vulgarly supposed, a mere childish tale, but a strange myth found among nearly all nations, savage and civilised. Among the Indians this story goes up to the Rocky Mountains at least, and, perhaps, further, in one guise or another, but little altered. "Knochan Hill," the scene of the Tsongeisth adventure, which they describe as the ropes coiled up, is an eminence at the head of the "Victoria Arm," and means, in the Tsongeisth language, "coiled up." It is, probably, this peculiarity that has suggested placing there the locale of the final catastrophe of the damsels.

Much of the Indian mythology is occupied with strange stories of what young hunters saw who "went out seeking their medicine." A hunter will wander for a long time, fasting and weary, until he dreams of something which is to be his guardian angel through life. No doubt these men dream strange dreams, and the overstrained nervous system helps to conjure up hobgoblins, suited to the wild scenery round. When the hunter wakes up at night the silent moon looks down upon him, and the stars are watching him with their twinkling eyes. Every wind that sighs through the forest bears the whispers of unseen spirits, and afar off he hears the spirits of the waterfalls. On the mountain-side he is alarmed by the blazing forest, ignited by sparks from his fire, or by two trees rubbing together. Besides, to an Indian, all the world out of sight of his village is an unknown land, full of wonders and wonder-workers, and the Indian traveller is not a little addicted to foster the belief that "cows afar off have long horns." This fasting is called in Chinook "making *tomana-was*,"[8] and the young man ambitious of this distinction must pass night after night away from his father's lodge, in some lonely place, without food, and with strict attention to chastity and personal cleanliness, until he dreams of something which is to become his *tomanawas*. This *tomanawas* is believed to descend from father to son. It is of much the same nature as "seeking his medicine." What follows sounds like a Scandinavian tale, the "Wehre Wolves," or some Arcadian story of the wolf-hunters.

THE WOLF-HUNTER SEEKING HIS MEDICINE[9]

Stuckeia (the wolves) were once a tribe of Indians, who were turned into their present form by Haelse for their evil deeds. One day a hunter of Quantlin [Fort Langley] went into the mountains to seek his medicine. He travelled all that day and all the next day, still he dreamt not of his medicine; but he resolved to find it, be a great hunter, or die. One night he saw the light of a great fire on the side of a mountain, and drew near. Round it were the wolves sitting in a circle, talking of the day's hunt. They had taken off their skins, and were drying them on sticks. Our hunter sprang within the light of the fire, and instantly the wolves jumped into their skins again, and howled round him, but the hunter moved not, and lay down and slept uninjured. That night he dreamt of his medicine, and next day he began to travel with the wolves, now his guardians, and did so for a long time, until his friends grieved for him and thought him dead. But one day a hunter saw him in the mountains travelling along the hill-side with the wolves. Sometimes he travelled on two legs—more often on all-fours. His face was bearded like that of a wolf, and he looked savage and fierce. So the young man went back to his village and told the story. "Ah," said the people, "that is his medicine; but we must bring him back again." So they took strong nets made of elk-sinew, and went out to find him. At last they sighted him, and finally caught him in this net, and brought him to Quantlin; but he could not speak, only howled like a wolf, and had lost all human attributes. He had found his medicine with a vengeance! He was not long in escaping again, and nobody went in search of him. Occasionally still he has been seen in the mountains travelling with the wolves. The last time he was sighted was about Fort Yale. Moral— "Evil communications corrupt good manners."

THE INDIAN CYCLOPS[10]

There was a widow who had three sons. One day the eldest said to her, "Mother, I must go and seek my medicine; make me a cloak of bird-skins." The mother tried to dissuade him, but in vain. So he went away and wandered through the woods until he came to a lonely lake surrounded by swampy marshes. The cry of the crane sounded lonely on this lake, and as he was wondering how he should cross it, the crane came up in her canoe and ferried him over. Now, on the other side of the lake lived a one-eyed giant, Netsachen, or Coquochem, whose servant the crane was. The crane invited him in to see his master, and as he passed the door, which opened with a spring, it shut after him so fast that, though he would willingly have retreated when he saw the giant, he could not. So the giant killed him, and took out his heart, and laid it on a bench beside his body. The widow grieved very much at her son not returning, until the second brother said, "Mother, I will go and seek my brother." So he went and travelled until he reached the same lake, when the crane ferried him over; and when he went in to see the giant he met the same fate; his heart was taken out and laid beside his body. Now the widow was very sorry at their not returning, but still she could not oppose the wish of the last son when he wished to go after his two brothers. The same incident happened to him. He was ferried over the lake, and his heart taken out by the giant and laid beside his body on the bench where already his two brothers were. Long and sadly cried the childless widow at the non-return of her sons, and as she cried her tears fell on the ground. Now an Indian is superstitious about tears or mucus gathering on the ground, so she took a little moss and wiped up the tears.[11] Her eyes were very dim with weeping, so that she could scarcely see, but as she looked down at the moss she was astonished at seeing a little child lying where the moss was. So she took it up and laid it on her couch. Next day he had grown up a big boy, and next day was a full-sized man. "Ah," said the people, "he is a great medicine-man." Still the poor widow cried bitterly for her lost sons, and one day when she was crying much, the "medicine-child" said, "Do not cry, mother! I will bring back your sons."

*"Oh no, you won't," the poor mother sobbed. But as the youth
insisted, she made him a cloak of woodpecker-skins which he
shot for the purpose; and, armed with a sword made of elk-
horn, he started off, and travelled until he came to the lonely
lake where the crane presented itself as ferryman. "Do you
know where my brothers are?" he asked. "Yes, they are over
seeing my master." So he crossed the lake and came to Coquochem's house. The crane, as before—for an Indian story always repeats itself—invited him in to see his master; but the
medicine-youth refused, and said, "No, your master must
come out to see me"; and as the giant came out, being a very
big man, he stooped, and as his neck bent the youth cut off his
head with the elk-horn sword; after which the crane, much
frightened, screamed and fled away. The youth now entered
the house, and found the three brothers lying on a bench with
their hearts beside them. So he took up their hearts and put
them again in the bodies and breathed on them; when they all
lived again, and were very happy, and came home in the
crane's canoe over the lake. Of course, their mother was very
glad to see them, and the medicine-youth was a great man.
The brothers were also very grateful, and paddled him about
in their canoe wherever he cared to go. This went on for a
while, until they began to forget their deliverer, and the youth
grew sad at this neglect. One day he lay in the lodge tired with
hunting, with his blanket covering his head, and the sons
were all sitting waiting for their meal of venison. The mother
called them when it was ready, but she forgot her medicine-
son, as the people called the strangely-come youth. At this he
must have been sad, for afterwards recollecting him, she
shook him, but the blanket fell in, and on taking it up she
found nobody there, only the tuft of moss with the tears from
whence he had sprung. Now they were all very sorry, for they
were no longer any better than other people; but he could not
be recalled: the medicine-youth had disappeared as strangely
as he came.*

It may not be unworthy of note that this continual use of a cloak of
bird-skins, and of feathers, occurs much in Indian mythology. At
feasts the chiefs scatter feathers over themselves, and at death the
dying person is strewed with them. While negotiations are going on

in the west coast, the negotiators will cover all their backs with
feathers, as if powdered, and when going among a strange tribe, an
Indian will often put white feathers in his cap. (In this, perhaps, the
Indian shows the "white feather" in more senses than one.) All over
the continent, chiefs and other great men wear eagles' feathers in
their hair and caps. Remarkably enough, the same idea is found in
Scandinavian mythology—apparently the same thought striking
semi-barbarous people in the same way. . . .

SKELECHUN, THE LIGHTNING-EYED[12]

*Skelechun was a poor man's son, who died when he was very
little, and he was brought up by his grandmother. He was,
moreover, a very little boy, with whom no one would play.
His head was full of vermin and scabs, and though his grandmother cried much for him, and often took him down to the
water and scrubbed him with sand, yet it was of little avail. In
course of time he grew up, and said to his grandmother,
"Grandmother, I think I will go away and seek my medicine."
So she made him a cloak of bird-skins for a blanket, and he
went away and travelled in the mountains. Many days and
many nights he travelled, but yet never dreamt of his medicine. One night he lay on the top of a high hill, and there was
a fearful storm of thunder and lightning: it was then that he
got his medicine. The lightning-birds took out his eyes, and
put in the lightning-serpent's instead, and every time he
opened his eyes he burnt up everything before him. Ah! it
was a great medicine! So he came home to his village again,
and when the boys jeered at him, and said, "Oh! ho! have you
got you [sic] medicine?" he just opened his eyes and burnt
them up. When he went into his grandmother's lodge she was
glad to see him again, and said, "Open your eyes; let me see
your pretty eyes"; but he did not dare, though opening them a
little away from her, she saw enough to frighten her, so that
she never asked him again. No longer was there want in
Skelechun's lodge. His grandmother became a great lady, and
this slave's son more than a chief. If any one disobeyed him,
he had only to open his eyes, and the lightning burnt them
up. Chiefs became his slaves, and chiefs' daughters his wives.
If they refused, he had only to open his fatal eyes, and there
was an end of them. When he went about, seven chiefs*

paddled him and his grandmother, another carried his platter,
and another his paddle or his blanket. Everybody was afraid
of him; everybody was his slave. He built a house on the top
of Salt Spring Island—a mighty lodge it was, and there daily
trains of slaves (once chiefs) toiled up, carrying bear and
beaver, salmon and porpoise, and gamass and clams—every-
thing good—to this Skelechun the Lightning-eyed. There,
with his grandmother, he sat in state, sleeping and eating like
any lazy chief, with nothing to do. If a slave offended him, he
had only to open one eye, and before he could wink it again a
slave lay dead! Who could resist such a power? But Squemet, a
Taitka, and his cousin, Clem-clem-alut,[13] *said one day, "It is*
not right that this slave's son should have all the chiefs'
daughters; let us try and kill him." So they made swords of
elk-horn, and concealed them in their blankets, when as usual
they toiled up the hill with bear and beaver, elk and porpoise
loads. His slaves were all standing in a row, chiefs and chiefs'
sons. Now Skelechun was afraid to lift up his eyes in case he
should destroy them all, so he always looked down, and called
Squemet to stir up the fire, but while Squemet was pretend-
ing to do so he struck heavily on Skelechun's bended neck, and
Clem-clem-alut helping him, before he could turn his light-
ning-eyes they killed him. So every chief took his wife and his
daughter, and they were (as fairy-stories end) happy for the
rest of their days.

Some of these stories are love-songs and tradition mixed,—how the
course of true love never runs smooth, but all goes well in the end.
Such a tale was the:—

Contest for the Chief's Daughter

There was once a great chief who had a very handsome
daughter, and all the young warriors, hunters, and fishers
came courting her; but her father said, "I will only give my
child to him who will split the tines of an elk-horn asunder
with his hands." So the news went forth, and the competitors
began to assemble until the lodge was full. The bears sat
growling in one corner and the wolves in another. The ra-
coons and the deer all came, but all tried in vain, and went
back disheartened. And after all had tried, Kewuk (the

salmon) came, and the lodge resounded with jeers and laughter at the bare idea of his attempting it after the flower of Indian athletes had failed. But Kewuk was the sweetheart of the girl, and had prayed to Haelse to put power into his arms; and Haelse, in pity, answered the love-sick pair, and the tines split asunder, and the bride was Kewuk's. Now all the rivals were bitter with envy, and went off to their lodges inflamed with malice and rage against all the salmon tribe. But the young wolf was worst of all, and determined to effect by foul means what he could not accomplish by fair. Watching his opportunity, while the young husband was absent for a few minutes, he seized the bride and fled with her. As he dragged her along through the bush, she tore off pieces from her blanket and tied them to the shrubs, and so marked her way till she arrived, disconsolate, at the wolf's lodge.[14] The salmon was sad, and pursued him, and escaped with his bride again; but he was no match for the young wolf and his father, and as he saw them gaining on him, he jumped into the river at hand, and Haelse turned him into the form of salmon,[15] and so he escaped the crafty Stuckeia.

This tradition has a smack of the old Roman mythology about it, and more learned mythologists than the present writer may decide how far its origin connects it with Asiatic myths. The Kootanie tradition about the origin of the Americans has a broad vein of humour in it, and shows their hatred of that nation—a hatred shared by all the Indian race, and more especially by those on the British frontier. Once on a time, the Indians say, they and the Pesioux (French Canadian voyageurs) lived together in such happiness that the Great Spirit above envied the happy condition of the Indian. So he came to the earth, and as he was riding on the prairies on the other side of the Rocky Mountains he killed a buffalo, and out of the buffalo crawled a lank, lean figure, called a "Boston man" (American), and from that day to this their troubles commenced, and there has never been peace for the Indian, and never will be, until they again go where their fathers are—they who lived so happily with the Pesioux and the fur-traders of King George.

Not a few of these myths have been invented to account for natural phenomena. Such is the story of the origin of the mosquitoes, and their mysterious appearance in the spring. Round the mouth of

Fraser River in British Columbia are extensive swamps, or marshy
flats, where the mosquitoes revel in superabundance. So terrible is
this pest that, though the land is clear, and for the most part good and
suitable for agriculture, yet it was until lately almost uninhabitable
during the summer and autumn months. The whole of the lower
parts of Fraser River are much troubled with these poisonous insects,
and especially wherever there are swamps or lowlands. Cattle are
equally tortured by them. When the Boundary Commission horses
were placed on the Sumas Prairie, the mosquitoes filled their ears,
until the horses, almost mad, jumped into the river, and many of
them were drowned.[16] Clouds of them rise off the swamps and hover
over the river. The tough skins of the Indians are even penetrated by
them, and it is almost impossible to persuade a native to accompany
you in exploring these places unless for enormous pay. Hence we may
well account for Indian imagination giving such an origin for the
mosquitoes as is evidenced in the story of:–

SLAL-ACUM-CUL-CUL-AITH
(THE EVIL WOMAN OF THE FRASER RIVER FLATS)[17]

Once on a time—a long time ago—two bad (slal-acum) *women lived on Fraser River. They are still remembered as Cul-cul-aith. They lived on young children, and travelled about from village to village, picking up their victims and pitching them into a basket woven of water-snakes, which they carried on their backs. They both came to an evil end, as might be expected, for an Indian hobgoblin story is as poetically just in its retribution as are such all the world over. One day one of the women went to the Lummi village, not far from Point Roberts, bent on her infamous trade. The men were all off fishing, and the women gathering clams on the shore at low tide, seeking gamass or berries, or sleeping in the lodges, while the children were disporting themselves on the beach. Cul-cul-aith came along, and snatching up the children one after another, pitched them into her snake-basket, and before their cries could alarm the sleeping village on that sleepy summer afternoon, she had escaped into the woods with them, and lay concealed in its dark recesses until nightfall, when she lit a fire. The children, with the elasticity of youth, had now recovered from their fright, and were intent on watching her operations. After heating some stones, she dug a hole and put them into it. The children now thought they had detected her designs, and that the stones were to broil them after the Indian fashion, by pouring water on the stones, and while the steam arose covering them with mats. "Shut your eyes, my little children," said the old hag, "and dance around me." They obeyed, but the younger ones were always peeping at odd times, until she put something on their eyes so that they could not open them. The elder ones were more cautious, and only occasionally peeped to see what she was about, and watching their opportunity, which at last occurred. Whilst she was stooping over the fire to arrange it, the children rushed behind her and pushed her into the hole she had dug for them, and there held her until she was burnt to ashes. But her evil spirit lived after that, for out of her ashes, blown about by the wind, sprang the pest of mosquitoes, which even now troubles mankind.*

The other witch died after this fashion. One day two young fishers were spearing salmon in Mud Bay, when they heard some one shouting to them on the shore. "Who can it be?" they cogitated, but as they paddled near they said, "Ah! it must be the Slal-acum Slane" (the bad woman), and they were afraid. "Our canoe is very leaky," they said. "Oh, never mind that, my sons; I do not care." But they still hesitated. "It is very small, and you will capsize it." "Oh no," she said, "I will lie very quiet. Do take me, I want to go back to my house and my little children." So the boys were forced to comply, and shoved the canoe ashore, and cut branches to keep her from the wet, until they were nearly level with the gunwale. They then told her to lay down carefully on the top. She did so, and when they got into deep water, by a rapid motion they capsized her out, and notwithstanding all her efforts, she was drowned. The Indian thinks that she yet lives at the bottom of the sea, and devours drowned men.

This story, in one form or another, is found among all the northern tribes, as far as Queen Charlotte Islands, or further. A Hydah chief, in crossing from these islands to the mainland in a large canoe, with some of his people, was in danger of being lost in a storm. One of the Indians told me that, handing him a pistol, the chief requested to be shot when the canoe was going to be capsized. He did not wish to be eaten by the bad woman at the bottom. The names of these women are the "Goody Two Shoes" of the Indian nursery, and mothers will quiet their children to sleep by telling them, "I will bring Cul-cul-aith to you," as Longfellow has represented old Nookoomis hushing the little Hiawatha to sleep by repeating an Indian legend of a similar character—

"Hush! the naked bear will get you!"[18]

Other myths are more palpably "myths of observations," such as the one I have already related in reference to the star-lovers and Knockan Hill. For instance, the Indians about Victoria say that Cedar Hill [Mount Douglas] was once the highest eminence in that district, but that quarrelling with Point Roberts, on the mainland, they commenced throwing stones at each other until Cedar Hill got lowered. Few of the stones came more than half way, which accounts for the numerous islands in the Haro Archipelago between British Columbia and Vancouver Island. On the Columbia River, just where the river bursts through the Cascades Mountains, there are certain broken rapids, well known as "The Cascades of the Columbia." These were formed by some of the volcanic convulsions of the region. Most of the peaks of the Cascades are still either active or bear evidence of being extinct or at least dormant volcanoes. The Indians have a tradition concerning Mounts Hood and Adams, the two nearest to the Cascades. They were once husband and wife, but they quarrelled, as (I am told) married people sometimes do, and commenced throwing stones at each other, and Mount Hood, who was the wife, determined, after the manner of womankind, to have the last word, and continued long after her husband had stopped. She still occasionally vents out her fury. This is, no doubt, a tradition of former severe eruptions of the mountain, when stones and ashes were thrown out.[19] They further say that once at the Cascades the rocks formed a bridge across, but that during one of these convulsions the bridge broke down and formed an islet in the middle of the Cascades, as at the present day.

I have little doubt of the probability of those traditions being tolerably correct history. They have, however, another story which goes off into the region of myths. Once on a time, they say, instead of cascades being here, there was a high fall which prevented the salmon from ascending to the Upper Columbia. Now, in a dream, a vision appeared to a great medicine-man, that some day the banks of the Upper Columbia would be peopled by numerous tribes of Indians,

and that the ascent of the salmon would be necessary to their existence. He, therefore, conceived the philanthropic project of converting these falls into cascades, but to effect this he had to go cautiously
about his task. The falls were guarded by two medicine-women, who
lived in a lodge by themselves, and who were nearly as powerful as
himself.[20] So he travelled up to the place, and while the women were
off gathering berries in the woods, he converted himself into a little
child. When the women came home, they found him crying in the
corner, and womanly instinct being strong even in witches, they took
good care of him. Every morning they went off gathering berries, and
as soon as they were out of sight he restored himself to his original
form, and commenced "prizing" away with a stake at the falls, and
before they came home was again a little child crying in the corner.
This went on for some days, until one evening, intent upon his
labours, he forgot about the women coming home, and was discovered. The witches gave a loud cry, and made for him, but just then the
falls gave way; the magician sprang into the river, and was soon
beyond the vengeance of the enraged witches. Since that date the falls
have ever since remained cascades, and many generations have
blessed the wisdom of the medicine-man—name unknown. I heard
the story in the summer of 1865, as I sat looking at the cascades—
scene of many a tale of bygone adventure and fur-trader's exploit. A
little block-house yet stands there, where several settlers were belea-
guered by the Indians in the war of 1853, until they were relieved by a
dashing lieutenant of dragoons, who afterwards rose to fame as
General Phil. Sheridan.[21]

The wild, romantic tale of how the Alberni Canal came to be
explored to the top by two hunters, and how they found a fine lodge,
with two bad women living in it, is also another of a similar character.[22] The story relates how the canal closed behind them as they
paddled up; a very natural appearance, for, as you round the bends and
points of this long narrow inlet of the sea, it seems to the eye as if the
canal was closely behind you. Crossing the wild, silent lakes of Vancouver Island, you often hear the strange cry of the loon, and it is then
that the Indian will tell you the story of the two halibut fishers, one of
whom stole the other's fish, and cut out his tongue, on the principle
that silent men tell no tales, and how the tongueless man was converted by Quawteaht, or Haelse, as the case might be, into this bird.
As his lonely cry is heard, the Indians will tell that this is the mangled
fisher trying to tell of his wrongs. Every hill has a tale attached to it;

every silent lake frequented by the Indian is the subject of a tradition, and the number of these stories is very great. On the Snoqualami Prairie, in Washington Territory, is a large rock, and the story connected with it is, that once on a time this rock was suspended from heaven, but the Great Spirit, offended at the improper conduct of some minor deity and his inamorata, cut the rope, when it dropped down on the prairie. Their gods are of like passions with themselves. This conversion of human beings into animals, already noticed, shows a striking similarity to Greek and Roman mythology, a great portion of which, again, came from Hindostan.

I do not think that the North-west American Indians have any decided theory on the subject of the creation of the world. The world was always as it is now—a big, flat plain, and if they have any further notions about it, I have not yet been able to clearly ascertain them. Most Indian tribes have some tradition or another about a great flood which once covered their country, but in most cases these are merely

30 Frederick Whymper, *Ouchucklesit Village. Barclay Sound* (Yale Collection of Western Americana, Beinecke Rare Book and Manuscript Library). On 3 October, the exploration party divided into two groups to explore rivers entering the Alberni Canal. Whymper was among those who went up Uchucklesit Inlet and Uchuck Creek to Uchuck Lake.

31 Frederick Whymper, *Falls and Indian Lodges. Ouchucklesit*
(PABC Pdp 106)

"myths of observation." They see shells, rolled stones, and bones of whales, or other marine animals, high on mountains, and they then set their wits to discover how they could possibly have come there. Knowing nothing of the gradual elevation of coasts, the most natural theory is that once there was a great flood, and in due course the minor incidents get worked in, until what was originally only an invention of some ingenious aboriginal philosophers, becomes part and parcel of their traditions. Again, we must be exceedingly cautious in receiving as native any of the pseudo-biblical tales, as I have found that in very many instances they can be traced to the teachings of missionaries, or other civilised men—either directly or indirectly— proximately or remotely. The tribe among whom a particular tradition is extant may be pagans, to whom no teacher of religion has come, but these people are so fond of mythological lore, that a curious

story of the great flood, and such like, will permeate from tribe to
tribe in a hundred conceivable ways, such as through intermarriages,
slaves, native traders, or intervisits at their great feasts or *potlatches*.
It will get twisted into the most aboriginal form imaginable, and it is
only by some trifle, such as a name, that you can detect its origin. An
eminent ethnologist once told me that, after great trouble, he had, at
least as he thought, got hold of a tradition of the flood among the
North-west American Indians, but he could only get it bit by bit out of
the old man who was the repositary of this and other such-like lore. It
cost my friend many blankets and other presents, and the labour of
hours to write it down from the aboriginal language. At last he came
to the finale. "Now what was the man's name who got away with his
wife in the big canoe?" The old Indian could not recollect, and went in
search of another who knew the name. The two came back in pride,
and related to my breathlessly eager friend, "His name was *Noah*!" It
was, of course, a Bible story, told them by the priests, and not understanding the value of myths, the old Indian innocently thought that it
must be just as novel to the ethnologist as to himself. He was, however, undeceived in a violent manner, as he was speedily landed on the
other side of the door, and will to the end of his life doubtless remember my friend on the rather forcible "ex *pede* Herculem" kind of
evidence which was so vigorously impressed on his retreating person.

The natives in Barclay Sound have a tradition of a great flood
which is certainly aboriginal, but whether this refers to a flood, or
only, apparently, to a great spring-tide, or earthquake tidal wave, it is
difficult to say. Though the tale has already appeared in print, yet, as I
heard it long ago, I think it is worthy of being given here in the words
of my note-book:—[23]

> *Generations back the Seshahts were unacquainted with the
> head of the Alberni Canal. They had two villages in the
> Sound, and used to migrate from one to the other. At that
> time a most curious phenomenon of Nature occurred. The
> tide ebbed away down the canal and left it dry, and the sea
> itself retreated a long distance. This continued for four days,
> and the Seshahts made light of the occurrence. There was,
> however, one Wish-pe-op, who had with him his two broth-
> ers, who did not do so. After mature consideration of the
> circumstances, he thought it probable that the ebb would be
> succeeded by a flood of unusual height. Accordingly, he and*

his brothers spent three days in collecting cedar-bark for a
rope, which when made was so large as to fill four boxes.
There was a rock near the Seshaht village, from the base of
which sprang a group of bushes. Wish-pe-op fastened one
end of the rope here, and the other to his canoe. In the canoe
were placed all his property, his wife, his brothers, and their
wives and children, and thus prepared they waited the result.
After four days the tides began to flow, and crept slowly up to
about half between the point of its furthest ebb and the
Seshaht houses. At this point its pace was considerably quick-
ened, and it marched up with fearful speed. The Seshahts
then rushed to their canoes; some begged to be attached to
Wish-pe-op's rope, but to this he would not consent, in case
his rope should be broken, and others would have given him
some of the women to take care of, but he would not receive
them. They were soon all caught in the rising tide, and while
Wish-pe-op rode safely at anchor, the Seshahts were unable
to resist its force, and drifted to distant parts. Finally, the
water covered the whole face of the country, except Quossakt,
a high mountain near the Toquahts' village, and Mount Ar-
rowsmith (Cush-cuh-chuhl). The Toquahts got into a large
canoe (Eher Klutsoolh), and paddled to the summit of Quos-
sakt, where they landed. At the end of four days the flood
began to abate; Wish-pe-op then began to haul in his rope,
and as the waters descended to the usual level, found himself
afloat near the site of the former Seshaht village. He then
built himself a small house with two compartments, one he
occupied himself, the other was tenanted by his brothers. One
day a Klah-oh-quaht canoe, manned by three Indians, ap-
proached the shore where the house was built. One of them
had with him a quantity of the medicine which they use to
make them successful in the capture of the whale (ehe-toop).
They brought their canoe close to the land, and when asked
what they wanted, they said, "We have come to see Wish-pe-
op's house." After some consideration, they were invited to
land, and, as the Indian manner is when friendship is in-
tended, assisted to pull up their canoe and offered sleeping
accommodation (chimoinlh). The Klah-oh-quahts, to show
their good-will, made a present of their whale medicine to
Wish-pe-op. After this Wish-pe-op proposed to make him-

self chief of the small household. This was finally agreed to, and the Klah-oh-quahts took each a Toquaht wife (for that tribe had returned from Quossakt), and this is the origin of the present tribe of Seshahts. The person who thus rose to dignity was the great-grandfather of Hy-yu-penūel, chief of Seshaht,[24] *and the present good understanding between the Klah-oh-quahts and the Seshahts is owing to this circumstance.*

From this it appears that this flood was of marine origin, very local, and of recent occurrence. There are many other such stories among the Carriere and other Indians in British Columbia, corresponding more or less to the Biblical version, but I think they must all be looked upon with grave suspicion, and we must put under the same ban the numerous South American flood-stories related by Humboldt and other travellers.

From *The Races of Mankind* (London: Cassell, Petter, and Galpin [1873]) 1, 130–46

NOTES

1 Eleanor C. Smyth was the daughter of Arthur Fellows, a Victoria hardware merchant, whose wife was the daughter of Sir Rowland Hill. Brown was acquainted with the family during his sojourn in Victoria and subsequently corresponded with Mrs. Fellows (Brown Collection: PABC III, 11).
2 *Scenes and Studies of Savage Life* (London: Smith, Elder & Co. 1868), 177. In *A Guide to B.C. Indian Myth and Legend* (Vancouver: Talonbooks 1982), Ralph Maud quotes Sproat's acknowledgment and notes that he has not located any publication of Brown on this topic (44n).
3 *Illustrated Travels: A Record of Discovery, Geography, and Adventure*, ed. H.W. Bates (London: Cassell, Petter, and Galpin [1869]), I, 276.
4 For another version, see Franz Boas, "Indian Legends of the North Pacific Coast of America," unpublished translation by Dietrich Bertz (1977), 100–2 of *Indianische Sagen von der Nord-Pacifischen Küste Amerikas* (Berlin 1895). Like Brown, Boas associated this legend with the Lekwungen or Songhees tribe, but he also noted that it "has an extraordinarily wide distribution" (573).
5 Brown footnotes: "The bulb of the *Gamassia esculentea*, Lindl." The camas bulb, used as a sweetener, was highly valued by the Coast Salish Indians.
6 Brown has previously remarked that Haelse (on the east coast of Vancouver Island) and Quawteaht (on the west coast) designate "the Supreme Being—the Originator of all things" (*The Races of Mankind* [London: Cassell, Petter, and Galpin [1873], I, 116).
7 Brown footnotes: "The reader will remember that women, to a certain extent,

can be initiated in the medicine rite mysteries." He is presumably recalling an earlier passage: "Medicine, understood as the physician's art, is chiefly in the hands of old women" (*Races of Mankind*, 122).

8 For an account of "The Tamahnous" contemporary with that of Brown and similar to it, see Ella E. Clark, "George Gibbs' Account of Indian Mythology in Oregon and Washington Territories," *Oregon Historical Quarterly* 47 (1956): 125–40. Gibbs wrote: "According to the Chinooks, every man has a good and a bad tamahnous, something analagous to an attendant spirit or angel who influences his fortunes and the character of his life, but as I understand it, in order to obtain control over these spirits the individual must go through a certain ceremony which comparatively few adventure" (126).

9 For another version, see Charles Hill-Tout, *The Salish People*, ed. Ralph Maud, 4 vols. (Vancouver: Talonbooks 1978), 4: 153–5.

10 For another version, see Hill-Tout, *Salish People*, 4: 135–7.

11 Brown footnotes: "Probably owing to the same reason that the New Zealander wipes up his saliva—viz., that no one can get hold of it to bewitch him with it." The animation of mucus occurs frequently in Indian tales, as noted by Boas, *Tsimshian Mythology* (Washington: Smithsonian Institute 1916), 734.

12 For other versions, see Boas, *Indian Legends* (Cowichan Section), 82 and Hill-Tout, *Salish People*, 4: 142–6.

13 Brown probably refers to the Tateke, a Cowichan tribe who lived on Valdes Island. The Clemclemalats are another Cowichan tribe: see p. 46 above.

14 Brown footnotes: "A similar method of marking the path occurs in German nursery-stories (vide Grimms Mythology)."

15 Brown footnotes: "Among other tribes the salmon was the *wife* of the raven, who, exasperated with losing at gambling, caught her by the gills, and beat her so sorely that she jumped into the river, and has remained there ever since."

16 C.W. Wilson, secretary of the British Boundary Commission, wrote in his journal of the extreme discomfort caused by mosquitoes during June and July 1859. Finally, he notes, "we had to turn them [the horses] out on the prairie & let them take their chance of living. I never saw anything like the state of their skins, one mass of sores" (*Mapping the Territory*, ed. George F.G. Stanley [Toronto: Macmillan 1970], 63).

17 For another version, see Boas, *Indian Legends*, 93–4, 145.

18 In Longfellow's poem, Nokomis, the grandmother of Hiawatha, "Stilled his fretful wail by saying, / 'Hush! the Naked Bear will hear thee!' "

19 Brown footnotes the following references: Rev. H.K. Hines, "Ascent of Mount Hood, Oregon," and Robert Brown, "A Journey across the Cascade Mountains in Eastern Oregon and a Description of Idaho Territory," *Proceedings of the Royal Geographical Society* 11 (1867): 80–4 and 84–97 respectively. For a legend concerning the eruptions of Mounts Ranier and St. Helens as a result of the jealousy of Mount Adams, see *Folk-Tales of the Coast Salish*, ed. Thelma Adamson (New York: American Folk-lore Society 1934), 258.

20 Brown footnotes: "This incident of two medicine women living in a lodge by themselves occurs in several Indian traditions."

21 An account of this engagement with the Yakimas and their allies is given in *Personal Memoirs of P.H. Sheridan* (London: Chatto & Windus 1888), I, 72–82. Sheridan subsequently distinguished himself during the American Civil War.

22 Brown is indebted for this tale to Sproat, *Scenes and Studies*, 181.

23 Brown again indebted to Sproat for the following tale; *Scenes and Studies*, 183–5.

24 Brown elsewhere notes that Ia-pou-noul had recently become chief of the Sheshahts, following the abdication of his father (Introduction, *The Adventures of John Jewitt* [London: Clement Wilson 1896], 23).

APPENDIX 1

Published Writings by Robert Brown Relating to the Northwest Coast

In response to a request from Dr. C.F. Newcombe that Brown send him copies of his articles on the northwest coast, Brown wrote in 1894: "I never kept any complete list." He did, however, provide the titles of ten scholarly journals to which he had contributed—journals which range over geography, geology, zoology, and botany. A more helpful guide to his publications is provided by *Testimonials in Favour of Robert Brown* (1868), the publication which accompanied his unsuccessful candidacy for the Chair of Botany at the Royal College of Science for Ireland. In the following checklist, I have indicated indebtedness to this source when I have been unable to check the reference independently. Brown remarks that the list in *Testimonials* is "exclusive of numerous purely literary articles, reviews, &c," and I have also extended the list by including these publications. In some instances—for example, the articles published in *All the Year Round*—authorship is not acknowledged, and attribution to Brown is on the basis of internal evidence or references in Brown's correspondence.

"Mr. Robert Brown's Botanical Expedition to British Columbia," *The Scottish Farmer*, 7 Oct. 1863

An abridgement of Brown's dispatch to the Botanical Association of Edinburgh (dated "Victoria, July 24, 1863") describing his travels on the west coast of Vancouver Island, 22 May–8 July 1863

[Travels on west coast of Vancouver Island], *Evening Express* [Victoria], 20 May 1864

An abridgement of Brown's dispatch to the British Columbia Botanical Association of Edinburgh dated "Barclay Sound V.I. November 4th, 1863"

"The Land We Live In," *Victoria Daily Chronicle*, 8 and 10 May 1864 See pp. 29–34 above.

Vancouver Island. Exploration. 1864 (Printed by authority of the Gov-

ernment by Harries and Company, Victoria, Vancouver Island 1864).
27pp.

"Catalogue of Trees, Shrubs, and Herbaceous Plants collected during
the year 1863." *The Scottish Farmer*. (*Testimonials* x, Number 14)
Further catalogues were published in *The Scottish Farmer* in 1864,
1865, and 1866: *Testimonials*, x, Numbers 15-19. These catalogues
were based on those printed by the British Columbia Botanical Association of Edinburgh and distributed with seeds to subscribers to the
expedition.

"The Lamp Fish." *All the Year Round*, 25 Mar. 1865: 199-201

"Narrative of a Botanical Expedition from Eugene, Oregon, over the
Cascade Mountains, to Rogue River Valley." *The Scottish Farmer*, 1
Nov. 1865.
An abridgement of Brown's letter to the Botanical Association of
Edinburgh (dated "Rogue River Valley, South Oregon, 26th August /
65")

"Narrative of a Journey from Rogue River to San Francisco and Vancouver Island." *Transactions of the Botanical Society* [Edinburgh]
(1866). (*Testimonials* x, Number 20)

"A Journey across the Cascade Mountains into Eastern Oregon and a
Description of Idaho Territory." *Journal of the Royal Geographical
Society* 12 (1867):84-97

"On the Physical Geography of the Cascade Mountains." *Transactions
of the Royal Physical Society* (1868). (*Testimonials* xi, Number 26)

"Contributions to the Seismology of North-west America." *Transactions of the Royal Physical Society* (1868). (*Testimonials* xi, Number
23)

"On the Natural History of the *Castor Canadensis* Kihl . . ." (Joint Authorship), *Transactions of the Royal Physical Society* [Edinburgh]
(1868). (*Testimonials* xii, Number 27)

"The Present State of Science on the North-Western Slopes of the
Rocky Mountains." *Journal of Travel and Natural History* 3
(1868):173-80

"A Monograph of the Coniferous Genus *Thuja*, Linn., and of the North
American Species of the Genus *Libocedrus* Endl. . . ." *Transactions of
the Botanical Society* [Edinburgh] 9 (1868):358-78

"On the Vegetable Products used by the North-West American Indians
as Food and Medicine, in the Arts and in Superstitious Rites." *Transactions of the Botanical Society* [Edinburgh] 9 (1868):378-96

"Observations on the Medicinal and Economic Value of the Oulachan
(Osmerus Pacificus Rich.)." *Pharmaceutical Journal and Transactions*
(1868):1-7

"Synopsis of the Birds of Vancouver Island," *The Ibis* 4 (1868):414-28

"Far-Western Newspapers." *All the Year Round*, 19 Sept. 1868:349–56
"Far-Western Judges and Juries." *All the Year Round*, 10 Oct.
    1868:428–32
"The Indians of Vancouver Island." *Journal of Travel and Natural History* (1868). (*Testimonials* xiii, Number 38)
"Das Innere der Vancouver-Insel," translation of "Memoir on the Geography of the Interior of Vancouver Island" (holograph, Brown Collection, I, 10, PABC), in A. Petermann's *Mittheilungen aus Justus Perthes' Geographischer Anstalt*, Jan. (1869), 1–10 and Mar. (1869), 85–95
"On the Geographical Distribution and Physical Characteristics of the Coal-Fields of the North Pacific Coast." *Transactions of the Geological Society* [Edinburgh] (1869):1–23
"On the Geographical Distribution of the Coniferae and Gnetaceae." *Transactions of the Botanical Society* [Edinburgh] 10 (1869):175–96
"On the War-Path." *The Cornhill Magazine* 20 (1869):313–26
"On the Physical Geography of the Queen Charlotte Islands." *Proceedings of the Royal Geographical Society* 13 (1868–9):381–92
"The Free Trapper." *All the Year Round*, 15 Jan. 1870:156–62
"A Winter Vigil." *All the Year Round*, 26 Feb. 1870:298–301
"The Avengers." *All the Year Round*, 5 Mar. 1870:328–30
"The Last of the Chiefs." *All the Year Round*, 12 Mar. 1870:345–7
"Saving a City." *All the Year Round*, 19 Mar. 1870:377–8
"Up a Tree." *All the Year Round*, 9 July 1870:127–32
"Mail Day in the West." *All the Year Round*, 4 Nov. 1871:534–9
"At Home among the Koskeemo Indians." *The Field Quarterly Magazine and Review* 3 (1871):180–6
"Winter Life on the Shores of the North Pacific." *The Field Quarterly Magazine and Review* 4 (1872):18–22, and (1872):88–93
"A Doctor's Life among the North-American Indians." *Illustrated Travels: A Record of Discovery, Geography, and Adventure*. Ed. H.W. Bates. London: Cassell, Petter, & Galpin [1869]: 1, 126–8; 2, 143–6
"The First Journey of Exploration across Vancouver Island." *Illustrated Travels*: 1, 254–5; 2, 274–6; 3, 302–4; 4, 349–51
"In Pawn in an Indian Village." *Illustrated Travels*: 3, 271–5, 338–43, 358–64
The Countries of the World: Being a Popular Description of the Various Continents, Islands, Rivers, Seas, and Peoples of the Globe. 6 vols. London: Cassell, Petter, & Galpin 1876–81. Brown abridges a number of the articles previously published in *All the Year Round*, and includes an account of his journey from Sooke to Victoria during the 1864 expedition (1, 271–82)
"The North-Western American Indians." *The Races of Mankind: Being*

a Popular Description of the Characteristics, Manners and Customs of the Principal Varieties of the Human Family. 4 vols. London: Cassell, Petter, & Galpin 1873: 1, 20–153
   A revised edition was published as *The Peoples of the World*. 6 vols. 1881–6
The Adventures of John Jewitt. Edited with introduction and notes by Robert Brown. London: Clement Wilson 1896

APPENDIX 2

The Drawings of Frederick Whymper

The exhibition of Whymper's drawings which opened in the Government Buildings on 28 November, 1864, contained thirty-three items, according to a receipt for them made out to Robert Brown by the Colonial Secretary on 6 August, 1866, shortly before Brown's departure for England (Brown Collection, III, 3, PABC). Twenty-three of these drawings (or copies of them made by Whymper) are now in the Beinecke Rare Book and Manuscript Library, Yale University, having formerly been in the possession of Robert Brown's son, Professor Thomas Rudmose-Brown, Trinity College, Dublin. The ten drawings not present in the Yale Collection are listed in the receipt made out to Brown as follows:

Cowichan Harbour
Qualis
Cowichan L[ake]. E. End
Junction of Brown's river with the Puntledge
Coal Seam [on Brown's River]
Puntledge Lake
Central Lake
Ouchucklesit Rapids
Henderson Lake
Head Waters. Chemainus river

Six drawings by Whymper are bound in with Robert Brown's *Vancouver Island. Exploration. 1864*, in the Library of the Royal Geographical Society, London (Numbers 7, 12, 15, 22, 27, 32, below). Some of these scenes are not represented by drawings in the Yale Collection, and since

the scenes are referred to on the receipt for the drawings that Brown
signed in 1866, it would appear that Brown donated them to the Society
(Numbers 22, 27, 32 below). In addition, one drawing (Number 6
below)—the subject of which is noted on Brown's receipt—is known
only by a version in the Scott Polar Institute, Cambridge, to whom it was
presented by Professor Rudmose-Brown.

Several drawings are now known only as engravings (Numbers 10, 13,
21, 28 below). Whymper had learned the technique of engraving from
his father, and his engravings often display details that are not present
in the drawings. The frequent use of pen and sepia in the drawings may,
in fact, suggest that Whymper planned from the outset to adapt his
drawings for engravings. By the close of the expedition Brown had
certainly come to recognize their potential, and he was later to use two of
them in his publications (Numbers 19, 21 below).

In the checklist of drawings and engravings that follows, measure-
ments of drawings give height before width. Whymper's spellings of
place-names in inscriptions have been retained, and currently accepted
spellings have been included within square brackets when they differ
significantly.

Checklist of Drawings by Frederick Whymper
Relating to the Vancouver Island Exploring Expedition,
Together with Related Engravings

1 *Victoria, Vancouver Island*, 165 x 241mm (6½ x 9½in) watercolour
   (National Archives of Canada C–1572)
2 *Comiaken—from M. Jean Compagnon's garden*, 105 x 152mm
   (4⅛ x 6in), watercolour (Yale University)
3 *Kakalatza and his hat-box*, 113 x 105mm (4⁷/16 x 4⅛in), pencil and
   watercolour (Yale University)
4 *Squitz [Skutz]. Falls of the Cowitchan River*, 120 x 178mm
   (4¾ x 7in), pencil, heightened with white chalk and black watercolour (Yale University)
5 *Squitz [Skutz]. Camp in deserted rancherie*, 105 x 152mm (4 x 6in),
   watercolour (Yale University)
6 *Qualis (the warm place). Cowichan River*, 190 x 260mm
   (7½ x 10¼in), watercolour (Scott Polar Institute, Cambridge)
7 *On the Cowichan River*, 155 x 105mm (6⅛ x 4in), pencil and wash
   (Yale University). There is a similar drawing: *Making a portage—
   on the Cowichan River*, 158 x 140mm (6½ x 5½in), pencil (Royal
   Geographical Society Library, London)
8 *Cowitchan Lake. 8th camp*, 202 x 298mm (8 x 11¾in) (irregular)
   (Yale University). There is a watercolour with the same composi-

tion: *Camp Cowitchan Lake*, 229 x 395mm (9 x 13in) (PABC–PdP 1704). In the latter drawing, Kakalatza is visible in the foreground in a reclining position identical with that in No. 3 above.

9 *"Quoitquot" or Foley's Creek. Cowitchan Lake, N. side*, 157 x 246mm ($6^3/16$ x $9^{11}/16$in), pencil and monochrome (Yale University)

10 *Camp with "blaze," or Camp-mark*, in F. Whymper, *Travel and Adventure in Alaska* (1868), 63

11 *Mt. Gooch and Nitinat River*, 105 x 152mm (4 x 6in), pencil and monochrome (Yale University)

12 *Descent of the Nitinat and Ascent of the Puntledge*, 255 x 160mm ($10^1/16$ x $6^5/16$in), pencil and monochrome (Yale University). There is a similar rendering of part of this drawing: *Ascent of the Puntledge River* 118 x 133mm ($4\frac{1}{4}$ x $5\frac{1}{4}$in), pencil (Royal Geographical Society).

13 *The Rampant Raft*, in F. Whymper, *Travel and Adventure in Alaska* (1868), 49 facing

14 *Head of Nitinat Inlet and Mouth of River*, 165 x 258mm ($6\frac{1}{2}$ x $10^3/$16in), pencil and ink (Yale University)

15 *Indian village. False Nitinat*, 185 x 315mm ($7\frac{1}{4}$ x $12^9/16$in), pencil and monochrome (Yale University). There is a similar drawing on a smaller scale: *Whyack. Nittinacht Village* 140 x 238mm ($5\frac{1}{2}$ x $9\frac{3}{8}$in), pencil (Royal Geographical Society Library, London). *Whyack Village, Vancouver Island*, was published in *Illustrated London News* 24 Nov. 1866:497.

16 *Aht Native, West Coast of Vancouver Island*, in F. Whymper, *Travel and Adventure in Alaska* (1868), 53 facing

17 *Patchinah [Pacheenaht] Indians*, 90 x 115mm ($3^9/16$ x $5\frac{7}{8}$in), watercolour and pencil (Yale University)

18 *Cooper's Inlet. Port San Juan*, 130 x 208mm ($5\frac{1}{8}$ x $8^3/16$in), watercolour (Yale University)

19 *Sooke Lake*, 180 x 260mm ($7\frac{1}{8}$ x $10\frac{1}{4}$in), pencil and monochrome (Yale University). *View of Sooke Lake* was published in R. Brown, *Countries of the World* (1876) II, 37

20 *Nanaimo*, 200 x 380mm ($7\frac{7}{8}$ x $14^{15}/16$in), pencil and monochrome (Yale University). There is a similar drawing in the Glenbow–Alberta Institute.

21 *Junction of Brown's River with the Puntledge* in *Countries of the World* (1876) I, 197

22 *Coal seam, Brown's river. Comox* 114 x 140mm ($4\frac{1}{2}$ x $5\frac{1}{2}$in), pencil (Royal Geographical Society)

23 *Falls. Puntledge River. Comox*, 205 x 290mm ($8\frac{1}{8}$ x $11^7/16$in), pencil and monochrome (Yale University). *The Laughing Waters Rapids,*

on the Puntledge was published in *Illustrated London News* 24 Nov. 1866:496.

24 *Upper falls. Puntledge River*, 185 x 170mm (7¼ x 10⅝in), pencil and wash heightened with black watercolour (Yale University)

25 *Cruickshank River. Puntledge Lake*, 150 x 190mm (5⅞ x 7½in), pencil, pen, and watercolour (Yale University)

26 *Young's Lake*, 195 x 248mm (7¹¹/₁₆ x 9¾in), watercolour (Yale University)

27 *The Central Lake* 140 x 235mm (5½ x 9¼in), pencil (Royal Geographical Society)

28 *View near Sproat's Lake*, in G.M. Sproat, *Scenes and Studies of Savage Life* (1868) xii

29 *Alberni*, 155 x 380mm (6⅛ x 14¹⁵/₁₆in), watercolour (Yale University)

30 *Alberni*, 174 x 296mm (6⅞ x 11⅝in), watercolour (Yale University)

31 *Ouchucklesit Village. Barclay Sound*, 170 x 250mm (6¹¹/₁₆ x 9⅞in), pencil and monochrome with wash (Yale University)

32 *Falls and Indian Lodges. Ouchucklesit*, 164 x 222mm (6⁷/₁₆ x 8¾in), watercolour (PABC–PdP106). There is a similar drawing: *Ouchucklesit Rapids Below Henderson Lake* 118 x 133mm (4¼ x 5¼in), pencil (Royal Geographical Society).

33 *Horne Lake*, 175 x 258mm (6⅞ x 10³/₁₆in), pencil and monochrome (Yale University)

INDEX